CHRISTIANS AND MOOR

C000076194

CHRISTIANS AND MOORS IN SPAIN

VOLUME III
ARABIC SOURCES (711–1501)

Charles Melville
and
Ahmad Ubaydli

Aris & Phillips Ltd – Warminster – England

© Charles Melville & Ahmad Ubaydli 1992. All rights reserved. No part of this publication may be reproduced or stored in a retrieval system or transmitted in any form or by any means including photocopying without the prior permission of the publishers in writing.

ISBNS   0 85668 449 X   (cloth)
         0 85668 450 3   (limp)
ISSN   0953 797 X

This book is dedicated to the memory of Martin Hinds

Printed and published in England by Aris & Phillips Ltd, Teddington House, Warminster, Wilts. BA12 8PQ

Contents

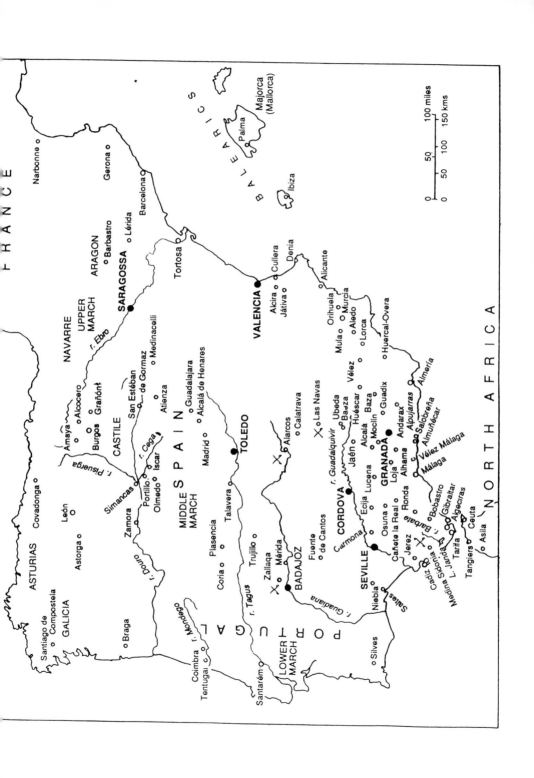

Acknowledgments

We would to thank the following for their help at various stages of this project: the Jafet Library (American University of Beirut), the Library of the Centre for Islamic Studies (Beirut), and Dr Martiniano Roncaglia, librarian in the German Orient-Institut der DMG (Beirut). We would also like to acknowledge the care and skill of Mrs Buthaina Fakhroo in preparing the Arabic texts for publication. Particular thanks also to Malcolm Lyons, John Mattock and Basim Musallam for their assistance with the translation of problematical passages. Last but not least, Colin Smith has read the final draft of the whole book and we are most appreciative of his valuable comments and encouragement.

C.M.
A.U.

Publishers note

The Publishers would like to thank all those who have given permission for the use of their copyright material; details can be found in the introductions to each entry and in the bibliography.

Introduction

By chance, the completion of this book coincides with the five-hundredth anniversary of the fall of Granada in 1492. Although at the time of writing a certain amount of attention has been paid to the Moors in Spain, 1492 is generally seen to mark the beginning of something, not the end. While this may be understandable, it deflects attention from the more remarkable fact that for nearly 800 years (over eight centuries of the Muslim lunar calendar), Spain was home to a people who came as invaders and stayed to foster a civilization that even in its decadence was capable of achievements of permanent and timeless splendour.

It is natural that this 'alien' presence should be regarded, from a Spanish nationalistic point of view, as an unwanted intrusion, and its durable influence resented where acknowledged. It is not difficult to regard the whole period of eight centuries as one long struggle between mutually hostile and incompatible forces. Superficially, the Arabic literature of Spain supports this view: the Christians are routinely cursed whenever they are mentioned. They are variously referred to as *rumi* (Roman), *'ajami* (non-Arab), *'ilj* (infidel, non-Arab) or *mushrik* (polytheist), the latter because the Christians associate God with partners (the Three in One). All these terms are either racial or sectarian in their application, and indicate that the official boundaries between the two cultures were clearly drawn. The Alfonsos and the Rodericks were designated as "the tyrant". Yet Jesus and David are mentioned with an automatic pious invocation (texts 73b, 81b, 96a). We are then reminded of intricate connections between these two great monotheistic religions, connections that were acknowledged at least by the Muslims, who extended to the Christians the protection and freedom of worship due to "People of the Book", that is, to monotheists with a revealed scripture. Following this precedent, the Christians too, until the bitter end, guaranteed the Muslims continuity of their traditional religious life, by the terms of the surrender treaties they agreed as the Reconquista gathered way.

It is not necessary to become embroiled here in a discussion of the relative merits of the two faiths and of the degree of toleration they displayed towards each other. There is little reason to suppose that the Mudejars were in practice much better or worse off in Christian territory than their Christian counterparts in the Muslim south. Nevertheless, it can be stressed that historically, Islam has been conspicuously tolerant towards Christian minorities within its midst, and that this unchanging and consistent attitude rests from an early date on their legal status as *dhimmis* (protected people). Killing the enemy abroad was one thing; forcibly converting them at home quite another. Islamic law and religion are almost inextricably mixed: both the legal and religious aspects of the faith coexist in the Qur'an, interwoven with each other. Provisions governing the subject population, the conduct of Holy War and the status of booty, regulated the Muslims' treatment of the Christians from the start (e.g. texts 74, 77, 81). Various passages included in these selections illustrate the punctiliousness with which the Muslim lawyers viewed the agreements made with the Christians (texts 85, 90, 99, 100); this doubtless goes some way towards explaining the outrage when the Christians violated the terms of their agreements (texts 100, 103, 105, 112). Throughout, there is a similar concern with the inviolability of safe-conducts, and it is generally recorded whether or not they were observed (e.g. texts 94, 105, 109). One must not over-sentimentalize this juridical virtue, for it guaranteed not only the existence, but also the subjugation, of Christian communities. The Christians in Muslim territory remained a subject people, second-class citizens and, with a few conspicuous exceptions, deprived of access to political power and influence. Nevertheless, they were left more or less undisturbed under the wings of their bishops.

The texts presented here are, of course, biased, for they are taken from the works of Muslim authors who impose their own view of things, even if unconsciously, on their narration of events or explanation of affairs. The Muslims are hardly going to depict themselves as treacherous. There is no deliberate attempt here to present, through the choice of passages, a particular attitude towards Christian – Moorish relations; rather, the texts speak for themselves. Nevertheless, in such an epic confrontation, which has aroused great passions, it is (and always has been) difficult not to take sides. At the end of the period covered by this volume, in 1502, a new decree called for the conversion or expulsion of all Muslims under the jurisdiction of the Crown of Castile. The final expulsions over a century later showed the failure of such a policy and the inability of the new Spain to prolong the symbiosis achieved in the old. There remains something peculiarly distasteful about the Christian form of moral superiority that emerged. By the time that centuries of dominance finally culminated in the overdue successes of 1492, the world was indeed on the point of a new departure. The long generations of familiarity had bred their contempt, and in 1492 a thrusting Christendom was on the eve of discovering the New World and its new god, Gold.

At the same time, we hope this book will encourage a more objective reading of the Muslim experience in Spain among modern Arab historians. Two main problems usually stand in the way of understanding how the Arabs retreated and lost their momentum. On one hand, the loss of the battle for al-Andalus is sometimes attributed to causes lying outside human control; on the other, some Arab studies of Islamic Spain are written in the context of a continuing confrontation with Europe. The following quotation may be taken as representative:

> Al-Andalus is the Paradise Lost for the Muslims, where the civilization of Islam reached a high level of evolution and prominence. Al-Andalus together with Sicily were the two main gates through which Islamic thought and Islamic civilization passed to Europe. [...] The tragedy of the fall of Islamic rule and Islamic presence in al-Andalus still evoke in our hearts deep sadness, because of the suppression, killing, eviction and torture which took place against the Muslims there, [and because] the great tolerance of Islam was met with the most violent wave of suppression and fanaticism by the Spaniards. (Hamadi, *al-Watha'iq al-siyasiyya wa'l-idariyya fi'l-Andalus wa shimaliyy Ifriqiyya*, Beirut, 1986, pp.7-8).

The statement at the end of the Fifth International Conference for Morisco and Andalusian Studies, held in Tunis in 1991 and dedicated to the five-hundreth anniversary of the fall of Granada, mentioned that the participants' call for the study of the Andalusian Moriscos and other similar minorities that have been suppressed in history, is not meant to revive struggle and resentment, but is part of a new "civilized and historical responsibility, which aims at purifying the present of all forms of suppression."

It is a positive sign, at least, that the need for a more objective understanding of the Muslims' retreat is recognized. In particular, a distinction must be made between those factors innate in Arab rule in Spain, and those arising from external causes and outside pressures, which are sometimes overestimated, or given a role that overshadows the internal causes of Muslim weakness.

'Umar ibn 'Abd Rabbihi of Cordova (d. 940), who compiled a famous anthology of Arabic literature, remarks in his introduction that "choosing words is harder than composing them"; to reinforce this, he cites a line of poetry: "We have known you through your choice, since one's choice is evidence of the soundness of his judgement". In fact, he chose to quote no compositions from al-Andalus other than his own, which indicates, among other things, how important the Islamic east remained to the Muslims of Spain.

Colin Smith's provocative remark in the introduction to his first volume in this series (p. v), that "history on a broad scale is too important to be left to the historians", might be adapted to suggest that the history of Islam in Spain is too important to be left to the Hispanists. Despite the example of Ibn 'Abd Rabbihi, there is a tendency for Islam in Spain to be viewed from an insular standpoint. Conversely, developments in Spain are generally ignored by students of the Middle East as being of marginal and peripheral interest. In fact, Spain saw one of the peaks of Islamic civilization and provides an illuminating example of the nature and concerns of political power in the mediaeval Muslim state. It gains a particular interest from the fact that Spain is the only territory acquired in the early Arab conquests, from which Islam was expelled, both as a religion and as a political entity, and replaced by the original culture.

Inevitably, Spanish Islam has been very much the preserve of Spanish historians and scholars, with many early and important contributions from France. English, or Anglo-American, is not well represented, although a number of recent publications go some way to redressing this imbalance. Despite the pioneering work of Pascual de Gayangos, who in 1840 was "impressed with the idea" of printing the historical writings of the Arabs "in the original with a literal translation", the relative dearth of material in English remains the main justification for adding this volume to those already published by Colin Smith. It would be gratifying if this small offering encouraged English arabists to pay more attention to the Muslim west and its place in the scheme of Islamic history.

As for choice, the Arabic literature of Muslim Spain is vast in its extent, despite being periodically reduced – by the destruction of the library of al-Hakam II at the hands of Ibn Abi 'Amir in the 960s, by the *auto da fé* in Granada authorized by Cardinal Jimenez in 1499, and by the fire in the Escurial in 1671. Fortunately, a large number of manuscripts found their way to North Africa, from a relatively early date (see text 106), and much remains to be done with the sources at our disposal. It is impossible to hope to survey such a large field for a small volume such as this, which could have been filled several times; and besides, we are not attempting a view of Spanish Islam as a whole. Relations with the Christians form a distinct, and always important, aspect of the Muslim experience in Spain, but one that is not particularly well-chronicled except in its military and, to a lesser extent, legal dimensions. One prerequisite for the choice of texts was that they should able to stand on their own, with a minimal commentary, as interesting and readable passages. This is not to be regarded as a source book of texts for the specialist historian, who might find that more significant passages could be sifted from the Arabic chronicles, or might choose to rely on more formal documents and fewer episodic accounts. Such texts would require a different treatment that would be inappropriate to the established format of these volumes.

The Arabic texts presented here are all selected from sources that have been edited and published, rather than from works still in manuscript. Many are quite well known: it is hardly surprising that suitable passages relevant to our theme have also been noticed by others. An earlier selection of texts concerned with Muslim Spain as a whole has been made by Claudio Sánchez-Albornoz (*La España musulmana*, 3rd ed. Madrid, 1973, 2 vols), in Spanish translation; another, treating the 11th and 12th centuries, by Pierre Guichard, has more recently appeared in French (*L'Espagne et la Sicile musulmanes aux XIe et XIIe siècles*, Lyon, 1990). However, there has been no previous selection in English, and none that deals exclusively with texts regarding the Christians and the Moors. In general, when a reasonably accessible English translation of a piece exists, it has been omitted here; this explains the absence (for example) of any selection from the Memoirs of 'Abd-Allah, the last Zirid ruler of Granada, which contain many oft-quoted passages of great relevance to our topic. The memoirs have recently been given a splendid and richly annotated translation by Amin T. Tibi (see the Booklist).

The underlying scheme of the book is to follow the pattern established by Colin Smith, and where possible to provide parallel Arabic accounts of the episodes covered in his selections. Obviously, a close match is made difficult, and even unrepresentative, simply by the course of history. In the first place, Christian sources are scanty for the early centuries, while the Muslim empire was at the peak of a flourishing literary culture. The book could have been filled with texts relating only to the period before A.D. 1000. Conversely, Christian sources increase while Arabic sources decline dramatically by the late 14th century, so that there is very little material in Arabic for the last century of Muslim rule. The advance of the Reconquista has the same see-saw effect in the spatial dimension. Arab writers at first are concerned with the whole Peninsula; their scope then shrinks to the mountain kingdom of Granada, in inverse proportion to the expanding outlook of the Christian authors. The pivotal point is the 11th century, and the centrality of this period is reflected in the fact that over a quarter of the selections belong to it. Our concern throughout is with the Muslim portion of the Peninsula, not with the fate of the Muslims in reconquered territory, unless incidentally. Though many excellent studies of the Mudejar communities have appeared, notably concerning Valencia (in the work of Burns, Lourie, Meyerson and others), it is noticeable how little they rely on Arabic material. Similarly, with the fall of Granada in 1492 and the official end of Islam in Spain shortly afterwards, it is not practicable to provide Arabic texts right through to the final expulsions of the Moriscos in the early 17th century. For a study of the Aljamiado literature of the Morisco period, see the work of Chejne mentioned in the Booklist.

Certain topics recur, unforced, in several passages, notably the question of the Moorish baths – viewed with righteous horror by the Christians, who were themselves regarded as filthy brutes (texts 83, 89, 91, 98, 110). Occasionally a striking image is created that encapsulates the whole nature of the rivalry between the two sides and even helps to explain its outcome. If the contrast of black and white in text 106 is commonplace, the picture of the Berber lord of Badajoz haggling over how much tribute he must pay, from the comfort of his boat, while his Castilian opponent sits implacably on his horse in the middle of the river (text 86), is an arresting one. In contrast to some of the Christian writings presented in the volumes by Colin Smith, there is little evidence of the supernatural at work. Allah (translated throughout as "God") and the Prophet Muhammad are omnipresent; God either assures or witholds victory (the very word for which in Arabic implies God's assistance), but not in a miraculous way. His lack of favour to the Muslims, when it occurs, is quickly recognized as being due to their sins and those of their rulers (texts 87, 92, 111). Several texts make direct quotations from the Qur'an, as is indicated where appropriate, though some such references have doubtless escaped notice.

The position of the Jews, which is the subject of another volume in this series, is mentioned only incidentally, and their only representative here gets murdered (text 89), though it is interesting to see how important they were to the Christian army (text 93). There is also little evidence in these selections of the enormous contribution of Moorish Spain to European civilization (though see text 96a). This is hardly surprizing. In contrast, there are a few indications that Islam itself was not water-tight. It is difficult to see how it could have been, with Christian marriages commonplace in the upper levels of society (for example, text 75), inter-communal romance perfectly natural (text 88), and everyone but the lawyers happy to join in celebrating the Christian festivals (texts 79, 98). Efforts were made to keep the urban Christian population in its place, but strictures against the Muslim purchase of meat and wine from the *dhimmis* (text 96) suggests that such regulations must have been honoured in the breach.

Despite the fraternization and occasional courtesies, the overall picture presented by these selections is one of hostility. The most newsworthy contact between the two sides was on the battlefield, and this is inevitably reflected in the sources. Despite a couple of striking victories (texts 93, 101), the trend of these selections is towards Muslim defeats (82, 86, 91, 94, 102, 104, 108, 109, 110). It would have been easy enough to provide accounts of more Muslim triumphs, particularly in the 9th and 10th centuries, when almost every year some new humiliation was inflicted on the Christian north, or even in the last years of Nasrid Granada. Text 78 stands alone to represent the successes of the early phase, which is also alluded to in text 84. This pattern is partly dictated by the framework established in the first two volumes, with the Muslim side of the see-saw tilted downwards. But the historical realities cannot be denied, and the Muslims, after all, were the final losers. This is no doubt partly why they have our sympathies.

The texts

These are reproduced as found, although it has occasionally been necessary to propose an alternative reading or correct a misprint. The more significant alterations are indicated by the use of square brackets. The passages are not all vocalized uniformly, as it seemed pointless both to remove vocalization from some texts and to add it to others. However, punctuation has been added where it was missing, and paragraphs inserted or altered when this has seemed appropriate. With two exceptions (Ibn 'Abd al-Hakam and 'Abd al-Basit, from Egypt), all the authors represented were writing in either Spain or

North Africa. The source of each passage is noted in the introduction to the text, and the authors and editors are listed in the index. We are grateful to all those who have kindly allowed the use of their copyright materials.

The numbering of texts (73-112) continues the sequence of the first two volumes (1-72).

The translations

All the passages have been newly translated. Occasionally, insertions have been made into the translations to clarify the meaning or assist the readability of the passage. These are placed in square brackets. No attempt has been made to supply a commentary, though particular points of interest or matters that need some explanation are mentioned in the introduction to each text.

It is reliably reported on a professorial *isnad* that R.A. Nicholson once observed that if there is not some insoluble crux on every page of mediaeval Arabic, then there must be something wrong with the text. Many of our texts have their fair share of difficulties; these have perhaps been highlighted by our efforts to provide as literal a translation as is readable. Translation is a risky undertaking, particularly so when the original text is printed on the facing page. Despite the assistance acknowledged above (p. viii), we have to accept sole responsibility for the errors that doubtless remain.

A note on transliteration

One of the advantages of having the texts alongside the translations is that it becomes unnecessary to resort to an elaborate system for transliterating Arabic names and technical terms. Since these put off the non-specialist, and are not needed by the specialist reader, we have avoided the use of macrons and diacritics throughout the book, and apologize to the purists for doing so.

A note on proper names

Muslim names have many components and the same person might appear in different guises. The basic form is "so-and-so son of (*ibn*) so-and-so", where ibn is generally abbreviated to b.. Some of the persons in these selections are known chiefly as Ibn so-and-so (e.g. the author Ibn al-Qutiyya). Others are known by their *nisba*, which describes their place of origin or some other characteristic (e.g. al-Marrakushi, the man from Marrakesh). Rulers generally adopted a "throne name" or honorific title, such as al-Mu'tasim or al-Nasir. Where necessary, all persons so named have also been given the other names by which they might be more familiar. Titles such as *Amir al-Muslimin* (Commander of the Muslims) have sometimes been translated and sometimes left as they stand.

The Arab authors tend to use the same system to refer to the Christian rulers, thus Ibn Ludhriq for "the son of Roderick". There is also a marked tendency for the Arabic authors to call all the Christian rulers Alfonso indiscriminately, for there was a good chance it would be right. In these cases, the correct name of the ruler has been identified and used in the translation. The word *qumis* is translated as Count, and *duna* as Don.

Although it has been convenient occasionally to speak of "the Moors", in this introduction and in the title of the book, the Arabs never referred to themselves as Moors, and the term Muslims is used throughout.

Arabic geographical names are transcribed on their first appearance, with the modern Spanish or anglicized equivalent (when identified) following in round brackets. Thereafter, the modern name is used. In the index, the modern name comes first, with the Arabic version in brackets. "Al-Andalus", the Arab name for Muslim Spain, is generally left untranslated; sometimes it refers only to the south (Andalusia), sometimes to the whole Peninsula, or even to the Christian north (e.g. in text 82). The word "al-Jazira" (literally, "the island"), is also used for the Peninsula as a whole. "Al-'Udwa" is generally translated as North Africa; Maghreb (the West, literally place of the setting sun), is also translated as North Africa, rather than Morocco, Algeria, etc.

Concerning Christian territory, the term "Jilliqiyya" as used by the Arabs does not refer solely to the modern districts of Galicia, but, at least from the late 9th century, includes the territory of León, and, until it became independent, Castile as well (see for example text 83). Jilliqiyya is therefore equivalent to the Christian kingdoms of the north; it has been variously translated as Christian or Northern Spain, or occasionally left untranslated.

A note on dates

Most dates in this book are given according to both the Muslim and Christian calendars. The Muslim era began on 16 July A.D. 622, when Muhammad left Mecca for Medina. The Muslim year is lunar and the new month officially began with the sighting of the new moon: a graphic example of this is found in text 82. The Muslim day begins at sunset and day follows night; this explains the frequent discrepancy of one day in conversions between the two calendars. All such conversions in this book have been calculated from the tables in G.S.F. Freeman-Grenville, *The Muslim and Christian calendars* (London, 1963). The Muslim date is given first, followed by the Christian equivalent.

The booklist

The booklist that follows inevitably duplicates some of the titles listed in Colin Smith's volumes, and conversely it omits others (such as the work of Glick) simply because they have already been listed there. It includes the books cited most frequently in the introductions to the texts, and also aims to provide the English reader with a selection of works covering the field, which in turn lead to the mass of specialized studies that are available. The *Encyclopedia of Islam* (1st and 2nd editions) is a valuable reference work for Muslim Spain and Islam in general. Scholars whose work is cited in the introductions to the texts are listed in the index. Unless otherwise stated, all references to Lévi-Provençal apply to his standard work, listed below.

THE BOOKLIST

Jamil M. Abun-Nasr, *A history of the Maghrib* (2nd ed. Cambridge, 1975).

Rachel Arié, *L'Espagne musulmane au temps des Nasrides (1232-1492)* (2nd ed. Paris, 1990).

Anwar Chejne, *Muslim Spain. Its history and culture* (Minneapolis, 1974).

Anwar Chejne, *Islam and the West. The Moriscos: a cultural and social history* (Albany, 1983).

Roger Collins, *The Arab conquest of Spain, 710-797* (Oxford, 1989).

Richard Fletcher, *The Quest for El Cid* (Oxford, 1989).

Pascual de Gayangos, *The History of the Muhammedan dynasties in Spain* (London, 1840-43, 2 vols) (a reorganised translation of al-Maqqari's *Nafh al-tib*).

A.A. El-Hajji, *Andalusian diplomatic relations with western Europe (A.H. 138-366/A.D. 755-976). An historical survey* (Beirut, 1970).

L.P. Harvey, *Islamic Spain, 1250 to 1500* (Chicago and London,1990).

S.M. Imamuddin, *Muslim Spain, 711-1492 A.D. A sociological study* (2nd ed. Leiden, 1981).

Ahmed Khaneboubi, *Les premiers sultans Mérinides (1269-1331). Histoire politique et sociale* (Paris, 1987).

E. Lévi-Provençal, *Histoire de l'Espagne musulmane* (Paris, 1950-53, 3 vols).

James T. Monroe, *Hispano-Arabic poetry. A student anthology* (Berkeley and London, 1974).

A.R. Nykl, *Hispano-Arabic poetry and its relations with the old Provençal troubadours* (Baltimore, 1946).

Henri Pérès, *La poésie andalouse en arabe classique au XIe siècle* (Paris, 1953)

Bernard F. Reilly, *The Contest of Christian and Muslim Spain, 1031-1157* (Oxford, 1992).

Abdulwahid Dhanun Taha, *The Muslim conquest and settlement of North Africa and Spain* (London, 1989).

Amin T. Tibi, The Tibyan. *Memoirs of 'Abd Allah B. Buluggin, last Zirid amir of Granada* (Leiden, 1986).

David Wasserstein, *The Rise and Fall of the Party Kings. Politics and Society in Islamic Spain, 1002-1086* (Princeton, 1985).

Kenneth Baxter Wolf, *Conquerors and chroniclers of early medieval Spain* (Liverpool, 1990).

THE TEXTS

73. The Muslim conquest of Spain (92/711)

The earliest surviving account of the Muslim conquest of Spain is provided by the Mozarabic chronicle of 754, probably written in Toledo, which is discussed at length by Collins, esp. pp.52-80 and Wolf, esp. pp.28-45 (see also text 3). The earliest Arabic account dates from about a century later, in the work of Ibn Habib (d. 238/852). The selections presented here are extracted from the chronicles of Ibn al-Qutiyya, Tarikh iftitah al-Andalus, *ed. J. Ribera (Madrid, 1926), pp.7-10 and Ibn 'Abd al-Hakam,* Futuh Misr wa'l-Maghrib wa'l-Andalus, *ed. A. Gateau (Algiers, 1947), pp.92-99. For a discussion of these and other Arabic sources, and of the Muslim conquest in general, the best study is the recent book by Abdulwahid Dhanun Taha.*

Ibn al-Qutiyya (d. 366/977) was, as him name indicates ("son of the Goth woman"), descended from Sara, grand-daughter of Witiza the Visigoth king. The extract gives a Muslim version of the foretelling of the invasion, both from the Visigoth and the Muslim side, and should be compared with text 2. For a recent treatment of these legends, see Julio Samso, "Astrology, Pre-Islamic Spain and the Conquest of al-Andalus", Revista del Instituto Egipcio de Estudios Islámicos, *23 (1985-86), 79-94. We may note, à propos the statue of Hercules at Cadiz, that it is also associated with a 12th-century prediction of the fall of al-Andalus to the Christians (see al-Himyari,* Kitab al-Raud al-mi'tar, *ed. E. Lévi-Provençal,* La Péninsule Ibérique au moyen age *(Leiden, 1938), p.176 of the*

(a)

وكان اجتماع طارق ولوذريق على وادي لكّة [بكة] من شُنُونة فهزم الله لوذريق.
وثقَّل نفسه بالسلاح وترمّى في وادي لكّة فلم يُوجد.

ويُقال انّه كان لملوك القوط بطليطلة بيتٌ فيه تابوت وفى التابوت الاربعة الانجيلة
التى يقتسمون بها وكانوا يُعظمون ذلك البيت ولا يفتتحونه. وكان اذا مات الملك منهم
كُتب فيه اسمه. فلما صار الملك الى لوذريق جعل التاج فانكرتْ ذلك النصرانية، ثم فتح
البيت والتابوت بعد ان نهتْ النصرانية عن فتحه. فوجد فيه صور العرب متنكبّة قسيها
وعمامها على روسها وفى اسفل العيدان مكتوب «اذا فُتح هذا البيت واخرجت هذه
الصور دخل الاندلس قوم فى صورهم فغلبوا عليها.»

وكان دخول طارق الاندلس في رمضان سنّة ٩٢ وكان سبب دخوله الاندلس ان
تاجراً من تجار العجم يُسمى يليان كان يختلف من الاندلس الى بلاد البربر وكانت
طنجة ... عليها وكان اهل طنجة على النصرانية ... ويجلب الى لوذريق عتاق الخيل
والبزاة من ذلك الجانب. فتوفّت زوجة التاجر وتركت له ابنة جميلة. فامره لوذريق

French translation). The passage also gives another version of the story of Count Julian (compare text 4). The invasion under Tariq is dated Rajab 92/April 711 in other Arabic sources, and the exact place of the decisive battle is also uncertain: Taha makes the plausible suggestion that there was a series of running battles in the Sidonia region. Lévi-Provençal, I, p. 21, has already demonstrated that the "Bakka" of the text should read "Lakka". Clearly, finally, Tariq did not penetrate as far as Galicia and Astorga in this first campaign.

Ibn ʿAbd al-Hakam (d. 257/871) was writing in Egypt, the base from which the conquest of North Africa was organized. His account relies on the reports of various oral sources, notably in this extract al-Laith b. Saʿd (d.175/791), who was also one of the main informants of Ibn Habib. The text gives an account of the booty captured by the Arabs, including the so-called Table of Solomon (al-maʾida), which was probably an altar from the Cathedral at Toledo. He also refers to the fact that the Muslims quickly penetrated southern France, a region that was to preoccupy successive governors perhaps to the exclusion of completing the conquest of the whole Peninsula. The Franks regained Narbonne in 759, when the inhabitants massacred the Arab garrison and put themselves under the protection of King Pepin.

(a)

The encounter between Tariq and Ludhriq (Roderick) took place in the Wadi *Lakka (Lago de la Janda) in Shudhuna (Sidonia). Allah put Roderick to flight. He was heavily encumbered with armour, and threw himself into the Wadi Lago; he was never seen again.

It is said that the Visigoth kings had a palace at Tulaitula (Toledo) in which was a sepulchre containing the Four Evangelists, on whom they swore their [coronation] oaths. The palace was greatly revered, and was never opened. When a king died, his name was inscribed there. When Roderick came to the throne, he put the crown on his head himself, which gave great offence to the Christians; then he opened the palace and the sepulchre, despite the attempts of the Christians to prevent him. Inside they found effigies of the Arabs, bows slung over their shoulders and turbans on their heads. At the bottom of the plinths it was written: "When this palace is opened and these images are brought out, a people in their likeness will come to al-Andalus and conquer it."

Tariq entered al-Andalus in Ramadan 92 (began 22 June 711). His reason for coming was as follows: One of the Spanish merchants called Yulyan (Julian) used to come and go frequently between al-Andalus and the land of the Berbers (North Africa). Tanja (Tangiers) was [one of the places he regularly visited]. The people of Tangiers were Christian....He used to bring back from there fine horses and falcons for Roderick. The merchant's wife died, and he was left with his beautiful daughter. Roderick ordered him to proceed to al-ʿUdwa (North

بالتوجه الى العدوة فاعتذر له بوفاة زوجته وانّه ليس له احد يترك ابنته معه. فامر بادخالها القصر فوقعت عينُ لوذريق عليها فاستحسن بها فنالها. فاعلمت اباها بذلك عند قدومه، فقال للوذريق «انى تركتُ خيلاً وبزاة لم تر مثلها» فاذن له في التوجه فيها وبعث معه المال وقصد طارقَ بن زياد فرغّبه في الاندلس وذكر له شُرفها وضُعف اهلها وانّهم ليسوا اهل شجاعة، وكتب طارق بن زياد الى موسى بن نصير يُعلمه بذلك فامره بالدخول فحشد طارق الخ.

فلما دخل السفن مع اصحابه غلبتْه عينُه فكان يرى في نومه النبى صلى الله عليه وسلم وحوله المهاجرون والانصار قد تقلّدوا السيوف وتنكّبوا القسىّ. فيمرّ النبى عليه السلام بطارق فيقول له «تقدّمْ لشانك» ونظر طارق في نومه الى النبى واصحابه حتى دخلوا الأندلس فاستبشر وبشّر اصحابَه الخ.

[فلما جاوز] طارق وصار بعدوة الاندلس كان اولَ ما افتتحه مدينة قرطجانّة بكورة الجزيرة فامر اصحابه بتقطيع من قتلوه من الاسراء، وطبخ لحومهم في القدور وعهد باطلاق من بقى من الاسراء فأخبر المنطلقون بذلك كل من لقوه فملا الله قلوبهم رعباً. ثم تقدّم فلقى لوذريق فكان ما تقدّم ذكره. ثم تقدّم الى استجة والى قرطبة ثم الى طليطلة ثم الى الفج المعروف بفج طارق الذى دخل منه جليقية، فخرق جليقية حتى انتهى الى استُرقة.

فلما بلغ موسى بن نصير ما تيسّر له حسده على ذلك وقدم فى حشد كثير ... به فلمّا صار في ساحل العدوة ترك المَدخل الذى دخل منه طارق بن زياد [وقصد] الموضع المعروف بمرسى موسى وترك طريق طارق واخذ فى ساحل شنونة وكان دخوله بعد طارق على سنة [وتقدّم الى شنونة ثم] الى اشبيلية فافتحها ثم قصد من اشبيلية الى لقنت، الى الموضع المعروف بفج موسى فى اول لقنت، الى ماردة [فقال بعض اهل العلم] ان اهل ماردة صالحوه ولم ياخذهم عنوةً وتقدّم جليقية من فج هو منسوب اليه فخرقها حيث دخلها ووافى طارقاً باستُرقة.

Africa), but Julian excused himself on the grounds that his wife had died and he had no-one with whom he could leave his daughter. He ordered her to be brought to the palace. When Roderick saw her, she pleased him greatly, and he took her. On his return, her father learned of this, and said to Roderick, "I have left behind horses and falcons such as you have never seen before." Roderick authorized him to go there and gave him money [to purchase them]. Julian went to Tariq b. Ziyad and excited his interest in al-Andalus, describing its fine points and the weakness of its inhabitants, and their lack of courage. Tariq b. Ziyad wrote to Musa b. Nusair with this information, and was ordered to invade al-Andalus. Tariq mustered the troops.

Once he was on board with his men, he couldn't keep his eyes open, and in his sleep he saw the Prophet (God bless him and grant him salvation), surrounded by the Muhajirun and the Ansar [see glossary] girded with their swords and with their bows slung over their shoulders. The Prophet (on whom be peace) passed in front of Tariq and said to him, "Pursue your business!" Tariq saw the Prophet and his companions in his sleep until they entered al-Andalus. He took this as a good omen, and encouraged his men with the good news.

So Tariq crossed over to the coast of al-Andalus and the first place he conquered was the town of Qartajanna (Carteya or Torre de Cartagena) in the district of al-Jazira (Algeciras). He ordered his men to chop up the captives whom they had killed, and to boil their flesh in cauldrons. The remaining captives were set free. Those who were released told everyone they met, and God filled their hearts with fear. Then he advanced, and met Roderick, with the result already mentioned. He pushed on to Astija (Ecija) and Qurtuba (Cordova), then to Toledo and the pass known as the Pass of Tariq, through which he entered Jilliqiyya (Galicia). He overran Galicia, ending up in Usturqa (Astorga).

When Musa b. Nusair heard how successful he had been, he became envious of him, and set off with a large force... When he came to the coast of North Africa, he left the point from which Tariq b. Ziyad had entered and went [instead] to a place known as Marsa Musa (the anchorage of Musa; near Ceuta). He avoided the route followed by Tariq and took the Sidonia coast. He arrived one year after Tariq, and proceeded via Sidonia to Ishbiliyya (Seville), which he conquered. From there, he went to Laqant (Fuente de Cantos), to a place called Musa's Pass at the edge of Fuente de Cantos, [and from there] to Marida (Mérida). Some scholars say that the people of Mérida surrendered on terms and were not taken by storm. Musa advanced into Galicia through the pass named after him, and overran the territory he entered, and appeared before Tariq in Astorga.

6

فلمـا جـاز طـارق تلقتـه جنـود قرطبة واجترؤا عليـه للذي رأوا مـن قلة اصحـابه، فاقتتلوا فـاشتد قتالهم، ثم انهزموا فلم يزل يقتلهم حتى بلغوا مدينة قرطبة. فبلغ ذلك لذريق فزحف اليهم من طليطلة فالتقوا بموضع يقال شنونة على واد يقال له اليوم وادي أم حكيم فاقتتلوا قتالاً شديداً، فقتل اللّه عز وجل لذريق ومن معه. وكان مغيث الرومي غلام الوليد بن عبدالملك على خيل طارق فزحف مغيث الرومي يريد قرطبة، ومضى طارق إلى طليطلة فدخلها، وسـأل عن المائدة. ولم له هم غيرها وهي مـائدة سليمـان بن داود التي يزعم اهل الكتاب. [...]

فتح لموسى بن نصير الاندلس فاخذ منهـا مـائدة سليمان بن داود عم والتاج. فقيل لطارق ان المائدة بقلعة يقال لها فراس مسيرة يومين من طليطلة وعلى القلعة ابن اخت للذريق فبعث اليه طارق بأمانه وامان اهل بيته فنزل اليه فـأمنه ووفى له طارق «ادفع الى المائدة»، فدفعها اليه وفيها من الذهب والجوهر ما لم ير مثله. فقلع طارق رجلا من ارجلها بما فيها من الجوهر والذهب وجعل لها رجلا سواها. فقومت المائدة بمائتي الف دينار لما فيهـا من الجوهر واخذ طارق مـا كان عنده من الجوهر والسلاح والذهب والفضة والآنية واصاب سوى ذلك من الاموال ما لم ير مثله فحوى ذلك كله ثم انصرف الى قرطبة واقام بها، وكتب الى موسى بن نصير يعلمه بفتح الاندلس وما اصاب من الغنائم. [...]

ويقال أن موسى هو الذى وجـه طارقاً بعد مـدخله الاندلس الى طليطلة وهي النصف فيمـا بين قرطبة وأربونة وأربونة اقصى ثغر الاندلس وكان كتاب عمر بن عبدالعزيز ينتهي الى أربونة، ثم غلب عليها اهل الشرك فهي في أيديهم اليوم. وان طارقا انما اصاب المائدة فيها. وكان لذريق يملك الفى ميل من الساحل الى ما وراء ذلك واصاب الناس غنائم كثيرة من الذهب والفضة. حدثنا عبدالملك بن مسلمة حدثنا الليث

(b)

When Tariq crossed over, the troops from Cordova went to meet him, and were scornful because they saw the small number of his followers. They fought a severe battle and were defeated; Tariq didn't cease slaughtering them until they reached Cordova. Roderick heard this and advanced from Toledo. They met at a place called Sidonia, on a river called today the Wadi Umm Hakim, and fought a hard battle. Almighty God killed Roderick and his men. Mughith al-Rumi, the slave of al-Walid b. 'Abd al-Malik [the Umayyad caliph, 705-15], was Tariq's cavalry commander and he marched on Cordova; Tariq went to Toledo. He entered it, and asked after the Table, which was the only thing that concerned him. The People of the Book [the Jews or Christians] assert that it was the table of Solomon son of David. [...]

[Tariq] conquered al-Andalus on behalf of Musa b. Nusair, and took from it the Table of Solomon son of David (on whom be peace!), and the crown. Tariq was told that the Table was in a fortress called Firas, two days' journey from Toledo, commanded by the son of Roderick's sister. Tariq sent him and his family a safe conduct; the prince came down [from the castle] and Tariq carried out his promise towards him. Tariq said, "Hand over the Table to me", which he did; it had gold decoration and precious stones such as he had never seen. Tariq removed one of its legs together with its ornamentation of gold and jewels, and made a replacement leg for it. The Table was valued at 200,000 dinars because of its precious stones. Tariq took all the jewels, armour, gold, silver and plate he found there, and besides that acquired wealth such as had not been seen before. He collected it all up and went to Cordova, where he made his base. He then wrote to Musa b. Nusair informing him of the conquest of Spain and of the booty that he had acquired. [...]

It is also said that it was Musa, after his arrival in al-Andalus, who sent Tariq to Toledo, which is half way between Cordova and Arbuna (Narbonne). Narbonne marks the furthest extent of al-Andalus and the limit of where the writ of 'Umar b. 'Abd al-'Aziz [Umayyad caliph, 717-20] was effective, before the polytheists overran it. It is still in their hands today. [It is also said that] it was only here that Tariq acquired the Table. Roderick was in possession of 2,000 miles of coast over and above that. [From these wide domains] the Muslims won great booty in gold and silver. 'Abd al-Malik b. Maslama told me, on the

بن سعد قال «ان كانت الطنفسة لتوجد منسوجة بقضبان الذهب تنظم السلسلة من الذهب باللؤلؤ والياقوت والزبرجد وكان البربر ربما وجدوها فلا يستطيعون حملها حتى ياتوا بالفاس فيضرب وسطها فياخذ احدهما نصفها والآخر نصفها لانفسهم وتسير معهم جماعة والناس مشتغلون بغير ذلك».

حدثنا عبدالملك بن مسلمة حدثنا الليث بن سعد قال لما فتحت الاندلس جاء انسان الى موسى بن نصير فقال «ابعثوا معى ادلكم على كنز» فبعث معه فقال لهم الرجل «انزعوا ها هنا» فنزعوا. قال فسال عليهم من الزبرجد والياقوت شىء لم يروا مثله قط. فلما رأوه تهيبوه وقالوا «لا يصدقنا موسى بن نصير»، فأرسلوا اليه حتى جاء ونظر اليه. حدثنا عبدالملك حدثنا الليث بن سعد ان موسى بن نصير حين فتح الاندلس كتب الى عبدالملك «انها ليست بالفتوح ولكنه الحشر».

authority of al-Laith b. Sa'd, "The carpets there were found [to be] woven with rods of gold, which formed a string of gold, pearls, rubies and emeralds. When the Berbers found one, and were unable to carry it away, they took an axe to it and cut it down the middle. Two of them took half each for themselves [and went off] together with a large crowd, while the troops were preoccupied with other things."

[The same authorities relate that] when al-Andalus was conquered, someone came to Musa b. Nusair and said to him, "Send someone with me and I will show you a [buried] treasure." Musa sent people with him and the man said to them, "dig here". They did so, and emeralds and rubies such as they had never seen before poured out over them. When they saw it they were overawed, and said, "Musa b. Nusair will never believe us." They sent someone to get him and he saw it for himself. [The same sources] relate that when Musa b. Nusair conquered al-Andalus he wrote to [the caliph] 'Abd al-Malik: "It's not a conquest, so much as the Day of Judgement."

10

74. A treaty with the ruler of Murcia (94/713)

*There are several versions of the text of this treaty; the one given here is taken from
the biographical dictionary of al-Dabbi, Kitab bughyat al-multamis (ed. Cairo, 1967), p.
274, under the name of one of the signatories of the treaty. Al-Dabbi's text appears to be
corrupt in one passage, and this has been supplemented by the reading from the version
in al-Himyari [in square brackets].*

*Habib ibn Abi 'Ubaida was a leading Arab amir in the post-conquest period, and
was among the conspirators who later murdered 'Abd al-'Aziz (see text 75). The latter*

حبيب بن أبى عبيدة، واسم أبى عبيدة مرة بن عقبة بن نافع الفهرى من وجوه
أصحاب موسى بن نصير الذين دخلوا معه الأندلس، وبقى بعده فيها مع وجوه القبائل
إلى أن خرجَ منها مع مَن خرج برأس عبدالعزيز بن موسى بن نصير إلى سليمان بن
عبدالملك، ثم رجع حبيب بن أبي عبيدة بعد ذلك إلى نواحي افريقية، وولى العساكر في
قتال الخوارج من البربر، ثم قتل في تلك الحروب سنة ثلاث وعشرين ومائة كذا قال
عبدالرحمن بن عبدالله بن عبدالحكم، وقال أبوسعيد بن يونس: توفى سنة أربع وعشرين
ومائة وثبت إسمه في كتاب «الصلح» الذى كتبه عبدالعزيز بن موسى بن نصير لتدمير
بن غبوش الذى سميت باسمه تدمير إذ كان ملكها، ونسخة ذلك الكتاب:

بسم الله الرحمن الرحيم

كتاب من عبدالعزيز بن موسى بن نصير لتدمير بن غبوش أنه نزل على الصلح،
وأن له عهد الله وذمته وذمة نبيه صلى الله عليه وسلم ألا يقدَّم له ولا لأحد من أصحابه
ولا يؤخر ولا ينزع عن ملكه، وإنهم لا يقتلون ولا يسبون ولا يفرق بينهم وبين أولادهم ولا
نسائهم، ولا يكرهوا على دينهم، ولا تحرق كنائسهم، ولا ينزع عن ملكه ما تعبّد ونصح
وأدّى الذى اشترطنا عليه وأنه صالح على سبع مدائن: أوريوالة، وبلنتلة، ولقنت، وموله،
وبقسره، وأيّه ولورقة. وأنه لا [يأْوى لنا أَبقا، ولا يأُوى] لنا عدواً، ولا يخيف لنا آمناً، ولا
يكتم خبر عدو علمه، وأن عليه وعلى أصحابه دينارا كل سنة، وأربعة أمدَاد قمح وأربعة
أمداد شعير، وأربعة أقساط طلاء وأربعة أقساط خَلّ وقسطى عسل، وقسطى زيت، وعلى

was sent by his father Musa to subdue the southeast, and reached an agreement with Theodemir, whose capital was Orihuela. The generous terms of the treaty suggest that Musa favoured a policy of cooperation with the indigenous population. The list of towns covered by the treaty varies in the different versions and there is some dispute as to their identification; for a map of the region, see Lévi-Provençal, I, p. 31. The list of signatories also varies; see the references cited by Taha, p.97.

Habib b. Abi 'Ubaida. Abu 'Ubaida's name was Murra b. 'Uqba b. Nafi' al-Fihri. He was one of Musa b. Nusair's leading followers who entered al-Andalus with him. He remained there with the tribal chiefs after he [Musa] had left, until he himself left al-Andalus together with those who went with the head of 'Abd al-'Aziz b. Musa b. Nusair to Sulaiman b. 'Abd al-Malik [Umayyad caliph, 715-17]. Then Habib b. Abi 'Ubaida returned to North Africa and commanded the troops fighting against the Berber *khawarij*. He was killed in these wars in 123/741, according to 'Abd al-Rahman b. 'Abd-Allah b. 'Abd al-Hakam. Abu Sa'id b. Yunus says he died in 124/742. Habib's name is attached to the peace treaty which 'Abd al-'Aziz b. Musa b. Nusair wrote to Tudmir (Theodemir) son of Ghabdush; he was king of Tudmir, which was called Tudmir (Murcia) after him. The text of the treaty:

In the name of God, the Compassionate, the Merciful: a written [agreement] from 'Abd al-'Aziz b. Musa b. Nusair to Tudmir b. Ghabdush, that he has entered a peace agreement, and has the covenant and guarantee of God, and of his Prophet (God bless him and grant him salvation!), that he will not introduce [anything new] with respect to him or to any of his people, and will not impede or take away his kingship. They [his subjects] will not be killed or taken captive, nor will they be separated from their children and women. They will not be coerced over their religious faith and their churches will not be burnt down, nor will their objects of worship be stripped from his kingdom. [So long as] he acts in good faith and fulfils the conditions that we have imposed upon him. He has agreed [surrender] terms covering seven towns: Uryula (Orihuela), Balantala (Valentilla), Laqant (Alicante), Mula, Baqasra (Bigastro), Ayyo (Ello) and Lauraqa (Lorca). [He has also agreed] that he will not give refuge to any of our runaway slaves, nor shelter any of our enemies, nor make anyone afraid who is safe with us; that he will not conceal information that he has acquired about [our] enemy; and that it is up to him and his people to pay one dinar every year, and four *mudd* (bushels) of wheat, four *mudd* of barley, four *qist* (measures) of thickened grape juice, four *qist* of vinegar, two *qist* of honey and two *qist* of oil.

العبد نصف ذلك. شهد على ذلك عثمان بن أبي عبدة القرشى وحبيب بن أبى عبيدة وابن ميسرة الفهمى، وأبو قائم الهذلى، وكُتِبَ في رجب سنة أربع وتسعين من الهجرة.

Slaves pay half that. Witnessed by 'Uthman b. Abi 'Abda al-Qurashi, Habib b. Abi 'Ubaida, Ibn Maisara al-Fahmi and Abu Qa'im ['Asim ?] al-Hudhali. Written in Rajab in the year 94 of the hijra (April 713).

14

75. The murder of 'Abd al-'Aziz (97/716)

When Musa b. Nusair was recalled to Damascus by the Umayyad caliph al-Walid, with the conquest of the whole Iberian Peninsula still incomplete, he left his son 'Abd al-'Aziz behind as governor. 'Abd al-'Aziz made Seville his capital and pursued a tolerant attitude towards the Christians (see also text 74); no doubt he was aware of his lack of real power, which rested in the hands of the Arab leaders and their Berber allies. This tolerant policy was among the factors that led to his assassination; another seems to have been the hostility of the new Umayyad caliph, Sulaiman. On the one hand, the tribal leaders wished to gain control of the conquered lands for themselves; on the other, the caliph was opposed to any attempts to make Spain independent of the governorship of North Africa and to withhold revenue. 'Abd al-'Aziz's opponents were thus able to strike without fear of retribution from the caliph.

وكان عبدالعزيز بن موسى بعد خروج ابيه قد تزوج امرأة نصرانية بنت ملك من اهل الاندلس يقال انها ابنة لذريق ملك الاندلس الذى قتله طارق. فجاءت من الدنيا بشىء كثير لا يوصف فلما دخلت عليه قالت «ما لى لا ارى اهل مملكتك يعظمونك ولا يسجدون لك كما كان اهل مملكة ابى يعظمونه ويسجدون له». فلم يدر ما يقول لها فأمر بباب فنقب له فى ناحية قصره وجعله قصيراً، وكان ياذن للناس فيدخل الداخل اليه من الباب حين يدخل منكساً رأسه لقصر الباب، وهى فى موضع تنظر الى الناس منه. فلما رأت ذلك قالت لعبدالعزيز «الآن قوى ملكك».

وبلغ الناس انه انما نقب الباب لهذا وزعم بعض الناس انها نصرته. فثار به حبيب بن ابى عبيدة الفهرى وزياد بن النابغة التميمى واصحاب لهم من قبائل العرب واجتمعوا على قتل عبدالعزيز للذى بلغهم من امره. واتوا الى مؤذنه اذن بليل لكى نخرج الى الصلاة فأذن المؤذن ثم ردد التثويب، فخرج عبدالعزيز فقال لمؤذنه «لقد عجلت وأذنت بليل» ثم توجه الى المسجد وقد اجتمع له اولئك النفر وغيرهم ممن حضر الصلاة فتقدم عبدالعزيز وافتتح يقرأ «اذا وقعت الواقعة ليس لوقعتها كاذبة خافضة رافعة» فوضع حبيب السيف على رأس عبدالعزيز، فانصرف هارباً حتى دخل داره فدخل جناحاً له واختبا فيه تحت شجرة. وهرب حبيب بن ابى عبيدة واصحابه واتبعه زياد بن النابغة، فدخل على اثره فوجده تحت الشجرة فقال له عبدالعزيز «يا بن النابغة نجنى

The pretexts used against 'Abd al-'Aziz are interesting, for they show the different attitudes to royal power on the part of the Christians and the Arabs. The Christian wife of 'Abd al-'Aziz is said by other sources to have been Egilona, the widow of Roderick. It should be noted that one of the assassins, Ziyad b. Nabigha, had also married a Christian woman. Such marriages subsequently became common. It is unlikely that 'Abd al-'Aziz, who was a devout Muslim and, as this extract shows, the prayer-leader (imam), had converted to Christianity, but the charge is not surprizing in the circumstances. After the murder of 'Abd al-'Aziz, the capital was moved to Cordova.

The version selected here is again taken from the chronicle of Ibn 'Abd al-Hakam (see text 73 for details), from pp.106-11.

After the departure of his father, 'Abd al-'Aziz b. Musa had married a Christian woman, the daughter of one of the Spanish kings; she is said to have been the daughter of Roderick, the king of al-Andalus, whom Tariq killed. She brought him worldly wealth beyond description. When she came to him, she said, "Why don't I see the people of your kingdom glorify you and prostrate themselves before you in the way that the people of my father's kingdom used to glorify him and bow down to him?" He didn't know what to say in reply, and gave orders for a door [to be built], which was punched through the side of his palace. He made it rather small. He would summon people, and anyone entering through the door would have to bow his head because the door was too low. She was placed where she could watch the people [entering] and when she saw this, she said to 'Abd al-'Aziz, "Now your majesty has become stronger."

The people heard that he had only made the door for this purpose, and some alleged that she had made him a Christian. Habib b. Abi 'Ubaida al-Fihri and Ziyad b. al-Nabigha al-Tamimi, together with their Arab tribesmen, rebelled against him and agreed to murder 'Abd al-'Aziz because of what they'd heard about him. They went to his muezzin and told him to call the night-time prayer, so that they could go to pray. The muezzin gave the call to prayer, and then repeated the formula "prayer is better than sleep". 'Abd al-'Aziz went out to pray, saying to the muezzin, "You're in a hurry with the night prayers". He went to the mosque, where those men and others were assembled for the prayers. Abd al-'Aziz went to the front and began to read "When the Terror descends, and none denies its descending, abasing, exalting..." [*Qur'an* 56: 1-3]. Habib struck him on the head with his sword, but 'Abd al-'Aziz escaped to his palace and ran to one of the gardens, where he hid under a tree. Habib b. Abi 'Ubaida and his men thereupon fled, but Ziyad b. al-Nabigha pursued ['Abd al-'Aziz] and followed his tracks till he found him under the tree. 'Abd al-'Aziz said, "Ibn

ولك ما سألت»، فقال «لا تذوق الحياة بعدها» فاجهز عليه واحتز رأسه وبلغ ذلك حبيبا

واصحابه فرجعوا.

-Nabigha, spare me and you shall have whatever you ask!" He replied, "You
ll taste no more of life after this", and he finished him off, cutting off his head.
hen Habib and his companions heard this, they returned.

76. Christian resistance begins (c. 117/735 and 136/753)

Pelagius and his importance for the ideology of the Reconquista need no length
discussion here. For a useful recent account of the Christian sources on the Asturic
revolt, see Collins, esp. pp.141-51. The Muslim sources are rather more subdued, ar
make no reference to a battle in 722 in Asturias, in which the Muslims were defeate
(see text 6). The first selection, however, shows that the legendary elements of the sto.
were not absent from later Arabic chronicles. The text is taken from al-Maqqari, Na
al-tib, ed. Ihsan 'Abbas (Beirut, 1968), III, p. 17. Although a late author, al-Maqqa
preserves many extracts from earlier works that are now lost, including the earlie
sections of the history of Ibn Hayyan cited here. The other source cited, Ibn Sa'id, is t
author of al-Mughrib fi hula al-Maghrib, *which is extant.*

According to this account, Pelayo's resistance occurred in the governorship
'Anbasa b. Suhaim (103-07/721-26), who was perhaps most concerned wi
strengthening the Muslims' hold on Narbonne and southwest France. Other Arat
sources indicate that Muslim expeditions against the Rock (i.e. Covadonga) intensifi
in the governorship of 'Uqba b. al-Hajjaj (116-23/734-41), who was able to pacify m
of northern Spain and Asturias with the exception of the Rock. During this period, t
Pelayo died in 737, to be succeeded after a brief interval by Alfonso I of Asturias (73
57).

(a)

وذكر ابن حيان أنّه في أيامه قام بجليقية عِلْجٌ خبيث يدعى بلاي، فعاب على

علوج طول الفرار، وأذكى قرائحهم حتى سما بهم إلى طلب الثار، ودافع عن أرضه،

ن وقته أخذ نصارى الأندلس في مدافعة المسلمين عمّا بقي بأيديهم من أرضهم

لحماية عن حريمهم، وقد كانوا لا يطمعون في ذلك، وقيل: إنّه لم يبق بأرض جليقية

ية فما فوقها لم تُفتح إلا الصخرة التي لاذ بها هذا العِلْجُ ومات أصحابه جوعاً إلى أن

ى في مقدار ثلاثين رجلاً ونحو عشر نسوة، وما لهم عيش إلا من عسل النحل في

باح معهم في خروق الصخرة، وما زالوا ممتنعين بوعرها إلى أن أعيا المسلمين

رهم، واحتقروهم، وقالوا: ثلاثون عُلجاً ما عسى أن يجيء منهم؟ فبلغ أمرهم بعد ذلك

القوّة والكثرة والاستيلاء ما لا خفاء به. وملك بعده أذفونش جد عظماء الملوك

شهورين بهذه السّمة.

*The second passage refers to later events in the north, which was settled
edominantly by Berbers. The latter revolted in the early 740s, first in North Africa
'e above, p.11) and then in Spain, because of Arab policies to lower their status, and
ainst this background their attachment to Islam may also have suffered. Our text
akes the interesting statement that many converted to Christianity, though some may
ve had little choice. These events occurred at the time of a great famine, which
ompted many Berbers to return permanently to North Africa. Both the terrain and the
mate of northern Spain proved disagreeable to the Berbers, as is often noted to
count for the Muslims' failure to occupy and settle the whole of the Peninsula. Abu 'l-
attar was sent as governor of al-Andalus (743-45) to restore order; he was defeated
d replaced by Thawab b. Salama al-Judhami (d. 129/746); see Taha, pp.218-23. The
t is taken from the anonymous (10th century) Akhbar majmu'a, ed. E. Lafuente y
antara (Madrid, 1867), pp.61-62.*

*The term "Jilliqiyya" (Galicia) refers to Northern or Christian Spain in general. At
s period the Christians were effectively restricted to Galicia, and the term has
netimes been retained here for convenience, but its wider significance should be
'ne in mind (see also text 83).*

(a)

Ibn Hayyan said, In the days of ['Anbasa b. Suhaim al-Kalbi] there arose in
liqiyya (Northern Spain) a vicious infidel called Balayo (Pelayo) who
ticized the infidels throughout the period of their flight, and kindled their
rits until he encouraged them to rise in revolt and defend his land. From that
1e the Christians of al-Andalus began to defend what land remained in their
nds and to protect their families against the Muslims, which they had not
:viously aspired to do. It is said that no single village, nor anything larger,
naained unconquered in the territory of Galicia, except a rocky outcrop on
ich this infidel took refuge. His companions died of starvation until only
rty men and about ten women were left. They had nothing to live on except
honey from some bees in hives that were there with them in the fissures of
rocks. They continued to defend their rugged ground until their efforts
1austed the Muslims, who viewed them scornfully and said, "Thirty infidels –
at could possibly come from them?" [But] after that they grew in power,
nbers and control of territory in such a way that it cannot be hidden. After
ayo their king was Alfonso, ancestor of the greatest and most celebrated
gs of that name.

قال ابن سعيد: فـآل احتقار تلك الصخرة ومن احتوت عليه إلى أن ملك عقبُ مَنْ كان فيها المدن العظيمة، حتى إن حضرة قُرْطُبة في يدهم الآن، جبرها الله تعالى، وهي كانت سرير السلطنة لعنبسة.

(b)

فثار اهل جليقية على المسلمين وغلظ امـر علج يقـال لـه بـلاى [...]. فـخرج من الصخرة وغلب على كورة واستورس. ثم غزاه المسلمون من جليقية وغزاه اهل استورقة زمانا طويلا حتى كانت فتنة ابى الخطار وثوابه. فلما كان فى سنة ثلث وثلثين هزمهم اخرج عن جليقية كلها. وتنصّر كل مذبذب فى دينه وضعف عن الخراج، وقُتل من قُتل صار فُلهم الى خلف الجبل الى استورقة حتى استحكم الجوع. فـاخرجوا ايضا المسلمين عن اسـتورقة وغيرهـا وانضّم الناس الى مـا وراء الدرب الاخر والى قـورية ماردة فى سنة ست وثلثين. واشتّد الجوع فخرج اهل الاندلس الى طنجة واصيلا وريف بربر ممتارين ومرتحلين. وكانت اجازتهم من وادى بكورة شـنونة ويقال له وادى برباط. تلك السنون تسمى سنى برباط فخفّ سكان الاندلس وكاد ان يغلب عليهم العلو الا ان الجوع شملهم.

Ibn Saʿid said, Contempt for that rocky outcrop and those who crawled about on it ended up with their descendants gaining possession of great cities; even the capital city of Cordova, which had been the centre of ʿAnbasa's government, is now in their hands (may God restore it [to Islam]!).

(b)

The people of Christian Spain rose in revolt against the Muslims and the position of the unbeliever Pelayo became strong. He left his rocky outcrop and conquered the district of Asturias. Then the Muslims of Galicia and the people of Astorga attacked him over a long period, until the time of the civil war between Abu'l-Khattar and Thawaba. In the year (1)33/750-51 he [Pelayo] defeated them and expelled them from the whole of Galicia. Everyone who was wavering in his faith or was too weak to pay tribute converted to Christianity; those who were killed were killed and the defeated survivors went over the mountains towards Astorga, until the famine took a firm hold. [The Christians] also expelled the Muslims from Astorga and elsewhere, and in (1)36/753-54 the people became concentrated in the region beyond the last mountain pass [beyond the Duero basin] and in Quriya (Coria) and Mérida. The scarcity intensified and the people of al-Andalus left for Tangiers and Asila and the Berber Rif, moving away and emigrating. They crossed over a wadi in the district of Sidonia known as the Wadi Barbat (río Barbate). These years were called the Years of Barbate [during which] the population of al-Andalus was diminished, and the enemy could almost have overcome them, had not the famine encompassed them also.

77. The price of peace (42/759)

Another early treaty with the Christians is found in Ibn al-Khatib's 14th-century History of Granada (the Ihata), *as reproduced by M. Casiri*, Bibliotheca Arabo-Hispana Escurialensis, II (Madrid, 1770), p.104, *citing the Escurial Ms. 1668. The text of the treaty comes in the biography of 'Abd al-Rahman b. Mu'awiya, the first Umayyad amir*

بسم الله الرحمن الرحيم. كتاب امان الملك المعظم عبدالرحمن للبطاركة والرهبان
والاعيان والنصاري الاندلسيين اهل قشتاله ومن تبعهم من ساير البلدان، كتاب امان
وسلام وشهد علي نفسه ان عهده لا ينسخ ما اقاموا علي تأدية عشرة الاف اوقية من
الذهب وعشرة الاف رطل من الفضة وعشرة الاف راس من خيار الخيل ومثلها من
البغال، مع الف درع والف بيضة ومثلها من الرماح، في كل عام الى خمس سنين. كتب
بمدينة قرطبة ثلثة من صفر عام اثنين واربعين وماية.

of al-Andalus, who by 142/759 had barely succeeded in imposing his authority in the region south of Toledo. This, and the reference to Castile, which did not exist at this period, make the text problematic, but it is nonetheless of interest. For the context, see Lévi-Provençal, I, pp.116-17 and Collins, pp.157-58.

In the name of God the Compassionate, the Merciful. [This is] a truce document of the great king 'Abd al-Rahman on behalf of the Patriarchs, monks, notables and Spanish (Andalusian) Christians of Qashtala (Castile ?), and those from other regions who adhere to them. A document [granting] security and peace: he has attested in person that his covenant will not be revoked so long as they pay ten thousand ounces (*wiqiya*) of gold, ten thousand pounds (*ratl*) of silver, ten thousand of the best horses and likewise of mules, one thousand coats of mail, one thousand helmets and likewise of spears, every year for five years. Written in the city of Cordova on 3 Safar 142 (5 June 759).

78. Campaigns against the Christians (193-94/809-10)

Arabic sources are rather uninformative about the activities of Charlemagne in northern Spain (see texts 7 and 8), and make no reference to the fall of Gerona in 785 (text 9). Nevertheless, the sources report the gradual erosion of the Muslim position in the northeast, culminating in the fall of Barcelona to Louis of Aquitaine, son of Charlemagne, in 185/801. After this, evidently, some of the Muslims not only stayed in Christian territory rather than crossing over to the Muslim side, but even engaged in military activity against their co-religionists. Barcelona remained in Christian hands except for a brief period in 856 and again in 985, when it was taken by Ibn Abi 'Amir al-Mansur (see also text 84).

The first of the campaigns mentioned in this selection was against Louis, whom the author calls Roderick, and who had also attacked Tortosa the previous year. The Umayyad amir al-Hakam (796-822) sent his son and future successor to fight Louis; 'Abd al-Rahman was joined by 'Amrus b. Yusuf, the muwallad governor of Saragossa, and 'Abdun b. al-Ghamr, the governor of Tortosa. Louis' retreat is also recorded in the Royal Frankish Annals, tr. B.W. Scholz, Carolingian chronicles (Michigan, 1972), p.82. Tortosa thereafter remained the Muslims' forward position against the Franks.

وفى سنة ١٩٣، خرج رُذَريق صاحب إفرَنجة الى جهة طرطُوشة، فأغزى الحَكَم ابنه عبدالرحمن فى جيش كثيف، وكتب الى عَمرُوس وعَبدُون عاملى الثَّغر بالغزو معه بجميع أهل الثغر. فتقدَّم عبدالرحمن بالجنود، وتوافت عليه الحشود، وحفّت به المُطَّوِّعة. فألفوا الطاغية خارجاً الى بلاد المسلمين. ودارت بينهم حروب شديدة، ثبّت اللهُ فيها أقدام المسلمين. فانهزم المشركون؛ وكانت فيهم مقتلة عظيمة؛ ففنى أكثرُهم.

وفى سنة ١٩٤، غزا الحَكَم الى أرض الشرك. وكان السبب فى هذه الغزاة أنّ عبّاس بن ناصح الشاعر كان بمدينة الفَرَج (وهى وادى الحِجَارة). وكان العدوُّ، بسبب اشتغال الحَكَم بماردة وتوجيهه الصوائف اليها مدَّةً من سبعة أعوام، قد عظمت شوكتُه، وقوى أمرُه. فشنَّ الغارات فى أطراف الثغور، يسبى ويقتل. وسمع عبّاس بن ناصح امرأةً فى ناحية وادى الحِجَارة، وهى تقول: «واغوثاه يا حَكَم! قد ضيَّعتَنا وأسلَمتَنا واشتغلتَ عنّا، حتى استأسد العدوُّ علينا!»

فلما وفد عبّاس على الحَكَم، رفع اليه شعراً يستصرخه فيه، ويذكر قول المرأة واستصراخها به؛ وأنهى اليه عبّاس ما هو عليه الثغر من الوهن والتياث الحال. فرثى

The story of the second expedition is told in several sources, but its exact date and identification are open to doubt. Most of al-Hakam's energies at this period were directed against a Berber and muwallad revolt in Mérida, which eventually submitted in 197/813. This would suggest a later date than the one given here by Ibn 'Idhari, who also mentions another raid in 196/812: possibly a duplication of the same event. Al-Hakam's main expedition against Asturias, in response to increasing Christian incursions over the northern marches, was in 200/816. The poet 'Abbas b. Nasih al-Jaziri was also a jurist, and was qadi of Algeciras. One version of the anecdote omits all mention of him, while another reproduces the first three lines of the poem he is said to have recited to al-Hakam (see al-Maqqari, ed. Ihsan 'Abbas, I, pp.343-44 and Gayangos, II, pp.105-06). All versions so far identified are late works, and although they doubtless refer to a genuine historical event, the story is recounted with an obviously literary structure. The text selected here is taken from Ibn 'Idhari, al-Bayan al-mughrib, ed. G.S. Colin and E. Lévi-Provençal, II (Leiden, 1951), pp.72-73.

In the year 193 (began 25 October 808), Roderick (Louis) the ruler of Ifranja (France) set out for Turtusha (Tortosa). Al-Hakam sent his son 'Abd al-Rahman on an expedition with a heavy force and wrote to 'Amrus and 'Abdun, the two governors of the frontier, with instructions to join the expedition with the frontier forces. 'Abd al-Rahman advanced with the regular army; the auxiliaries were mobilized for him and volunteers flocked to him. They found the tyrant leaving for Muslim territory and heavy fighting took place between them, in which God enabled the Muslims to stand firm; the polytheists were defeated and put to the slaughter, so that most of them perished.

In 194 (began 15 October 809), al-Hakam campaigned in the land of polytheism. The cause of this expedition was the poet 'Abbas b. Nasih [who] was at Madinat al-Faraj, which is Wadi al-Hijara (Guadalajara). Because of al-Hakam's preoccupation with Mérida and his despatch of summer campaigns there for the last seven years, the enemy's power was growing and his position was strengthening. He [the enemy] despatched raids into the border territories, taking prisoners and killing people. 'Abbas b. Nasih heard a woman in the region of Guadalajara saying, "O Hakam, our succourer, you have let us perish and given us up and ignored us for other concerns, so that the enemy has become courageous as a lion against us!"

When 'Abbas came to see al-Hakam, he addressed a poem to him, calling for his help and mentioning the words of the woman who had cried for his assistance. 'Abbas informed him of the weakness and confused circumstances that prevailed on the frontier. Al-Hakam felt sorry for the Muslims and yearned

الحَكَمُ للمسلمين، وحمى لنصر الدين، وأمر بالاستعداد للجهاد، وخرج غازياً الى أرض الشرك؛ فأوغل فى بلادهم، وافتتح الحصون وهدم المنازل، وقتل كثيراً، وأسر كذلك، وقفل على الناحية التى كانت فيها المرأة، وأمر لأهل تلك الناحية بمال من الغنائم، يصلحون به أحوالهم ويفدون سباياهم؛ وخصَّ المرأة وآثرها، وأعطاهم عدداً من الأسرى عوناً. وأمر بضرب رقاب باقيهم، وقال لأهل تلك الناحية وللمرأة: «هل أغاثكم الحَكَمُ؟» قالوا: «شفا والله الصُّدُورَ، ونكى فى العدوِّ، وما غفل عنّا إذ بلغه أمْرُنا! فأغاثه الله وأعزّ نصره!»

ardently to help the faith to victory. He gave orders for the troops to be made ready, and set off on campaign towards the land of polytheism. He penetrated deeply into their territory, captured strongholds, destroyed settlements, killing many people and likewise taking captives. He came to the region in which that woman lived and ordered the inhabitants to be given money from the spoils of war, with which they could make good their affairs and ransom their prisoners. The woman was given special and preferential treatment. [Al-Hakam] gave them a number of the prisoners of war to assist them, and ordered the rest to be executed. He said to the inhabitants of the region and to the woman, "Has al-Hakam come to your help?" They said, "by God, he has restored [our] hearts and harmed the enemy; when he heard of our circumstances he did not neglect us. May God come to his help and cherish his support!"

79. Muslims celebrate Christian festivals (mid 9th century)

Incidental light is cast on the position of the Christians during the Umayyad amirate, and on their continuing freedom to practise their own religion, by the evidence that Christian religious festivals were celebrated by Spanish Muslims (see also text 98).

The text presented here is taken from the collection of legal judgements, called Kitab al-mi'yar al-mu'rib, *by the late 15th-century author, al-Wansharishi (d. 914/1508), a native of Tlemcen who worked in Fez. The text comes from the Rabat edition of 1981, XI, pp.150-52. For a study of al-Wansharishi's voluminous work, see E. Amar, "Consultations juridiques des faqihs du Maghreb", in* Archives Marocaines, *12 (1908) and 13 (1909), and the paper by H.R. Idris, "Les tributaires en occident musulman médiéval d'après le "Mi'yar" d'al-Wanšarīšī",* Mélanges d'Islamologie, *ed. P. Salmon (Leiden, 1974). The question of Christian festivals is considered by Fernando de la Granja, "Fiestas cristianas en al-Andalus",* Al-Andalus, *34 (1969), 1–53 and 35 (1970), 119–42, where al-Wansharishi's text is also to be found, together with a Spanish translation (pp.133–38).*

The jurist questioned on the legality of Muslims celebrating Christian festivals, Abu'l-Asbagh, has not been identified with certainty. A marginal note gives his name as Musa b. Muhammad al-Tutili. Ibn Bashkuwal, Kitab al-sila (Cairo, 1966, 2 vols), p. 434, gives a biography of a certain Abu'l-Asbagh Isa b. Muhammad of Cordova, who died in Rajab 402/February 1102. His identity is not, however, vital, for he cites in his answer the opinion of Yahya b. Yahya al-Laithi, the well-known jurist of Berber origin, who plotted against the Umayyad amir al-Hakam I (796–822) and yet retained a position of influence over his successor, 'Abd al-Rahman II (822–52). Yahya was instrumental in establishing Maliki law as the official legal school in al-Andalus, before his death in 234/849. 'Uthman b. 'Isa b. Kinana was a disciple of Malik and died in Medina in about 185/901. Reference is also made to Malik b. Anas himself, the founder of this school of law (d. 795).

The passage therefore concerns the first half of the 9th century, during the period when Malikism, with its rigorous and rather conservative attitudes, was spreading in

الإحتفال بفاتح السنة الميلادية

وسُئل أبو الأصبغ عيسى بن محمد التميلي عن ليلة ينير التي يسمونها الناس الميلاد ويجتهدون لها في الإستعداد، ويجعلونها كأحد الأعياد، ويتهادَون بينهم صنوف الأطعمة وأنواع التحف والطرف المثوية لوجه الصلة، ويتركُ الرجالُ والنساء أعمـالهم صبيحتها تعظيماً لليوم، ويعدّونه رأس السنة.

أترى ذلك أكرمك اللّه بدعة محرّمة لايحل لمسلم أن يفعل ذلك، ولا أن يجيب أحداً من أقــاربه وأصــهــاره إلى شيء من ذلك الطعـام الذي أعـده لهـا؟ أم هـو مكروه ليس

Spain, and doubtless found much of which to disapprove. This was only shortly before the wave of martyrdom that washed over the Christians of Cordova between 850 and 859 (see text 10). It is one of the paradoxes of the mingling of two strong cultural and religious traditions at the popular level, that sectarian prejudices could be fanned into uproar just as easily as the two communities could rub shoulders in the common enjoyment of theoretically exclusive festivals and holidays.

A further example of this process of acculturation is provided by the so-called Calendar of Cordova, a work written in Arabic and Latin, which has survived as a sort of combination between an Arab astronomical almanac and Christian liturgical calendar. January 1st is correctly defined as the Feast of the Circumcision, not as Christmas Day; al-'Ansara is Midsummer's day (24 June), which was also celebrated as the Feast of St John the Baptist; see the edition by Ch. Pellat, Le Calendrier de Cordoue *(Leiden, 1961), esp. pp.26, 100, 183. This goes some way towards explaining the reference to Zakaria (Zacharias), the father of John the Baptist (Qur'an 19: 2–7), although the feast day celebrates his birth, not his martyrdom. These dates (1 January and 24 June) appear to have become associated in Spain with the ancient Persian festivals of Nauruz and Mihrajan, respectively the Spring and Autumn equinox, Nauruz being the Persian New Year's day. See Lévi-Provençal, III, pp.435–39 on these festivals, and Pérès,* La poésie, *pp.303–05, on their celebration in poetry. For some of the water rites associated with al-'Ansara, and to which an allusion is made here, see the article in the* Encyclopedia of Islam, *2nd ed., I, p.515.*

The ruling, which clearly considers women to be the main offenders in introducing these practices, goes on to enjoin them not to respect Saturdays and Sundays or to take holidays on the Christian festivals. Women should work on Fridays until the call to prayer, and then pray, and then return to the business of looking after their husbands and children. The only days off work should be the two main Muslim festivals of the 'id al-fitr (breaking the fast of Ramadan) and the 'id al-adha (the feast of the sacrifice at the end of the pilgrimage). For the legal terminology, see the Glossary, and also text 98.

The celebration of the beginning of the Christian year.

Abu'l-Asbagh 'Isa b. Muhammad al-Tamili was asked about the eve of January, which the people call the Birth [of Jesus], for which they work so hard over the preparations, and which they consider one of the great feast days. They give each other different foods, various presents and novelties exchanged by way of gifts, and men and women abandon their work that morning because of the importance they attach to the day. They consider it to be the first day of the year. [The text of the question is:]

"Do you think (may God be generous to you!) that it is a forbidden innovation, which a Muslim cannot be permitted to follow, and that he should not agree to [accept] from any of his relatives and in-laws any of the food that he prepared for [the celebration]? Is it disapproved of, without being

بالحرام الصراح؟ أم مستقل؟ وقد جاءت أحاديث مأثورة عن رسول الله صلى الله عليه وسلّم في المتشبهين من أمته بالنصارى في نيروزهم ومهرجانهم، وأنهم محشورون معهم يوم القيامة. وجاء عنه أيضاً أنه قال: «مَنْ تَشَبَّهَ بِقَوْمٍ فَهُوَ مِنْهُمْ». فبيّن لنا ماصح عندك في ذلك إن شاء اللّه.

فأجاب: قرأت كتابك هذا ووقفت على ماعنه سألت وكل ماذكرته في كتابك فمحرّمٌ فعلُه عند أهل العلم. وقد رويت الأحاديث التي ذكرتها من التشديد في ذلك ورويت أيضاً أن يحيى بن يحيى الليثي قال: لاتجوز الهدايا في الميلاد من نصراني ولامن مسلم، ولا إجابة الدعوة فيه، ولاستعداد له. وينبغي أن يجعل كسائر الأيام، ورفع فيه حديثاً إلى النبي صلى الله عليه وسلّم أنه قال يوماً لأصحابه: «إنَّكُمْ مُسْتَنْزَلُونَ بَيْنَ ظَهْرَانِيْ عَجَمٍ، فَمَنْ تَشَبَّهَ بِهِمْ في نِيْرُزْهِمْ وَمَهْرَجَانِهِمْ حُشِرَ مَعَهُمْ». قال يحيى وسألت عن ذلك ابن كنانة، وأخبرته حالنا في بلدنا فأنكر وعابه وقال: الذي يثبت عندنا في ذلك الكراهية، وكذلك سمعت مالكاً يقول: لقول رسول الله صلى الله عليه وسلم «مَنْ تَشَبَّهَ بِقَوْمٍ حُشِرَ مَعَهُمْ».

قال يحيى بن يحيى: وكذلك إجراء الخيل والمبارة [المباراة؟] في العنصرة، لايجوز ذلك وكذلك مايفعله النساء من وشئي بيوتهن يوم العنصرة، وذلك من فعل الجاهلية. وكذلك إخراج ثيابهم إلى النَّدَى بالليل ومكروه أيضاً تركهُنَّ العملَ في ذلك اليوم، وأن يجعل ورق الكرنب، والخضرة، واغتسالُهُنَّ بالماء ذلك اليوم لايحلُّ أصلاً إلا لحاجة من جنابة.

قال يحيى بن يحيى: ومن فعل ذلك فقد أشرك في دم زكريا وقد جاء عن النبي صلى اللّه عليه وسلّم أنه قال: «مَنْ كَثَّرَ سَوَادَ قَوْمٍ فَهُوَ مِنْهُمْ». ومن رضي عملاً كان شريك من عمله، هذا فيمن رضي ولم يعمله فكيف من عمله وسنَّة سنة. والله نسأله التوفيق.

unambiguously forbidden? Or is it absolutely [forbidden]? There are traditions handed down from the Prophet of God (may God bless him and grant him salvation!) concerning those of his community who imitated the Christians in their [celebration] of Nauruz and Mihrajan, to the effect that they would be mustered with the Christians on the Day of Judgement. It is also reported that he said, "Whoever imitates a people, is one of them." So explain to us – may God be generous to you – what you consider correct in this matter, if God wills."

He answered: I have read this letter of yours and have understood what you are asking about. It is forbidden to do everything that you have mentioned in your letter, according to the 'ulama. I have cited the traditions that you mentioned to emphasize that, and I have also cited Yahya b. Yahya al-Laithi, who said, [Receiving] presents at Christmas from a Christian or from a Muslim is not allowed, neither is accepting invitations on that day, nor is making preparations for it. It should be regarded as the same as any other day. He produced a *hadith* on this subject going back to the Prophet (may God bless him and grant him salvation), who one day said to his Companions, "You will become settled amongst the non-Arabs; whoever imitates them in their [celebration] of Nauruz and Mihrajan will be mustered with them." Yahya also said, I asked Ibn Kinana about that, and informed him about the situation in our country, and he disapproved and denounced it. He said, Our firm opinion about that, is that it is *makruh* (repugnant). Similarly, I have heard Malik say, In the words of the Prophet, may God bless him and grant him salvation, "Whoever imitates a people, will be mustered with them."

Yahya b. Yahya said, It is similar to racing horses and holding tournaments on al-'Ansara (Midsummer's Day); that is not permitted, likewise what women do to decorate their houses on Midsummer's Day. That is an act of the period of pre-Islamic ignorance, as is the way they take out their clothes at night to be soaked by the dew. Abandoning their work on that day is also disapproved of, as is preparing cabbage leaves and greens [i.e. vegetarian food]. That women should wash themselves in water on that day is also absolutely forbidden, unless it is for [normal reasons such as] a ritual impurity.

Yahya b. Yahya said, Whoever does this has shared in [spilling] the blood of Zakaria (Zacharias). It is related that the Prophet, may God bless him and grant him salvation, said, "Whoever multiplies the number of a people is one of them." Whoever is content with an act is a partner of the person who did it. If this is so for someone who approved but did not perform an action, what about the person who did it and made it his custom?! We ask God for success.

80. A Muslim renegade (early 10th century)

The most serious expression of the loss of authority of the Umayyad amirate in Cordova was the revolt of the muwallad leader, Ibn Hafsun, in southern Spain. The revolt started in 265/879, and was not finally crushed until the fall of the rebel stronghold, Bobastro, in 315/928. The population of the south was very largely made up of Berbers and muwallads, and there must have been many Christians too; their presence in the region continued at least until the mid 12th century (see text 100). Ibn Hafsun's decision to embrace Christianity signifies from where he expected to derive his support, but it had the effect of alienating Muslim adherents. Ibn Hafsun, who adopted the new name of Samuel, died in 305/917, bloodied but unbowed, and the revolt was carried on by his sons. Only after their defeat and the fall of Bobastro did 'Abd al-

(a)

فيها أظهر اللعين عمرين حفصون النصرانية وباطن العجم نصرى الذمة
واستخلصهم بالكلمة وأيدهم وفضلهم وتعصب على المسلمين وأساء الظن بهم. فنابذه
عند ذلك عوسجة بن الخليع التاكرني ظهيره وانحرف عنه وأظهر الميل إلى الطاعة وانتبذ
إلى حصن قنيط فصار حربا لابن حفصون والياً عليه. وخرج عليه أيضا يحيى بن أنتلة
صاحبه الأثير عنده في جماعة من المسلمين فتمرس منه. فانكشف للناس الآن ردته
ورأوا فرضاً عليهم حربه واطردت مغازي السلطان عليه وعلى أشياعه صوائف وشواتي
على يدي قائده أحمد بن محمد بن أبي عبدة. فجرت له وعليه معه أمور طويلة.

(b)

وكان طريق الناصر لدين الله إليها على أسجه إلى مدينة أشونة. فاحتلّ بمدينة
بَبَشْتَر يومَ الأحد لعشر بَقِينَ من المُحرّم منها، فدَخَل المدينة وجال في أقطارها، وعايَن
من شَرَفها وحَصانتها ، وعلُوِّ مُرْتَقاها وانْقطاع جَبَلها من جميع جِهاتها ما أيْقَن معه ألا
نظيرَ لها بأرض الأندلس حَصانة ومَنَعة واتُّساع قَراره واجْتِماع مَنافع وإراضة بَسيطه،

Rahman (III) consider himself sufficiently in control of al-Andalus to arrogate the title Caliph, with the name al-Nasir li-Din Allah, thus inaugurating a new and more glorious phase of Umayyad rule in Spain. For a full account of this whole episode, see Lévi-Provençal, I, pp.300 ff, 368 ff, and II, pp.6-22.
  Both passages are taken from Ibn Hayyan's chronicle, al-Muqtabis: *(a) ed. Melchor M. Antuña (Paris, 1937), p.128; (b) ed. P. Chalmeta et al. (Madrid, 1979), pp.215-17, from the annal for 316/928.* The poet mentioned in this piece was said to have been responsible for introducing the new poetic form of the *muwashshahat. The Threshold (or Barrage) Gate in Cordova opened onto the Rasif, the esplanade that ran along the right bank of the Guadalquivir downstream of the bridge, a popular place for the public exposure of rebels' corpses, cf. Lévi-Provençal, I, pp.260-61.*

(a)

In the year 286 (began 17 January 899) the accursed 'Umar b. Hafsun openly professed Christianity, the non-Arab (*'ajam*) having inwardly confided in the Christian *dhimmis*. He favoured them with his words, supported them and preferred them. He became fanatical against the Muslims and formed an evil opinion of them. Thereupon, his partisan 'Ausaja b. Khali' from Takoronna opposed him and turned away from him, and instead showed an inclination to return to obedience [to Cordova]. He withdrew to the castle of Qanit (Cañete la Real) and took it over, and began to fight Ibn Hafsun. Yahya b. Antala (Anatole), his favourite companion, also declared against him together with a large number of Muslims and was at odds with him. Once his apostasy was out in the open, the people realized it was a religious obligation to fight against him. The sultan's campaigns against him and his adherents continued uninterruptedly with raids in the summer and the winter under the command of his general, Ahmad b. Muhammad b. Abi 'Abda. Long drawn-out events happened both for and against him [in Ahmad's dealings] with him.

(b)

Al-Nasir li-Din Allah's route there was through Ecija to Madinat Ushuna (Osuna). He alighted in Bubashtru (Bobastro) on Sunday 20 Muharram [316] (Saturday 15 March 928). He entered the town and wandered through its districts. He inspected its elevation, its impregnability, the height of its ascents and the inaccessibility of its mountain [location] from every side, whereby he became certain that it had no peer in the land of al-Andalus for impregnability, strength, the expanse of its base, the combination of resources and the wide

فـأكثـر حَمْد الله تعالى على مـا أُتيح له منها ويسَّر له فيها، والتَزَم الصَّوْم أيّام مُقامـه وأنعم تَصفُّح آثار الطّواغيت الذين اقتَفَوها، ماحياً آثارها، طامساً أعْلامها، ومشى إلى مَسْجدها الأقْدَم المهجور منهم، فصلّى فيه، وأمَر أن تُوصَل فيه الصَّلَوات المفروضة التي كانت ممنوعة منه.

وكشَف الله من غَيْب المُلْحِد عُمَر بن حَفْصُون، مُتَبوِّئ هذه القَلعة لضلاله، وأبان من تَذَبْذُبه بَعْد إظهار الإسلام، وتَشبُّثه بالنصرانيّة والتباس أمْره على مَرّ الأيّام، مـا حَمَله على نَبْش صداه من مَرْمَسه واستثارة رِمّته على قُرْب عَهْده، فانكَشَفَت دفنة جُثّته الخبيثة عن سُنّة مَدْفوني النّصارى غَيْر شكّ، لأنّه أُصيب مُلْقى على ظَهْره، مُستقبلاً وَجْهَ المَشرِق بوَجْهه، موضوعًا ذراعه على صَدْره، كَما يتَدافَن النّصارى، عاينه على تلك الهَيْئـة الخَلْق من أهل العَسكَر وغَيرهم، وشَهد بهَلاك المُشرِك على دين النّصرانيّة لا مَحالةً، فهَتَك الله بذلك سِتْره، وفَضَح شِرْكه.

وأمَر الناصِر لدين الله باستثارة صداه الخبيث من مَلْحَده، وبحَمْل أوصـاله الخبيثة النّجسة إلى باب السُدّة بقُرْطُبة، ورفعه هُنالك في أعلى الجُذوع المُنيفة، مُعتَبِرًا لعُيـون النّاظرين إذ لاحَتْ جَليّة أمْره عن ارتداده عن الإسلام الذي وُلِد عليه واعْتِقـاد النّصرانيّة، وأبانَتْ عن سُوء النّيّة، فنُفِّذَ ذلك، ورُفِع شِلو عُمَر الخبيث في أعلى جِذْع، واسِطًا مـابَيْن جِذْعَي ابنَيْه الصليبيَّيْن هُنالك قَبْلَه، حَكَم وسُلَيْمان، قد تَكَنَّفاه من جانبَيْه، وأناف جِذْعه عليهما، عظةً للنّاظرين وقُرّةً لقُلوب المُسلمين، فلم تَزَل جُنوعهم مُقيمة هُنالك ومالة قَصْد أعْيُن النّاظرين من وقت تَوافيهم عليها إلى سنة احدى وثلاثين وثلاث مائة، فإن مَدّ النّهْر المُوافي في تلك السنة طما، فذَهب بجُذُعهم.

وكان من عجيب الإتّفاق، في اجْتِماع عُمَر وابنَيْه، حَكَم وسُلَيْمان، في الصَّلْب على باب السُلطان، أن حقّق القَضاء من ذلك ما قد تَفاءَل به عليهم مُقدَّم بن مُعافَى الشاعر قَبْلَ ذلك بدَهْر طويل، وعُمَر في رَيْعان غِوايته وعُنْفوان شَرَّه، إذ يقول في مَدْح القائد

extent of its territories. He greatly praised Almighty God for what had been vouchsafed for him and facilitated for him there. He undertook a fast during the days of his stay, and pondered over the remains of the tyrants who had made it their capital, wiping out their traces and effacing the signs of them. He walked to its oldest mosque, abandoned by them, and prayed in it, and ordered that the obligatory prayers which had been forbidden there should be restored.

God revealed the secret of the heretic Ibn Hafsun, who had taken possession of this castle to [promote] his error, and [God] made manifest his vacillation after he had professed Islam, his attachment to Christianity, and the ambiguity of his dealings over the passage of days, which led [al-Nasir] to dig up his corpse from his grave and to remove his rotting remains [which had been buried only] a short time ago. The burial of his vile body was found to be according to the custom of Christian burials, beyond a doubt, because he was laid out on his back, lined up with his face pointing east and his arms folded on his chest, just as the Christians bury their dead. Many people in the army, and others, observed him in this position, and all the jurists who were accompanying al-Nasir li-Din Allah on this expedition witnessed this. They were all convinced that the polytheist ['Umar b. Hafsun] had died in the Christian faith, without question. God thereby ripped aside his veil and disclosed his polytheism.

Al-Nasir li-Din Allah ordered his vile corpse to be brought out of its burial place, and his filthy and impure limbs to be carried to the Threshold (or Barrage) Gate in Cordova, and hung up there on the highest of tall stakes, as an example for the eyes of the beholders. For the matter of his apostasy from Islam, into which he had been born, and his adherence to the Christian faith, were made clear and the evil of his intentions was plain. This [order] was carried out. 'Umar's vile remains were raised on top of a stake, in between the stakes of his two sons who had been crucified there before him, Hakam and Sulaiman. They surrounded him on both sides, but his stake was higher than theirs. This was a warning for the beholders, and a cause of joy in the heart of the Muslims. Their stakes remained standing there, in the full gaze of those who looked on, from the time they were raised up until the year 331 (began 15 September 942). The rise of the river that year caused a great flood, which carried the stakes away.

One extraordinary thing about the crucifixion of 'Umar and his two sons Hakam and Sulaiman, all together at the gate of the sultan's [palace], was that it fulfilled a prophecy about them made by the poet Muqaddam b. Mu'afa a long time beforehand, when 'Umar was at the height of his error and in the bloom of his evil. He [Muqaddam] wrote a poem in praise of the general Ahmad b.

أحمد بن محمّد بن أبي عَبْدة، وهو مُنازِل لابن حَفْصون بِبَلَدة، في شِعر له، أوّله (وافِر):

حَلَلْتَ بِبَلْدةٍ في عَسْكَرَيْنِ   مُقِيـــــــمًا لِلْعَدُوّ قِيامَتَيْنِ

كَأنّي بِابْنِ حَفْصُونٍ وَشِيكًا   عَلى جَرْداءَ بَيْنَ دِعامَتَيْنِ

وَقَدْ أضْحـــــى خُتَيْنِصاهُ مِنْهُ   عَلى مَتْنِ الرُّصيفِ بِجانِبَيْنِ

وأُقيمَت الدَّعْوة للناصر لدين الله بجامِع بُبِشْتَر المُعَطَّل، واتّصلَت فيه الصَّلَوات والخُطَب، وعُمِرَتْ فيها المَساجِد المقفرة، وهُدِمَتْ منها الكنائس المَعْمورة، وقد كان حُسْن عِمارة هذه الكنائس واتِّصالها بِقَصْر اللعين عُمَر، وإقفار المَساجِد بها واستيلاء الدُّور عليها ووَحْشتها مِمّن يُعمِّرها مِن أقْوى الأدِلّة على رِدّة اللعين عُمَر وأقْطَعها بكُفْره.

Muhammad b. Abi 'Abda, who was besieging Ibn Hafsun in Balda (Belda), which begins:

> You stopped at Belda at the head of two armies, setting up a double overthrow for the enemy;

> It is as though I will soon see Ibn Hafsun on a smooth pole between two pillars.

> His two piglet [sons] already on display beside him in the middle of the Rasif.

Prayers were held for al-Nasir li-Din Allah in the Friday mosque of Bobastro, which had been shut down; prayers and sermons continued uninterruptedly. The neglected mosques were restored and the flourishing churches were destroyed. The fine repair of these churches, and their connection to the palace of the accursed 'Umar, as well as the impoverishment of the mosques and their lapse into oblivion, and their abandonment by those who might have kept them in good condition, were [all] among the strongest proofs of the apostasy of the accursed 'Umar and categorical evidence of his unbelief.

81. The Christians in Cordova (early 10th century)

As seen in the previous selection, the early years of ‘Abd al-Rahman III (912-61) were dominated by revolts in the neo-Muslim, muwallad population, particularly in the south. The extracts that make up this selection date from the last years of the resistance of Hafs b. ‘Umar b. Hafsun, which gives a particular point to the hajib's evident desire in text (a) not to alienate the Christian leaders of the area. It is not entirely clear whether these men had been involved in the recent rebellions, or whether their claims rested on their capitulation at the time of the original conquest, on terms (sulh) that were doubtless similar to those negotiated in the case of Theodemir of Murcia (see text 74), and which allowed them considerable religious freedom. Either way, these ‘ajamis had their own rights and the government in Cordova recognized the need to tread warily. The conflict of rights arises here because it was illegal under Muslim law for a free Muslim woman to be held against her will by a Christian. Badr b. Ahmad was the chief minister (hajib or chamberlain) to the amir ‘Abd-Allah (888-912) and continued to serve his successor, ‘Abd al-Rahman III, until his death in 309/921.

(a)

أخبرني من أثق به من أهل العلم قال: كان بقرطبة رجل أعجمي ممن استنزل من
الحصون المخالفة، وكانت له امرأة حرة مسلمة فاستجارت بالقاضي أسلم بن عبدالعزيز
فأجارها وبدأ بالنظر في أمرها. وكان في ذلك الوقت الحاجب بدر بن أحمد يحل من
أمير المؤمنين رحمه الله محلا لطيفا فلم ينشب القاضي أسلم. وأتاه يعلى عن الحاجب
بدر فقال له: «الحاجب يقرأ عليك السلام ويقول لك: إن هؤلاء العجم إنما استنزلناهم
بالعهد، ولا يحل الحقد بهم وأنت أعلم بما يجب من الوفاء بالعهود فدع بين فلان
العجمي وبين الأمة التي في يديه». فقال أسلم ليعلى: «الحاجب أرسلك بهذا؟» قال:
«نعم».

قال: «فأخبره عني الأيمان كلها لازمه لي، لا نظرت بين إثنين حتى أنفذ على
العجمي ما يجب عليه من الحق في هذه الحرة المسلمة التي في يديه».

فذهب عنه يعلى ثم رجع إليه فقال: «الحاجب يقرأ عليك السلام ويقول إني لا
أعترضك في الحق ولا أستحل سؤال ذلك منك وإنما أسألك التثبت في ما يجب من حق
هؤلاء المعاهدين فقد علمت ما يجب من رعايتهم وأنت أعلم بالواجب».

The first two passages are taken from the biography of Aslam b. 'Abd al-'Aziz given by al-Khushani (d. 361/971), Qudat Qurtuba *(Cairo, 1966), from pp.106-09. Aslam was chief qadi in Cordova from 300 to 309/913-22, and again from 312 to 314/924-26, early in the reign of 'Abd al-Rahman III; he died aged 60, in 929.*

The second and third passages illustrate a persisting religious mentality that harked back to the desire for martyrdom witnessed in the middle of previous century (see text 70). In addition to the references given by Smith, there is a full treatment of the martyrs of Cordova in Norman Daniel, The Arabs and Mediaeval Europe *(London, 1975), chapter 2. It is not entirely clear whether the text is referring to the teachings of Jesus, or to his example of sacrificing himself for others. The third passage is taken from al-Wansharishi (for which see above, text 79), II, p. 344. The most notable of the members of the council of Cordova whose opinion is cited in text (c), Muhammad b. 'Umar b. Lubaba, lived from 225 to 314/839-926.*

(a)

A scholar in whom I have confidence told me that there was in Cordova one of those non-Arabs ('*ajami*) who had been made to surrender the rebel strongholds. He had a free Muslim woman, who sought refuge with the qadi Aslam b. 'Abd al-'Aziz. He allowed her suit and began to investigate her case. At that time the hajib, Badr b. Ahmad, enjoyed the high esteem of the Amir al-Mu'minin ['Abd al-Rahman III], whereas Qadi Aslam was not secure [in his position]. Ya'la came to him on behalf of the hajib and said, "The hajib sends you greetings and says to you, We have only secured the surrender of these '*ajamis* by agreement [not by force], and it is not right [to stir up] resentment in them. You know better than anyone about the need for honouring agreements. So put aside this case between such and such an '*ajami* and the woman who is in his hands." Aslam said to Ya'la, "The hajib sent you with this message?", to which he replied, "Yes."

"Then tell him from me", said the qadi, "that all oaths are binding on me; I will not judge between any two parties until I have enforced on the '*ajami* what is legally required of him in respect of this free Muslim woman who is in his hands."

Ya'la left him and then returned to say, "The hajib sends you greetings and says, I am not opposing you on a matter of law nor regarding it as legitimate to question you about it, only I am asking you to consider carefully the rights of these people who have negotiated agreements. You know how they have to be taken into consideration, and understand best what is necessary".

(b)

وسمعت من يحكى أنه جاء رجل من النصارى مستقتلا لنفسه فوبّخه أسلم وقال: «ويلك من أغراك بنفسك أن تقتلها بلا ذنب»، فبلغ من سخف النصرانى وجهله إلى أن انتحل له فضيلة لم يقرا لمثلها لعيسى بن مريم صلى الله على محمد وعليه، فقال للقاضى: «وتتوهم إذا قتلتنى أنى أنا المقتول؟» فقال له القاضى: «ومن المقتول» فقال له: «شبهى يلقى على جسد من الأجساد فتقتله وأما أنا فأرفع فى تلك الساعة إلى السماء».

فقال له أسلم: «إن الذى تدعيه من ذلك غائبا عنا والذى يخبرك به من تكذيبك غائب عنك، ولكن ثم وجه يظهر صدقه لنا ولك». فقال له النصرانى: «وما هو؟» فالتفت أسلم القاضى إلى الأعوان ثم قال: «هاتوا السوط»، ثم أمر بتجريد النصرانى فجرد، ثم أمر بضربه فلما أخذته السياط جعل يقلق ويصيح فقال له أسلم: «فى ظهر من تقع هذه السياط؟» فقال: «فى ظهرى» قال له أسلم: «وكذلك السيف والله فى عنقك تقع فلا تتوهم غير ذلك».

(c)

من سبّ الله ورسوله قتل مسلماً كان أو كافراً

وسئل شيوخ الشورى بقرطبة عن نصرانية تسمت بدلجة زعمت انها نصرانية، فاستهلت بنفي الربوبية عن الله عز وجل، وقالت إن عيسى هو الله، تعالى الله عما قالت علواً كبيراً، وخرجت إلى أن قالت وإن محمداً كذب فيما ادعاه من النبوّة صلّى الله عليه وسلّم.

فأجابوا: ما قالت المرأة الملعونة المتسمّية بدلجة وما شُهد به عليها من نفيها الربوبية عن الله عز وجل وقولها إن عيسى هو الله، وتكنييها بنبوّة محمد صلّى الله عليه

(b)

I heard someone relate that one of the Christians came seeking his own death. Aslam rebuked him with the words: "Poor wretch, who incited you against your life, that you should want to take it when you have committed no crime?" It was due to the imbecility and ignorance of the Christian, who thought he would thereby acquire merit, [although] no such example could be found in [the teachings attributed to] Jesus son of Mary (may God bless Muhammad and him!). He said to the qadi, "Do you suppose that when you have killed me, I shall be dead?" The qadi replied, "Then who will be the dead man?" "My likeness will light upon any old body, and it is that that you will kill; as for me, I shall immediately rise up into the heavens."

Aslam said to him, "The one whom you call upon to do this is not here with us, and the one by whom you could be made fully aware of your error is not with you now. But there is a way to reveal the truth both to you and to myself." "What is that?", said the Christian. Qadi Aslam turned to his assistants and told them to bring the lash. Then he ordered the Christian to be stripped, which was done. He gave the signal for him to be whipped, and when the lashes overcame him, he began writhing about and shouting. Aslam said to him, "Whose back are these lashes falling on?" "On mine!", he said. "And so it would be with the sword falling upon your neck, by God", said Aslam, "so don't imagine otherwise."

(c)

Whoever blasphemes against God and his Messenger should be killed, whether he is a Muslim or an infidel.

The shaikhs of the Council in Cordova were questioned concerning a Christian woman called Dalja, who asserted that she was a Christian, and began to deny the divinity of Exalted and Glorious God. She said that Jesus was God – God is sublimely above what she said! She went so far as to say that Muhammad (may God bless him and grant him salvation!) lied in claiming the prophethood.

They replied: We consider that what this accursed woman named Dalja has said, and her denial of the divinity of Exalted and Glorious God, her statement that Jesus is God, and her lies about the prophethood of Muhammad (may God bless him and grant him salvation!), which have been testified against her, make

وسلّم، فالذي نراه قد وجب عليها القتلُ وتعجيلها إلى النار الحامية، عليها لعنة الله. قال بذلك عبيد الله بن يحيى، ومحمد بن لبابة، وسعد بن معاذ، وابن وليد، وأحمد بن يحيى.

her deserving of death, and of being brought quickly to the blazing fire, may God's curses be upon her! This was agreed by 'Ubaid-Allah b. Yahya, Muhammad b. Lubaba, Sa'd b. Mu'adh, Ibn Walid and Ahmad b. Yahya [members of the Council of Cordova].

82. The reverse at Simancas – Alhandega and the return of al-Nasir's Qur'an (327-30/939-41)

While 'Abd al-Rahman was consolidating his rule in the south, the kingdom of León was busy with its own internal difficulties, which were finally resolved by the accession of Ramiro II (931-50), son of Ordoño II. During the early tenth century, the Leonese began to resettle the Duero river basin, and to establish a line of fortifications from Zamora upstream towards San Estéban. Ramiro II undertook many successful raids along this frontier, and also enticed Muhammad b. Hashim, the ruler of Saragossa, to join him in alliance with Navarre against the caliph. This aberration was quickly dealt with by 'Abd al-Rahman, and in this selection we see Muhammad b. Hashim once more fighting, apparently wholeheartedly, alongside the caliphal army. The Simancas campaign, designed to knock out this active military centre and dismantle the Christian border fortresses, was undertaken as a reaction to the growing threat posed by the Leonese ruler. The serious reverse that followed marked the end of 'Abd al-Rahman III's personal involvement in campaigns against the Christians, which were henceforth left to his generals.

The text is taken from Ibn Hayyan, al-Muqtabis, V, ed. P. Chalmeta, F. Corriente et al. (Madrid, 1979), pp.432-36, 475-76. The relatively recent discovery of this portion of Ibn Hayyan's chronicle, which preserves the much earlier account of the historians 'Isa b. Ahmad al-Razi (d. 989) and his father Ahmad b. Muhammad (d. 955), allows a better understanding of these events than has previously been possible. The importance of Ibn Hayyan's material was recognized by Pedro Chalmeta, who has presented a detailed analysis in his articles, "Simancas y Alhandega", Hispania 133 (1976), 359-444 and

قـال عيـسى بن أحمـد [الرازيّ]: لمّا عَزَمَ الناصـر لدين الله على غَزْو أعْداء أهل جِلِّيقيّة، أهلكهم الله، بصـائفة هذه السنة، وقد فَرغ لهم ممّن كان يُسرّحِـهم من مِراسـه، من الناكثين على جَماعة المُسلمين الخالعين للطاعة، تَقدّم في الاستِعْداد لها قَبْلَ أوانها، فـجَبى وبالَغ في حَشْد أهل الاندلس، وتَخطّاهـم إلى أهل ولايتـه من أهل الحَضَر منهم، وقبائل البَرْبَر البادية، فبَثّ كُتُبه إليهم يَحُضّهم على الجهاد، ويَستَنْفِرهم له، ويُرغّبهم فيه، ويَضْرب لهم في التَراقي إلى الأندلس في المَسير معـه مَوْعِداً واسعـاً، لن يُخْلفه، ويُشدّد على عُمّاله في الاندلس في ابتِعـاثِ مَن قِبَلهم، وتَضـييق المَعاذير عليهم، والأحتفال في إزعاجهم، وضمّن كُتُبه النافذة إليهم فَصْلا، تَشاهَره الناس يَوْمئِذٍ وبَعْدَه، نصّـه: «وليَكُنْ حَشْدك حَشْرا لا حَشْداً».

Después de Simancas -Alhandega. Año 328/939-940", Hispania 144 (1980), 181-98.
)n the basis of this material, and particularly the uncertainly-located "Q.shtr.b",
halmeta seeks to identify the fateful "ditch" of Alhandega (or La Hoz) as one of the
eep gorges in the wild terrain between San Estéban de Gormaz and Atienza.

The chronology of the campaign, as reported by Ibn Hayyan, is not entirely
ccurate: he gives inconsistent dates for the period the caliph spent in Toledo, which
an be resolved by a minor textual amendment to the date given for his arrival.
hereafter, Ibn Hayyan's dates are internally consistent, though possibly not completely
orrect: he records a solar eclipse on Saturday 30 Ramadan (= Sunday 21 July 939),
hich actually took place on Friday 19 July (see Oppolzer's Canon of eclipses, *no.*
102). This passage provides a very circumstantial illustration of the workings of the
lamic calendar: as a result of the eclipse, the army did not see the full moon that
gnalled the start of the new month and the end of the month of fasting, so they fasted
nother day, whereas in Cordova, to the south, the moon was visible and Shawwal
arted on the Sunday (i.e. at sunset on Sunday 21 July). Throughout, there is one day's
isparity between the Christian and Muslim calendars; this is common, and it should be
emembered that the Muslim day starts at sunset. The duration of Muhammad's
nprisonment in León is calculated with total accuracy (according to the lunar
alendar).

The retrieval of al-Nasir's precious Qur'an makes a pleasant sequel to this episode;
e sources go to great pains to emphasize what a serious blow its loss was.

'Isa b. Ahmad (al-Razi) said: When al-Nasir li-Din Allah ('Abd al-Rahman I) determined to make the enemies of God, the northern Christians (Leonese) – ay God destroy them! – the target of his summer campaign this year 27/began 29 October 938), and was free to turn his attention to them and away om those whose treachery towards the Muslim community and renunciation of bedience had been allowing them [the Christians] to slip from his leash, he roceeded to make preparations for the campaign in good time. He raised taxes id went to great lengths to muster the people of al-Andalus, reaching out nong the people under his rule to both the settled inhabitants and the Berber bes in the countryside. He despatched letters to them, inciting them to idertake *jihad*, calling them to fight for him and arousing their ardour for ing so. He fixed a broad rendezvous for them to join his route on the advance to [Christian] Spain, but one which he would not change, and exerted pressure a his agents in al-Andalus to send those whom they had, to over-ride their cuses and make difficulties for them [until they went]. He included in his tters that went out to them a passage that became famous both then and

وتقدّم الناصر [لدين الله] بَعْدَه في عَساكر الصائفة، قاصداً سبيل جِهاده، حتى وافى بمَحَلَّته مدينة طُلَيطِلَة يومَ الخميس لتسع [لسبع] بَقِينَ من شَهْر رَمَضان، فأقام بها ستة أيّام. ثم رَحَل عنها يومَ الخميس لاثنيتَيْن بقِيتا منه، إلى حِصْن وَلَمش، ويومَ الجُمعة بَعْدَه إلى قَلْعة خليفة، وكَسَفَت الشَّمْس في ذلك النَّهار ضَحْوة، فعَمَّ كُسوفُها أجْمَعَها، وغَمَّ قُرْصها، إلّا طَرَفاً يسيراً من شِقّه، في رأي العَيْن. ويومَ الأحَد إلى مَحَلّة فَجّ حُمَيْد، واعتُدّ هذا النَّهار في العَسكر يَوْماً من شَهْر رَمَضان لإغماء اشتَمَل جميع الهلال عن المُرتقبين له، فأكمَلوا به عدّة شَهْرهم وأفطَروا يومَ الاثنَيْن بَعْدَه، وكُشِف هلال شَوّال لأهل قُرْطُبة وغَيْرهم، فأفطَروا يومَ الأحَد قَبْلَه.

واقتَحَم الناصر لدين الله بعَساكره أرضَ العَدُوّ، فجال فيها أيّاماً، من مَحَلّة إلى أخرى، مُتتبِّعاً لِما ألفاه لهم، مُدمِّراً لنِعَمهم، إلى أن احتَلّ على مدمه يومَ الخميس لخمس خَلَوْن من شَوّال منها، فأصابها خالية قد فَرّ أهلها عنها، وغادَروها مُتْرَعة بالنعَم والأقوات، فأتَهَب المُسلمون جميع ذلك كلّه، وجَمَعوا أيْديهم على إخرابها، فسُوّيَ أعْلاها بأسْفَلها، ووجَدوا في مَطاميرها عَدَداً من أسرى المُسلمين، فخلّصوهم. وأكبَّ المُسلمون عليها يومَيْن، ثُمّ انتَقَل عنها إلى حِصْن إشكر، فأُصيب خالياً فغرّبه المُسلمون، وانتَسَفوا مَعايش أهلها. ومنها إلى القَصرَيْن، فانتُسِف زُروعه، وغَيّر أعلامه، وطَمَس آثاره، ومنها إلى المَحَلّة على نَهْر جِيقة، ومنها إلى حِصْن بُرْتِيل عاصم، وذلك يومَ الجُمعة لثلاث عشرة خَلَتْ من شَوّال، وشَرَع المُسلمون في مُنازَلة أهلها.

وكان محمّد بن هاشم التُّجيبيّ، صاحب سَرَقُسْطة، قد تَقدّم بقطيع من الخَيْل، فأجاز نَهْر شَنْت ما نْكَش المعروف [ب] بِشُورْقة، وهو دون المدينة، فلاقى العَدُوّ وراء النَّهْر، وهم بجَمعهم في البَطحاء التي بَيْن مَدينتهم وشاطِئ نَهْرهم بِشُورْقة، واشتدّت الحَرب بَيْنه وبَيْنهم، فاستَظْهَر محمّد بن هاشم عليهم، وأخرَجهم من البَطحاء مقهورين،

afterwards, which read, "But your mustering is more like the Resurrection (*hashr*) than a mobilization (*hashd*)."

[...] Al-Nasir li-Din Allah set off after this [i.e. after the despatch of a diversionary force to the western frontier] at the head of the summer campaign, intending to fight his Holy War. He arrived at his encampment at Toledo on Thursday 21 Ramadan (12 July [actually a Friday]) and stayed there six [full] days, departing on Thursday 28 (19 July) for the castle of Wulmush (Olmos) and the next day, Friday, reaching Qal'at Khalifa (Calatalifa). Here, an eclipse of the sun occurred during the [following] morning [30 Ramadan/21 July]. It was a total eclipse in which the whole disc was obscured but for a small part to one side which one could see with one's own eyes. On Sunday [he went] to camp at Fajj Humaid (Puerto de Tablada) and spent this day in preparation with the army, as though it were still Ramadan, because of the darkness that had completely obscured the new moon from the gaze of those who were watching out for it. They thereby completed their month [of Ramadan] and broke their fast on the following Monday, [whereas] the new moon of Shawwal was visible to the people of Cordova and elsewhere, who [therefore] broke their fast on the Sunday.

Al-Nasir invaded enemy territory with his troops and for a few days roamed freely through it from one place to the next, following whatever [route] he could find that led to them and destroying their possessions, until on Thursday 5 Shawwal (Friday 26 July) he occupied Madmah (Olmedo ?), which was empty because its inhabitants had fled, leaving it full of their possessions and of provisions. The Muslims plundered the whole of this, and then set about destroying the place. They flattened it, and [in so doing] discovered in its underground storehouses a number of Muslim prisoners, whom they released. The Muslims broke their journey there for two days, then moved to Hisn Ishkar (Iscar), which they found empty. The Muslims wrecked it and destroyed the livelihoods of its inhabitants. Thence to al-Qasrain (Alcazarén), where they destroyed the crops, transformed its appearance and obliterated all traces of it. Then on to a halt on the river Jiqa (Cega), and so to Hisn Burtil 'Asim (Portillo 'Asim); that was on Friday 13 Shawwal (Saturday 3 August). The Muslims then began to take the field against their people.

Muhammad b. Hashim al-Tujibi, ruler of Saraqusta (Saragossa), had gone ahead with a detachment of cavalry and crossed the river Shant Mankish (Simancas), known as the Bushurqa (Pisuerga), below the town. He encountered the enemy on the other side; they had gathered on the level ground between their town and the Pisuerga river. There was fierce fighting between the two forces and Muhammad b. Hashim was victorious, driving them defeated from the

فـالتَجَئُوا إلى [قَصر] مدينتهم، واقتَحَم محمّد بن هاشم عليهم، فتَذامَروا على حَرْبه، وعَطفوا عليه وعلى مَن معه، فدارت بَينهم حَرْب صَعْبة، حتّى نُكِب محمّد بن هاشم عن فَرَسه، وتَرجّلَ فانْكَشف عنه مَن كان معه، ولم يَسْتقلّ إلى فَرَسه، وتَكاثَر أعداء الله عليه، ولم تتلاحَق الخيل به، فمَلَك أسيراً في يَوْم الثُلاثاء المذكور، فاشْتَدّ على السلطان وعلى المُسلمين أسْرُه وفَتّ في أعْضادهم.

وكَسَر العَسْكَر على باب شَنْت مانْكَش يَوْم الأربعاء بَعْدَه، ثُمّ صابَحهم الحَرْب يوم الخَميس لإحدى عشرة لَيْلة بقِيت من شَوّال، فجـالت بَيْن الفريقَين بأشْدّ مـا يَكُون وأصْعَب، ثُمّ ناجَزوا الحَرْب يَوْم الجُمْعة بَعْدَه، فصابَروا المُسلمين صَبْراً عظيماً إلى أن تَوجّهت عليهم كَسرة، ثُمّ كانت لهم كَرّة انحاز لها المُسلمون، فانْكَشفوا انْكِشافاً قبيحاً، نِيل فيه منهم مَنال مُمِضّ، وألجَاهم العَدُوّ في انْحيازهم إلى خَنْدق بعيد المَهْوَى، إليه تُنْسَب الوَقْعة، لم يَجِدوا عنه مَحِيداً فتَردّى فيه خَلْق، وداس بعضهم بعضاً، لكَثْرة الخَلْق، وفَيْض الجُموع، فدَخلَ بهم السلّطان مُضْطَراً، ونفَذ في أجْنَاده، وتَرَك سَواده بما فيه، فمَلَكه العَدُوّ، وآل الناصر [لدين الله] إلى كُفف من الجَمْع تَخَطّتهم الركَبة، فضَم كَشْفهم، واحْتَلّ بهم بأعْلى نَهر بشَنُورقة، وقد أقْصَر العَدُوّ عن اتْباعه، فاضْطَرب هُنالك يَوْمـه، مُوقِناً بتَمحيص الله المُسلمين، ثُمّ رَحل قافلاً، حتى خَرَج إلى مدينة الفَرَج المُسمّاة وادي الحِجارة، فأراح هُناك، ثُمّ تَقدّم إلى قُرْطُبة.

وأقام محمّد بن هاشم في الأسْر، بيَد رُذْمير بن أردُون الطاغية، قد شَدّ يداً به، وغالى في سَوْمه، والناصر لدين الله لا يأتَلي في السَعْي لافْتِكاكه، إلى أن تَهيّأ له ذلك بالبَذْل الرغيب والحِيَل المُرْهفة، فوافى إلى قُرْطُبة طليقاً يومَ الخميس لسِتّ خَلَوْن من صَفَر سنة ثلاثين وثلاث مائة، فكان من يَوْم أسْره إلى يوم دُخوله طليقـاً إلى قُرْطُبـة سنتان وثلاثة أشْهُر وثمانية عشر يوماً.

plain. They fled to the citadel of the town, where Muhammad b. Hashim led an assault against them. They urged themselves to fight him and turned against him and those who were with him. A tough fight ensued, until Muhammad b. Hashim was knocked off his horse. He got to his feet [but], left exposed by those with him, was unable to remount. The enemy pressed on him in large numbers and the cavalry did not catch up with him. He was taken prisoner that day, which was a Tuesday. His capture weighed heavily on the sultan and the Muslims, and sapped their strength.

On the next day, Wednesday, the army forced open the gate of Simancas and fighting [continued] on the Thursday morning, 19 Shawwal (Friday 9 August) involving both sides in the utmost efforts. The battle raged throughout the following Friday. The Christians withstood the Muslims with great fortitude until they were faced with the prospect of defeat. Then they launched a charge, at which the Muslims were overrun, and were disgracefully exposed, by which the Christians achieved their grievous objective: the enemy forced them to withdraw towards a very deep trench (*khandaq*), to which the name of the battle (Alhandega) refers. They [the Muslims] were unable to avoid it and a large number fell in. Some were trampled by others, thanks to the crush of people and the weight of the throng, into which the sultan was carried willy nilly. He fought his way through with his troops and abandoned his camp and what was in it, which the enemy seized. Al-Nasir li-Din Allah eventually came upon a troop of men who had been sent out as a raiding party; he collected these forces together and stopped with them above the river "Q.shtr.b". The enemy had already cut short their pursuit. He spent the whole day there in agitation, sure that God was putting the Muslims to the test. Then he rode home, setting out for Madinat al-Faraj which is called Wadi al-Hijara (Guadalajara), where he rested. Then he proceeded to Cordova.

Muhammad b. Hashim remained in captivity, in the hands of the tyrant Ramiro son of Ordoño. His hands were bound and the price demanded for him was excessive. Al-Nasir li-Din Allah did not fail in his efforts to ransom him, until that was made possible by heavy expenditure and burdensome expedients. He was delivered to Cordova, a free man, on Thursday 6 Safar 330 (31 October 941; a Sunday), two years, three months and eighteen days having elapsed since the day he was captured.

50

استعادة مُصحَف الناصر

وفي صَفَر منها صُرِف على الناصر لدين الله مُصحَفه الذي كان ضاع بجلّيقيّة في الهزيمة الخَنْدَقيّة، وكان مُجَزّأً على اثنَي عشر جُزْءاً، أنصاف أسداس، وله من نَفسه مكان مكين، اشتَدّ له قَلَقه وندَمـه على تَغريره به، في إدخـاله إلى دار الحَرْب، خلافـاً لسنّته، لم يَزَل مُستغفراً الله، خالقه، من تلك الحَوْبة، باذلاً في افتكاكه كُل رغبة، وكان قد رُدَّت عليه أكثر أجزائه دَفعاً، إلا قليلاً، أعيا على المُلتمسين لها بجلّيقيّة وجُدانها، فتضاعف وَجده بها، ومَضى على رأيه في البَحْث عنها والتَقصّي عليها والبَعثرة دُونَها بكل جهة، حتى عَثَر عليها الطاغية رُذمير في بعض زوايا جلّيقيّة، فأرسلها إلى الناصر لدين الله، فكَمِلت بها مَسَرّته، وصار عليه في افتكاك مُصحَفه هذا مال جسيم.

وذكَر أحمد بن محمّد الرازيّ أنّ الطاغية رُذمير بن أرذُون، أهدى هذا المُصحَف أجمَعه إلى الناصر لدين الله، فكَمِلت به مَسَرّته، في جُملة هَديّته التى هاداه بها أثَر انعقاد سِلْمه، ووَرَد عليه بهَديّته تلك رَسُوله فَتْح، المعروف بالحجرمله، وحريز، صاحبه من أهل سَمُّورة، في صَفَر المُورّخ به هذه السنة، ومع هَديّته تلك ثلاثون أسيراً من المُسلمين وألطاف كـثـيـرة، وخَصّ ابنه، ولي عَهْده، الحَكَم، ابن الناصـر لدين الله، بهَديّة أُخرى حَسَنة، عَظم سرور الناصر لدين الله بها.

كانت أثَر مـا أهداه إليه بما جَمَعه الله له من حِفْظ أجزاء هـذا المُصحَف، الذي كان يَخْشى الجَرْح فـيـه، إلى أن جَمَعه الله عليه، فكافـأ العِلْج رُذمير عن هَديّتـه هذه بضِعف قيمتها، جُزْلاً باستِنْقاذ كِتاب الله تعالى، وفَعَل ذلك ابنه الحَكَم، وصَرَف رَسُوله إليه بَعْد أن قَرَن به جَعْفَر بن يَحْيى بن مضم (؟)، للقاء العِلْج رُذمير بما أمَره به.

The recovery of al-Nasir's copy of the Qur'an (330/941)

In Safar this year (began 26 October 941) the copy of the Qur'an that was lost in Northern Spain in the defeat at Alhandega was delivered to al-Nasir li-Din Allah. It was divided into twelve parts, or six volumes of two parts each. It had a special place in his affections. He felt a strong concern for it and regretted having exposed it to danger by taking it with him into enemy territory (*dar al-harb*), contrary to his usual habit. He did not cease asking God his Creator for forgiveness for this offence, expending all his energy on ransoming it. Most of the volumes had been handed over to him, but for a small portion which those searching for it in Christian territory had been unable to find. His emotions towards the [missing portion] redoubled and he pursued his undertaking to search for it, enquiring after it and turning everything upside down for it in every region, until the tyrant Ramiro came across it in a corner [*zawiya* also means a religious cell] in Jilliqiyya. He sent it to al-Nasir li-Din Allah, thereby perfecting his happiness. He spent a vast fortune on retrieving this Qur'an of his.

Ahmad b. Muhammad al-Razi said that the tyrant Ramiro son of Ordoño presented the complete Qur'an to al-Nasir li-Din Allah, thereby completing his joy, as part of the presents which he gave him following the peace agreement [of the preceding year]. These presents were brought by his envoy, Fath, known as al-Hajramala (?) and his companion, Hariz (?) from Sammura (Zamora), in Safar this year. Accompanying this present [of the Qur'an] were thirty Muslim prisoners and many fine things. He [Ramiro] singled out [the caliph's] son and heir, al-Hakam b. al-Nasir li-Din Allah, with another splendid present, which caused al-Nasir li-Din Allah great pleasure. [...] The most precious present he gave him was the parts of the Qur'an that God had brought together safely for him, and which he had feared had become spoiled, so that the whole was reassembled. He paid the Christian Ramiro double its value in compensation for his gift, in consideration of the recovery of the Book of God Almighty; and so did his son al-Hakam. He then despatched his envoy back to him, together with Ja'far b. Yahya b. Mudm (?), who was to meet the Christian Ramiro as he had been ordered.

83. A description of Christian Spain (10th century)

*This passage is taken from the work of al-Bakri, al-Masalik wa'l-mamalik, ed. A.A.
el-Hajji (Beirut, 1968), pp.71-73, 80-81. The author was the son of the last independent
ruler of Saltes, before the town was swallowed up by the 'Abbadids of Seville in 1052.
Al-Bakri himself died in 487/1094, but his description of Christian Spain probably refers
to an earlier period. His source for the second part of this description, Ibrahim b.
Ya'qub al-Isra'ili al-Turtushi, was a Jew from Tortosa, who probably wrote down his
travels in the 960s, and presented them to the Caliph al-Hakam II (d.976), as suggested
by El-Hajji in his* Andalusian diplomatic relations, *esp. pp.228-37. Al-Bakri is
extensively quoted by later geographers, such as al-Himyari: see Lévi-Provençal, La
Péninsule Ibérique, pp.66, 249.*
*As noted earlier (see p.xv), the Muslim writers' use of the term "Jilliqiyya" refers to
the Christian north in general. From about the reign of Alfonso III of Asturias, at the*

قَسَّمَتْهُ الأوائل على أربعة أقسام: فالقِسْمُ الأولُ هو الذي [يلي] الغربَ وينحرف
الى الجَوْف، وساكنوه هم الجَلالِقَة وَمَوْضِعُهم جِلِّيقِيَّة. وكانوا حَوالَيْ مدينة بُرَاقَرَة التى
هي مُتوسِّطةُ الغرب.

ومدينةُ بُرَاقَرَة هي مدينةٌ أَوَّلِيَّةٌ من بُنْيانِ الروم وقواعدِهم، وتَوُرُ مملكتهم شبيهةٌ
من مدينة ماردة في إتقانِ بنيانِها وصِنْعَةِ أسوارِها، وهي اليوم مهدومةٌ الأكثر خالية،
هَدَمها المسلمون وأجْلَوْا أهلَها.

والقِسم الثاني: هو المُسَمَّى بـ «حَوْز أشْتُورِش»، وسُمِّيَ بذلك بوادٍ يقال له
أشترو، منه شُرْبُ جميعِ بلادِهم.

والقِسم الثالث: ماكان مِن جِلِّيقِيَّة بين الغَرب والقِبْلَة، ويُسَمَّى أهلُه البُرْتُقَالِش.

والقِسم الرابع: ما كان بين الشرق والقِبْلَة، ويُسَمَّى «قَشْتِيلَة»، وقَشْتِيلَة القُصْوى
وقَشْتِيلَة الدنيا. فالأدنى من حُصُونها: غَرْنُونُ والقُصَيْر وبُرْغُش وأمايَة.

قال إبراهيم: بَلَدُ الجِلِّيقِيِّين سهلٌ جميعُه، والغالبُ على أرضِهم الرملُ، وأكثرُ
قُوتِهم الدُّخْنُ والذُّرة ومُعَوَّلُهُم في الأشربِة على شَرابِ التُّفَّاح [والبُشْكَة]، وهو شَرابٌ

end of the ninth century, it signifies the territories of León and Castile, as here. The reference to the lack of washing highlights one of the more striking contrasts in the manners and outlook of the two rival communities in Spain. The dirtiness of the Christian crusaders was also noticed by the Muslims in the Holy Land, whereas the Christians viewed the Muslim baths as sinks of iniquity and dens of vice (a view not totally unjustified, in view of the events narrated in text 89, and a view seemingly shared by some Muslim religious scholars, as in text 98). Poetic celebrations of the delights of the baths in Spain are analysed by Pérès, pp.383-43. On this topic, see S.M. Imamuddin, pp.207-10, and J.F. Powers, "Frontier municipal baths and social interaction in thirteenth-century Spain", American Historical Review, *84 (1979), 649-67. See also text 58, for the end of the baths in Granada.*

Early authorities divided Jilliqiyya into four parts; the first part is that which lies to the west and faces to the north. Its inhabitants are the Galicians [Leonese] and their territory is Galicia [León]. They [are found] around the city of Braqara (Braga), which is in the middle west.

The city of Braga is one of the first cities founded by the Christians and [one of] their capitals. The localities in this country are like Mérida in the the skilful way in which they are built and in the construction of their walls. Nowadays it is ruined and mostly empty; the Muslims destroyed it and drove away its inhabitants.

The second division is the one called "the district of Ashturish" (Asturias), so-called because of the river there called Ashtru, which waters all their country.

The third division is the south and west of León, whose inhabitants are called the Burtuqalish (Portuguese).

The fourth division is to the south and east and is called Qashtilat al-quswa and Qashtilat al-dunya (Outer and Inner Castile). Its nearest castles [to Muslim territory] are Ghamun (Grañón), al-Qusair (Alcocero), Burghush (Burgos) and Amaya.

Ibrahim (al-Turtushi) said: The whole of Jilliqiyya is flat and most of the and is covered in sand. Their foodstuffs are mainly millet and sorghum and their normal drinks are apple cider and bushka, which is a drink made with flour

يُتَّخَذُ مِن الدقيق. وأهله أهل غَدْرٍ ودناءةِ أخـلاقٍ، لا يَتَنَظَّفـون ولا يَغْتَسِلُون في العـام إلاّ مَرّة أو مَرّتين بالماء البـارد، ولا يَغْسِلُون ثيـابهم مُنْذُ يَلْبَسُونهـا إلى أنْ تَنْقَطِعَ عليـهم، ويَزْعُمون إنّ الوَسَخَ الذي يعلوها من عَرَقهم تَنْعُم به أجسامُهم وتَصِحُّ أبدانُهم. وثيابُهم أضْيَقُ الثياب، وهي مُفَرّجَة يبدو من تَفاريجها أكثر أبدانهم. ولهم بأسٌ شديد، لا يرون الفرارَ عند اللقاء [في الحرب] ويَرَوْنَ الموتَ دونه.

(meal). The inhabitants are a treacherous people of depraved morals, who do not keep themselves clean and only wash once or twice a year in cold water. They do not wash their clothes once they have put them on until they fall to pieces on them, and assert that the filth that covers them thanks to their sweat is good for their bodies and keeps them healthy. Their clothes are very tight-fitting and have wide openings, through which most of their bodies show. They have great courage and do not contemplate flight when battle is joined, but rather consider death a lesser evil.

84. The dying regrets of Ibn Abi 'Amir al-Mansur (392/1002)

This review of the career of al-Mansur (Almanzor) touches on several aspects of his relations with the Christian powers not only in Spain but elsewhere, and includes some interesting observations on his border policies. Al-Mansur is perhaps most famous for his long sequence of devastating raids on Christian territory, over fifty summer and winter campaigns being credited to him. These expeditions not only brought back great booty to Cordova, but emphasized the power of the Umayyad caliphate and kept the northern Christians in a state of greater subjection than had been achieved at any time since the original conquests. Among his most famous exploits are the sack of Santiago de Compostela in 387/997 (see text 15), and his recovery of Barcelona in 375/985 (see above, p.24). Our historian is wrong in asserting that count Borrell (II) of Barcelona was killed in this campaign, since Borrell actually died in 992, having regained Barcelona within two years.

The text also refers to embassies from the Byzantine Emperor (Basil II, 976-1025) and the Holy Roman Emperor (Otto III, 996-1002). Such missions, the last of which was in 1006, had been a feature of the reigns of 'Abd al-Rahman III and his successor, al-Hakam II (d. 976); see for example, text 14, and the work of El-Hajji. Allusion is made to al-Mansur's building projects in Cordova, where, apart from his own palace complex at Madinat al-Zahira, the final phase of the expansion of the Great Mosque was started in 377/988. For the latter project, he used Christian captives as labourers, as alluded to here; see Lévi-Provençal, III, p. 394.

Al-Mansur came to power in the reign of Hisham II, whom he quickly dominated; our author remarks that Ibn Abi 'Amir left Hisham only his name in the Friday prayers and on the coinage, all other powers being arrogated to himself. Kauthar was a Slav imported from eastern Europe, one of the two groups (the others being Berbers) whom al-Mansur used to underpin his own authority, both in the administration and the army,

ثم سمت به همته وشجاعته إلى قود العساكر التى هى فى طاعته، وغزو بلاد

الروم، إلى أن ذلل منها كل صعب غير مروم، ففتح الله على يديه، وفتح برجلونه ملكها

بريل، وسبى أهلها وخربها وغنم منها غنائم كثيرة من عبيد وخدم ومال وسلاح وثياب

وبهائم، وآب إلى قرطبة سالماً غانماً ظافراً. ثم غزا عدة غزوات، وفتك فى الروم جملة

فتكات حتى دانت له أقاصى بلاد الشرك، ودخلت له بالسلم تحت الملك إلى أن وافاه

رسول صاحب القسطنطينية العظمى، ورسول صاحب رومة وقشتالة بهدايا وألطاف،

وغرائب اتحاف، وكلهم يخطب أمانه ويطلب أن يحاشى من معارته مكانه.

وأقام على هذه الحال مع هشام ثمانياً وعشرين سنة، فلما حضرته الوفاة بكى

فقال له حاجبه كوثر الفتى «مم تبكى يا مولاى؟ لا بكت عيناك». فقال «مما جنيت على

hereby excluding native Andalusians from the sources of power. What is unusual about the passage is the suggestion that al-Mansur pursued a policy of settlement in the border zones between the Muslims and the Christian north, whereas his raids are normally seen to have undone the repopulation of León that had taken place in the 9th and early 10th centuries and to have left the whole of Extremadura devastated. However, al-Mansur did install a Muslim population in Zamora on his campaign of 389/999, and leave a strong garrison there. In fact, a policy of settling population should have been more successful, as demonstrated by Ferdinand I and Alfonso VI of León and Castile, whose resettlement of the trans-Duero region and of the districts north of Toledo helped to bring these areas more permanently under Christian control.

The text is taken from Ibn Kardabus, Kitab al-iktifa fi akhbar al-khulafa, ed. A.M. al-Abbadi, Revista del Instituto Egipcio de Estudios Islámicos, 13 (1966), pp.63-65. The author (d. around 570/1174) is benefitting from a certain amount of hindsight – it is most unlikely that a Christian resurgence was really considered a possibility at the death of al-Mansur, though events then moved with remarkable speed, and the dying hajib might have found other aspects of his policies to blame for the hollow centre of the seemingly mighty Muslim state. Al-Mansur's anxieties about the capability of his sons is not, however, entirely misplaced; the first, 'Abd al-Malik al-Muzaffar (1002-08) successfully continued his father's policies, but the folly of the second, 'Abd al-Rahman "Sanchol" (so-called by his Christian mother), precipitated the fall not only of the Amirids but also of the Umayyad caliphate, thereby presenting the Christians with a golden opportunity to intervene (see text 85). For al-Mansur's political testament to his sons, see Ibn al-Khatib, Kitab a'mal al-a'lam, ed. E. Lévi-Provençal (Beirut, 1956), pp.81-82.

Then his ambition and courage led him to take command of the army, which was obedient to him, and he raided the Christian territories and surmounted every unattainable objective there. God conquered at his hands. He took Barjiluna (Barcelona) and killed its ruler, Boryel (Borrell II), captured its inhabitants and destroyed it. He took a great haul of plunder, [consisting of] slaves, servants, wealth, weapons, clothing and livestock, and returned safely and in triumph to Cordova, weighed down with booty. Thereafter he made numerous raids and caused total devastation in Christian territory, until the farthest parts of the realms of polytheism yielded to him, and came in peace under his dominion. Even ambassadors from the ruler of Constantinople the Great (Basil II), and of Rome (the Holy Roman Emperor, Otto III), as well as from Castile, came into his presence, with marvellous gifts, all of them proposing peace with him and seeking to turn away his wrath from their lands.

He carried on like this for 28 years under Hisham. When he was on the point of death he began to cry. His hajib, the slave Kauthar, said to him, "Why are you crying, master – you never cry?" [Al-Mansur] said, "Because of the evil I have

المسلمين، فلو قتلونى وحرقونى ما انتصفوا منى». فقال له «وكيف ذلك؟ وأنت أعززت الإسلام وفتحت البلاد وأذللت الكفر وجعلت النصارى ينقلون التراب من أقصى بلاد الروم إلى قرطبة حيث بنيت بها جامعها».

فقال له: «لمَّا فتحتُ بلاد الروم ومعاقلهم عمرتها بالأقوات من كل مكان وسجنتها بها حتى عادت فى غاية الإمكان، ووصلتها ببلاد المسلمين وحصنتها غاية التحصين فاتصلت العمارة. وهأنا هالك وليس فى بنى من يخلفنى، وسيشتغلون باللهو والطرب والشرب، فيجىء العدو فيجد بلاداً عامرة وأقواتاً حاضرة فيتقوى بها على محاصرتها، ويستعين بوجدانها على منازلتها فلا يزال يتغلبها شيئاً فشيئاً، ويطويها طياً فطياً حتى يملك أكثر هذه الجزيرة، ولا يترك فيها إلا معاقل يسيرة. فلو ألهمنى الله إلى تخريب ما تغلبت عليه وإخلاء ما تملكت، وجعلت بين بلاد المسلمين وبين بلاد الروم، مسيرة عشرة أيام فيافياً وقفاراً، لا يزالون لو راموا سلوكها حيارى، فلا يصلون إلى بلاد الاسلام، إلا بمشقة وكثرة الزاد وصعوبة المرام».

فقال له الحاجب: «أنت إلى الراحة إن شاء الله أقرب، فتأمر بهذا الذى رأيت». فقال له «هيهات! حال الجريض دون القريض، والله لو استرحت، وأمرت بما ذكرت، لقال الناس: مرض ابن أبى عامر فأورثه مرضه جنوناً ومساً تمكن من دماغه، فخرب بلاد المسلمين وأجلاهم وأقفرها».

nflicted on the Muslims – if they killed and burned me, they would only be aking just vengeance on me." [Kauthar] replied, "How so? – you have glorified slam and conquered the country, humbled unbelief and made the Christians arry earth from the furthest Christian territories to Cordova, while you have uilt its great mosque there."

[Al-Mansur] answered, "When I conquered the Christian lands and their trongholds, I brought in provisions from all sides and kept them there until they vere restored to a state of great strength, and rejoined them to Muslim territory, ortifying them to the utmost degree and linking them to surrounding ettlements. But now here I am dying, and none of my sons can succeed me, for ney are preoccupied with wine, women and song. The enemy will come and ind a flourishing, well-provisioned and populous land; he will be provided with ne resources to blockade it and will be helped by its riches when attacking it. Ie will continue to overcome it piece by piece and envelop it in his folds, until e possesses most of this Peninsula and only a few strongholds remain [in Muslim hands]. If only God had inspired me to destroy what I conquered and to eave it empty, and to create a zone of deserts and wastes ten days' journey wide etween Muslim and Christian territory, they would always have been at a loss vhen trying to find ways through it, and they would only have entered the Muslim realms with difficulty, by bringing many supplies with them and by tubborn persistence in their objective."

The hajib said to him, "You are nearer to finding peace, God willing! Give rders for what you think best to be carried out." He replied, "Time is running ut [literally, choking has prevented poetry, i.e. when one is dying one does not ave to think of rhyming]; by God, if I put my mind at rest and ordered what I ave just mentioned, the people would say, Ibn Abi 'Amir is ill, and his illness as caused him to go mad and fantasy to take possession of him: he has estroyed the lands of the Muslims and evacuated them and left them waste."

85. Castilian involvement in the fall of Cordova (400/1009)

The decade that followed al-Mansur's death saw the release of the tensions burie *beneath the outward glory of the 'Amirid dictatorship. The competing elements were th* *Umayyad family, largely dispossessed by al-Mansur, the Berbers and the Slavs, and th* *people of Cordova, who detested their alien masters, particularly the Berbers. It was n* *long before these various groupings looked to the Christian north for the additiona* *resources needed to give them an edge over their rivals. The story of these turbulen* *years is narrated in detail by Lévi-Provençal, II, pp.297 ff., and more recently b* *Wasserstein, pp.55-81.*

This selection concerns the brief reign of Muhammad II (al-Mahdi), who had secure *the support of the 'Amirid Slav general, Wadih, governor of the Middle March. Th* *Berbers, driven from Cordova, had acquired their own Umayyad protégé, Sulaiman b.* *al-Hakam. Both parties sought the assistance of Sancho García, Count of Castile (995* *1017), called here Ibn Mama Duna, after his great-grandmother, Mumma Domn*

وكان عند محمّد بقرطبة بليق غلام واضح فاتّخذ له محمّد جيشا وسار به الى

واضح ونادى منادي واضح في سائر الثغور، من حمل شيئا من الطعام الى محلّة

البربر فقد حلّ ماله ودمه. فأقاموا خمسة عشر يوماً يعيشون بحشيش الارض، فلما

اشتدّ ذلك عليهم أرسلوا الى ابن مامة النصرانيّ يقولون له «قد علمتَ ما بيننا وبين

واضح وابن عبدالجبّار فان انت رغبت في صلحنا ومسالمتنا فنحن معك عليهما»، فمضت

رسلهم الى ابن مامة دونه فوجدوا عنده رسل ابن عبدالجبّار ورسل واضح يسألانه

الصلح معهما على ان يعطياه ما أحب من مدائن الثغر، وحملا اليه هديّة منها خيل

بغال وكسى وما لا يحصى من الطرائف والتحف. فأجاب ابن مامة دونه للبربر على ان

يعطيه البربر اذا ظفروا ما أحبّ من مدائن الثغر فقبلوا ذلك منه وردُّ رسل واضح وابن

عبدالجبّار دون شيء. ثمّ أرسل الى البربر ألف عجلة من الدقيق والعقاقير وأنواع المآكل

ألف ثور وخمسة الاف شاة وجميع ما يصلحهم حتى الفحم والعسل والسروج والشقق

لباسهم وغير ذلك الى ما دونه من الحبال والاوتاد فعاش البربر بذلك وقويت نفوسهم.

ثمّ سار ابن مامة دونه بنفسه اليهم في جمع كثيف من النصارى فلما وصلوا الى

مدينة سالم أرسلوا الى واضح يرغبون اليه في الصلح كراهية في القتال، واقامة الحجّة

عليه وعلى [من اتى] به العون لابن عبدالجبّار، فأبى وامتنع، فساروا كلهم يومئذ الى

ancho García had revolted against his father, García Fernández, at the instigation of
al-Mansur, an action which led to García Fernández's capture and death in 995. The
new developments in Cordova gave Sancho the opportunity to recover some of the
border fortresses lost to al-Mansur's endless incursions. The presence of Castilian
troops in Cordova was a foretaste of things to come; the following year, it was the turn
of the Catalans to intervene.

Sancho García's contempt for the people of Cordova shows how quickly the
Christians' sense of inferiority could be dispelled; in a text that is clearly related, the
Cordovans are said to have been amazed at the "wisdom" of Sancho – see the Primera
crónica general de España, ed. R. Menéndez Pidal (Madrid, 1955), chapter 766.

The text is taken from Ibn 'Idhari, al-Bayan al-mughrib, III, ed. E. Lévi-Provençal
(Paris, 1930), from pp.86-91, 103-04.

Muhammad (b. 'Abd al-Jabbar, al-Mahdi) had with him in Cordova Biliq,
the ghulam (slave) of Wadih. Muhammad supplied him with some troops, with
whom he went to Wadih. Wadih's herald proclaimed in all the border regions
that the goods and the life of anyone bringing food to the Berbers' camp could
be lawfully taken. They [the Berbers] stayed for a fortnight living off grass.
When things became desperate they sent to Ibn Mama the Christian (Count
Sancho), saying to him, "You know what has arisen between us and Wadih and
Ibn 'Abd al-Jabbar; if you want peace and agreement with us, then let us act
together with you against them." Their messengers went to Count Sancho, where
they found messengers from Ibn 'Abd al-Jabbar and from Wadih, who were
asking him to make a treaty with them, by which they would give him any
border towns that he wanted, and bearing him gifts of horses, mules, garments
and countless precious and rare presents. Count Sancho replied favourably to the
Berbers, on condition that in the event of a victory they would give him the
border towns he wanted, which they accepted. The envoys of Wadih and Ibn
'Abd al-Jabbar returned empty-handed. Count Sancho thereupon sent 1,000
cartloads of flour, medicaments and different types of foodstuffs, 1,000 oxen,
1,000 sheep, and everything else that was agreed between them, even charcoal,
honey, saddles and strips of cloth, right down to other things such as ropes and
tent pegs. The Berbers lived off that and regained their strength.

Then Count Sancho came to them in person with a strong force of Christians.
When they reached Madinat Salim (Medinaceli), they sent messengers to Wadih
encouraging him to make peace, out of dislike for fighting and to give him and
the others who had assisted Ibn 'Abd al-Jabbar the chance to avoid it; but he
refused and rejected [these overtures]. Then they all proceeded to Sharnaba

شرنبة فحشر لهم واضح أهل الثغور وأرسل اليه ابن عبدالجبار غلامه قيصرا بالعسكر فنزل واضح وقيصر على البربر بشرنبة فاقتتلوا فانهزم واضح وأسر البربر من كان معه، فقتلوا منهم من أحبوا وعفوا عمن أحبوا. وكانت الوقعة بقرب قلعة عبدالسلام فنصب البربر الرؤوس عليها وكان وصول المنهزمين من أصحاب واضح وقيصر الى قرطبة يوم الأحد في أواخر ذي حجة من السنة. ...

وحدث من سمع ابن مامة النصراني صاحب العسكر الذي كان مع سليمان والبربر يقول «كنا نظن ان الدين والشجاعة والحق عند اهل قرطبة، فاذا القوم لا دين لهم ولا شجاعة فيهم ولا عقول معهم، وانما اتفق لهم ما اتفق من الظهور والنصر بفضل ملوكهم فلما ذهبوا انكشف أمرهم، أما العقول فان البربر قتلوهم يوم السبت والبلاء والخوف قائم بهم ثم أتوا اليهم يوم الاثنين على البغال مقصفين فما كان يؤمنهم ان يقتلهم سفهاؤهم، وأما الشجاعة فانهزم جندهم وملوكهم وجميعهم من أقل من مائتي فارس ليس فيهم رئيس ولا مذكور، وأما الدين فان أصحابي هؤلاء يعني النصارى يغيرون ويسرقون بغير أمر ثم يأتي أهل قرطبة فيشترون منهم نهبهم وأموال أصحابهم المسلمين فلا يرجع عنها أحد منهم فليس في القوم عقل ولا شجاعة ولا دين.»

وركب القومس ابن مامة الى القصر فأكرم وخلع عليه وعلى أصحابه ثم عاد الى معسكره وطلب من البربر ان يعطوه الحصون التى شرط عليهم فقالوا: «ليست الآن بايدينا فاذا تمهد سلطاننا أنجزنا لك ما وافقناك عليه.» ورحل يوم الاثنين لسبع بقين من ربيع الأول وبعث سليمان والبربر معه من يشيعه حتى أخرجوه من أرض الاسلام وبقي من أصحابه مائة أنزلوا في منية العقاب.

وأتى رسل ابن مامة القومس زعيم نصرانيته يستنجزون تسليم الحصون اليه على ألا يعذرهم ولا يتعرض لشيء من ثغورهم فرضوا بهذا.

(Jaramá), where Wadih assembled the men from the Marches. Ibn 'Abd al-Jabbar sent his ghulam Qaisar with the army. Wadih and Qaisar fell on the Berbers at Jaramá and fought them; Wadih was defeated and the Berbers captured those who were with him. They killed whom they liked and pardoned whom they liked. The battle took place near Qal'at 'Abd al-Salam (Alcalá de Henares, near Madrid). The Berbers raised up over it the heads [of the slain]. The defeated troops of Wadih and Qaisar arrived in Cordova on the Sunday at the end of Dhu'l-Hijja [399] (21 August 1009).

[...In Rabi' I, 400/November 1009 the Berbers entered Cordova in triumph after winning another bloody battle...]

Someone who heard Sancho the Christian, leader of the troops who were fighting along with Sulaiman and the Berbers, reported him as saying, "We used to think that the people of Cordova were men of religion, bravery and truth, yet here they are, lacking religious faith and bravery, with no intelligence among them. The triumphs and victories they have enjoyed have only occurred through the virtue of their kings. Now they [the kings] have gone, the truth of the matter has been revealed. As for their intelligence, the Berbers killed them [in the fierce fighting] on Saturday, when disaster and dread overcame them. Then on Monday they rode cheerfully out on mules, and the silly idiots had no guarantee that [the Berbers] would not kill them [again]. As for bravery, their army, their kings and their hosts have been put to flight by fewer that 200 knights, with no great leader nor anyone of importance at their head. As for their faith, these men of mine, the Christians, have been raiding and stealing without orders, then along come the people of Cordova to buy their plunder from them, and the possessions of their fellow Muslims. Not one of them has refrained from this. There is neither intelligence, bravery or religion among these people".

[...The Berber leader Zawi b. Ziri then entered the citadel and installed Sulaiman on the throne with the honorific title al-Musta'in...]

Count Sancho García rode to the citadel, where he and his men were honoured and presented with robes. Then he returned to his camp and asked the Berbers to give him the fortresses that they had stipulated, but they said, "they are not at present in our hands. When our sultan has got himself organized, we will recompense you as we agreed." He departed on Monday 23 Rabi' I, 400 (14 November 1009). Sulaiman and the Berbers sent someone to escort him and see him out of Muslim territory; [but] 100 of his men stayed behind and were settled in Munyat al-'uqab (a suburb of Cordova). [...]

[In 401/began 15 August 1010], messengers arrived from Count Sancho the Christian leader, asking for the fulfilment of the agreement to hand over the fortresses to him, with the conditions that he would not let them make any

ولما وصل الرسل الى قرطبة حضر الفقهاء والقاضي والعدول وكتبوا كتابا بالشروط وتسليم الحصون للنصارى وقريء على الناس بحضرة هشام وواضح وشهد فيه جميع من حضر وخرج القوم من القصر مستبشرين بما كان. فكان الذي صار لابن مامة [جميع الحصون التي كان أخذها] الحكم بن عبدالرحمن ومحمّد بن أبي عامر وابنه المظفّر كلُّ ذلك استخفافا من هشام.

... وسمع اللعين ابن شانجة ايضا بما سلّم الى اللعين ابن مامة دونه من الحصون فكاتب يطلب حصونا أخَر وتوعّد وتهدّد فأُجيب الى ما سأل من ذلك، وكُتب بتسليمها اليه وهذا كلُّه لجاجا في ألاّ يُصالح البربر.

excuses, and would not embark on any [hostile] activity on their borders. They [the Muslims] were satisfied with this [request]. [...]

When the messengers arrived in Cordova, the jurists, authorized witnesses (notaries public) and the qadi presented themselves and drew up a document covering the conditions and the surrender of the fortresses to the Christians. This was read out to the people in the presence of Hisham [II, restored in 1010] and Wadih, and all those present bore witness to it. The people then left the palace, happy at what had been done. The castles which passed to Sancho were all those which al-Hakam b. 'Abd al-Rahman and Muhammad b. Abi 'Amir and his son al-Muzaffar had captured – all of which Hisham made light of. [...]

When the accursed son of Sancho (of Navarre) heard of the fortresses that had been handed over to Sancho García, he wrote demanding other fortresses [for himself], with threats and menaces. He was given what he asked for, and a document was drawn up to make them over to him. All this was done out of a stubborn insistence on not making peace with the Berbers.

86. Ferdinand captures Coimbra (456/1064)

Christian resurgence in the 11th century reached an early peak in 1064, which saw two major successes, namely the fall of Coimbra in modern Portugal, and the sack of Barbastro in the northeast (see text 87). The first of these exploits was the achievement of Ferdinand I (1038-65), who succeeded in combining the kingdoms of Galicia, León and Castile. This gave him a firm base from which to operate against his divided neighbours, and in the last ten years of his reign he devoted himself to the reconquest of the Peninsula.

This text demonstrates the twin arms of his policy, which he seems to have employed with peculiar efficiency. On the one hand, as in the case of Santarém, he extracted large annual tributes from the Muslim rulers; on the other, where the costlier alternative of fielding a large expedition proved likely to be rewarding, he sought to extend Christian territory by direct annexation. The campaign against Santarém was possibly part of the great expedition of 1063 directed against Seville and Badajoz, which weakened the capacity of these two Ta'ifas to respond to the Coimbra campaign of the following year. Ferdinand's campaigns in Portugal are reported in the Historia Silense, *ed. J. Pérez de Urbel and A. González Ruiz-Zorilla (Madrid, 1959), pp.188-94, which amalgamates the*

ولم يزل أمر العدوّ يقوى ويظهر على ملوك ثغور الاندلس الى أن خرج الطاغية فرذلند بن شانجه ملك الجلالقة بأرض الاندلس بجيوشه النصرانيّة الى ثغر المسلمين بأرض الجوف قاصداً. وضمّ محمّد بن مسلمة بن الافطس لما منعه الاتاوة من بين جميع أمراء الثغور، فعاث في بلاد المسلمين وفتح حصونا كثيرة وكانت خيله تزيد على عشرة آلاف فارس معهم من الرجال أكثر من مثليهم، واتّصل خلال ذلك بالامير ابن الافطس أنّ عدوّ الله جرّد من خيله سريّة ثقيلة أمرهم بقصد مدينة شنترين. إذ كانت مدينة شنترين أفضل ذلك الثغر. فقضى الله أن لحق بشنترين أميرهم المظفّر بن الافطس قبل أن يأتيهم عدوّ الله وقد كان خامرهم الجزع فقالوا لاميرهم لقد هممنا أن نستسلم للعدوّ ولو لم تأتنا لضعفنا عن دفاعه.

وقصد هذا القومس لعنه الله الى شنترين للوجهة التى وجّهه لها أميره فرذلند أمير الجلالقة، فأرسل ابن الافطس اليه ليجتمع معه فيكلّمه في أمره، فالتقيا في الماء بنهر شنترين، ابن الافطس في زورق والعلج راكب فرسه في الماء الى صدر فرسه، وتكلّما طويلا فيما عرضه من السلم والاتاوة فامتنع المظفّر من ذلك الى أن وافقه بعد جهد ومشقّة على خمسة الاف دينار يؤديها اليه في كلّ عام من أوّل هذه الهدنة.

different campaigns into one account. This source also refers to the appointment of the Mozarab, Sisnando Davídiz, as governor of Coimbra by Ferdinand (see below, p.87). Haggling over the level of tribute (called parias *by the Christians) became a normal fact of life for the Party Kings of al-Andalus, as is mournfully attested in the contemporary memoirs of the Zirid ruler of Granada, 'Abd-Allah. The processes by which Christian aggrandizement was taking place were only too clear, yet the Muslims seemed unable to do anything to regain the initiative.*

The account of the fall of Coimbra is included in Ibn 'Idhari's section on the Aftasids, a dynasty of Berber origin who came to power in the region of Badajoz, on the Lower March, on the collapse of the Umayyad caliphate in Cordova. The Aftasid ruler in 1064 was Muhammad b. 'Abd-Allah b. Maslama, al-Muzaffar (1045-68). With the loss of Coimbra, which had been captured by al-Mansur in 987 (sic.), the whole region between the Douro and the Mondego was acquired by the forces of the Reconquista. The statement made here, that Ferdinand refused the defenders a safe conduct, is contradicted by the Christian sources (see also text 16).

The text is taken from Ibn 'Idhari, al-Bayan, III (ed. Lévi-Provençal), pp.238-39.

The enemy's position continued to strengthen and to prevail over the kings of the frontiers of al-Andalus, until the tyrant Ferdinand son of Sancho, ruler of the Galicians [Leonese], set out with his Christian troops for the Muslim frontier to attack the northern territories. Muhammad b. Maslama b. al-Aftas's fate was sealed when he, among all the amirs of the Marches, refused to pay [Ferdinand] tribute. He caused havoc in the Muslim territories and captured many castles. His forces numbered more than 10,000 horsemen, with more than double that number of infantry. Meanwhile, the amir Ibn al-Aftas heard that God's enemy had despatched a heavy detachment of his troops with orders to attack Shantarin (Santarém). Santarém was the best town in that March. God decreed that their amir al-Muzaffar b. al-Aftas reached Santarém before the enemy of God arrived. They [the inhabitants] had been seized with anxiety and told their amir that they had thought of surrendering to the enemy were it not for his arrival, because of their inability to defend themselves against him.

This Count, God curse him, headed for Santarém with the aims that his ruler, Ferdinand the king of Christian Spain, had given him. Ibn al-Aftas sent word to him that they should meet to discuss his business. They met in the middle of the river of Santarém, Ibn al-Aftas in a boat and the Christian sitting on his horse, with the water coming up to the horse's chest. They had a long discussion about his proposals for peace and the payment of tribute, which al-Muzaffar resisted, until after the greatest difficulty and effort he agreed to [a payment of] 5,000 dinars, which he would hand over every year on the anniversary of this armistice.

ولم يزل عدوٌ الله فرذلند يقوى والمسلمون يضعفون بغرم الجزية للنصارى الى أن نزل اللعين على مدينة قلمريّة وكان الذي فتحها المنصور بن [أبي عامر سنة] خمس وسبعين وثلاثمائة. فحاصرها الآن اللعين فرذلند حتّى فتحها وذلك أنّ قائدها في هذا الوقت كان عبدا من عبيد ابن الافطس يسمّى رانده فخاطب فرذلند في السرّ أن يؤمنه في نفسه وأهله ويخرج اليه من البلد ليلا، فأعطاه اللعين الامان فخرج اللعين سرًا الى عسكر النصارى، وأصبح أهل البلد وقد أخنوا أهبة القتال فقال لهم النصارى «كيف تقاتلونا وأميركم عندنا؟» ولم يكن لأهل المدينة علم بذلك فلمّا لم يجدوه وعلموا صحّة خبره طلبوا من العلج الامان فلم يجبهم اليه ونفدت أقواتهم وعلم عدوُّ الله ذلك منهم، فجدّ في حربهم حتّى دخلها عنوة فقُتل الرجل وسبى الحريم والذريّة وذلك في سنة ست وخمسين وأربعمائة، وانصرف غلام ابن الافطس الى مولاه فوبخه على فعله الذميم ثمّ أمر بضرب عنقه فكانت مدة بقاء هذه المدينة للمسلمين بضعا وسبعين سنة.

ولم يزل ثغر الاندلس يضعف والعدوُّ يقوى والفتنة بين أمراء الاندلس قبحّهم الله تستعر، الى أن كلب العدوُّ على جميعهم وملَّ من أخذ الجزية ولم يقنع الاّ بأخذ البلاد وانتزاعها عن أيدي المسلمين.

Ferdinand the enemy of God did not cease to become stronger and the Muslims to become weaker through the payment of tribute (*jizya*) to the Christians, until the accursed one descended on Qulumriyya (Coimbra), which al-Mansur b. Abi 'Amir had conquered in 375 (985). The accursed Fernando now besieged it until he captured it. This happened because its governor at that time was one of the slaves of Ibn al-Aftas, called Rando, who corresponded secretly with Ferdinand, asking for safe conduct for himself and his dependents if he left the town by night to go to him. The accursed one gave him safe conduct and the accursed [Rando] set out in secret for the Christian camp. In the morning the inhabitants of the town got ready to fight, when the Christians said to them, "How can you fight us when your leader is with us?" The people knew nothing about this, but when they couldn't find him, and knew the truth of the matter, they sought a safe conduct from the Christian. He would not grant them one; the enemy of God knew that their provisions were exhausted and he made great efforts to fight them until he entered [Coimbra] by storm. The men were killed and the women and children made captive. This was in 456/1064. Rando, the slave of Ibn al-Aftas, returned to his master, who rebuked him for his reprehensible action and ordered his decapitation. The town had remained in Muslim hands for about 90 [lunar] years.

The borders of al-Andalus continued to weaken, while the enemy grew stronger as the discord between the rulers of al-Andalus blazed fiercely (may God revile them!), so that the enemy eyed them all greedily; he wearied of taking tribute and was only satisfied by the seizure of the country and wresting it from the grasp of the Muslims.

87. The Crusade against Barbastro (456/1064)

As noted by Smith (see text 17), it is misleading to regard the campaign against Barbastro as a forerunner of the true Crusades initiated by Pope Urban II in 1095. Nevertheless, Pope Alexander II's approval and support for what was essentially a standard holy war against the heathen had the effect of giving it a more international character than had been the case in earlier expeditions. The invading force, composed mainly of Normans as well as Catalan and Aragonese troops, was led by William of Montreuil among others; it is not clear who is meant by the name al-Biyutbin (perhaps Albitush/Alvitus) preserved in our text. The Christian troops sacked and looted the city in a particularly savage and systematic manner. Arabic accounts express great shock and outrage at the Christian behaviour in the town; this in turn gives rise to some wild variations in the estimates of the victims of the massacre that was perpetrated, figures ranging from about 6,000 to 100,000. The number of Muslim women sent into captivity also varies between five and seven thousand. The story of their despatch to the Byzantine

(a)

مَدِينة بَرْبَشْتُرُ: بَرْبَشْتُرُ من بلاد بَرْبَطَانِية، وبعضها في ملك المسلمين وبعضها للعجم اليوم. وحصن بَرْبَشْتُرُ على نهر إبْرُه [؟]. ويَرْبَشْتُرُ من أمّهات مدن الثغر الفائقة في الحصانة البائنة في الإمتناع.

وقد غزاها، على غِرّة [وقلة عدد من أهلها] وعُدّة، أهل غاليش والروذمانون، وكان عليهم رئيس يسمى البِيُطبين، وكان في عسكره نحو أربعين ألف فارس، فـحصرها أربعين يوماً حتى افتتحها وذلك سنة ست وخمسين وأربعمائة، فقتلوا عامة رجالها سبوا فيها من ذراري المسلمين ونسائهم مالايحصى [كثرة]. ويذكر أنهم اختاروا من أبكار [جواري] المسلمين وأهل الحسن منهن خمسة آلاف جارية وأهدوهن إلى صاحب القسطنطينة؛ وأصابوا فيها من الأموال والأمتعة مايعجز عن وصفه.

وفتحها بعد ذلك أحمد بن سليمان بن هود صاحب سَرَقُسْطَة مع أهل الثغور، استنجد بخلفائه من رؤساء الأندلس. وأدخل منها سَرَقُسْطَة نحو خمسة آلاف سبية مختارة ونحو ألف فرس وألف درع وأموالاً كثيرة وثياباً جليلة. وكان افتتاحه لها لثمان خلون من جمادى الأولى سنة سبع وخمسين وأربعمائة. ومن ذلك تسمى أحمد بن سليمان «المقتدر بالله».

Emperor (Constantine X Ducas, 1059-67) reveals how the Muslims viewed the international dimensions of these events, and were aware of the interest shown by the whole Christian world in the reconquest of Spain. For discussions of the different perceptions of the fate of Barbastro, see Daniel, pp.83-84 and Wasserstein, pp.276-78. The ruler of Saragossa responded by ceasing payment of the parias, and permitting a slaughter of Christians in the city in January 1065, before regaining Barbastro later in the year. The number of female slaves he in turn brought home made the scores even.

The account selected is that of al-Bakri, which is also cited by later writers, such as al-Himyari; among other details, the latter adds the poem by Ibn al-'Assal (d. 487/1094), which is given in passage (b). Another contemporary account is given by Ibn Hayyan (d. 469/1076); this has been translated by Gayangos, II, pp.265-70, in the version preserved by al-Maqqari (for the Arabic text, see vol.IV, pp.449-54 in the edition of Ihsan 'Abbas).

Text (a) is taken from al-Bakri, al-Masalik wa'l-mamalik, pp.92-95; text (b) is extracted from al-Himyari, al-Raud al-mi'tar, ed. and tr.E. Lévi-Provençal, La Péninsule Ibérique (Leiden, 1938), pp.40-41.

(a)

Barbashtru (Barbastro) is one of the towns of Barbitania, part of which is in the domains of the Muslims and part of which today belongs to the non-Muslims. The castle of Barbastro is on [a branch of ?] the river Ibruh (Ebro), and is one of the key cities on the upper frontier in view of its unusual defensive strength.

The people of Ghalish (Southern France) and the Normans raided it unexpectedly, due to its small number of defenders and their lack of readiness. Their leader was called al-Biyutbin (?), who commanded an army of about 40,000 knights. They besieged it for 40 days, until they captured it. This was in the year 456 (August 1064). They massacred the men and took a countless number of Muslim children and women as prisoners. It is related that they picked out 5,000 Muslim virgins and beauties and sent them as a present to the ruler of Constantinople. [The French] gained so many goods and possessions in Barbastro that it beggars description.

After that, Ahmad b. Sulaiman b. Hud, the ruler of Saragossa, recaptured Barbastro with the frontier forces; he sought help from his deputies among the rulers of al-Andalus. He brought back to Saragossa from there about 5,000 choice female prisoners and 1,000 knights, 1,000 coats of armour, great wealth and splendid clothing. Ahmad b. Sulaiman's recapture of Barbastro was on 8 Jumada I, 457 (17 April 1065); thereafter he was known as "al-Muqtadir bi-llah" (Powerful in God).

72

(b)

وفى ذلك يقول الفقيهُ الزاهدُ ابن العسَّال من قصيدة [كامل]:

لـم يُخْطِ لكن شأْنُهَا الصَّمـــــــاءُ	وَلَقَدْ رَمَانَا المُشركُونَ بِأَسْهُم
لـــــم يـــــبقَ لاَ جَبَلٌ وَلاَ بَطْحَاءُ	هتكُوا بخَيْلِهم قـصـــودَ حـريمهـا
فى كـلّ يَوْمٍ غـــــــــارةٌ شَعْراءُ	جـــاسُوا خِلالَ ديارِهِمْ فَلَهُمْ بهـــا
فـــحـــــمـــــاتُنا فى حَرْبِهم جُبَناءُ	باتَتْ قُلُوبُ المسلمين برعـــــبِهِمْ
طفلٌ ولا شـــــيخٌ ولا عـــــذراءُ	كَمْ مَوْضِعٍ غنمــــوه لـم يُرْحَمْ به
فلهُ إليــــهـــــا ضَجَّةٌ وبغـــاءُ	ولَكَمْ رضيـعٍ فَرَّقُوا مـن أُمِّهِ
فَوْقَ التُّرَاب وفَرْشُهُ البـــــيْداءُ	وَلَرُبَّ مــــــولـودٍ أبُوه مُجَدَّلٌ
قـد أبْرَزُوها مَا لَهَا اسـتـخـفـاءُ	ومـصـونةٍ فى خِدْرِها مـحـجـوبةٍ
فـعـلَيْهِ بَعْدَ العِزَّةِ اسـتـخـذاءُ	وعـزيزِ قـــومٍ صـــارَ فى أيديهِمْ
ركـبـوا الكبائر مـا لهُنّ خَفَاءُ	لَوْلا ذنوبُ المسـلـمـين وأنَّهُمْ
أبداً عليـــهـــم فـــالذنوبُ الداءُ	مـا كـان يُنْصَرُ للنَّصارى فارسٌ
ومـــــلاحُ مُتَّحلى الصّلاحِ رياءُ	فـشرارُهم لا يـخـتـفـون بشرِّهم

(b)

The jurist and ascetic, Ibn al-'Assal, wrote a poem about [the Christian sack of Barbastro], some of which goes:

1. The polytheists have shot arrows at us, and they have not missed – they struck like hard rocks.
2. They have attacked its inviolable palaces with their cavalry; neither mound nor hollow remains.
3. They have pried around in their [sic.?] territories and every day they have made an abominable raid.
4. The hearts of the Muslims have passed the night in fear of them and our defenders have been cowardly in fighting them.
5. How many places have they plundered where neither a child, an old man nor a virgin has been shown mercy;
6. How many suckling babes have they separated from their mother, while they cry and long for her,
7. Many a child whose father has been knocked to the ground, lying in the dust with the desert for a mattress,
8. And [many a] chaste girl, closeted in her boudoir, whom they have brought out into the open – there is no concealment for her.
9. [Many a] great man has fallen into their hands – after enjoying greatness, he has now suffered humiliation.
10. Were it not for the sins of the Muslims – they have committed great sins, which cannot be hidden –
11. No knight would ever be able to give the Christians victory over them, but these sins are the malady;
12. The wicked ones among them do not keep out of sight to work their evil, while the virtue of those who profess virtue is hypocrisy.

88. Forbidden love (about 1075)

One of the chief glories of the Ta'ifa kings was their patronage of poets an
scholars, at courts that were miniature replicas of the caliphal court in Baghdad. Th
phenomenon goes some way to explaining the apparently paradoxical flowering c
Islamic civilization in Spain during the eleventh century, at a time when the Muslim
were politically degenerate and in military retreat. The 'Abbadid court in Seville i
perhaps the most renowned, but the arts flourished in lesser centres too.

Abu 'Abd-Allah b. Haddad was a native of Guadix, but spent most of his life i
Almería, at the court of al-Mu'tasim the Tujibid (443/1051-484/1091). The poet die
around 480/1087. The poem that follows refers to the time of his youth, and is one c
several that speak of his passion for a beautiful Christian girl of Guadix, called Jamila
but whom the poet addresses as Nuwaira ("little light"). Ibn Haddad is discussed b

رَهــينُ لُوْعـــاتٍ ورَوْعـــاتِ	قـــلـــبــى فــى ذاتِ الأُثَيْلاتِ
وإن بَغَوْا قِبلهُ بُغَـــيــاتى	فــوجّهــا نحـــوَهم إنّهُـمْ
بالهــــضَبـــاتِ الزَّهَرِيّاتِ	وعـــرّسَا مـن عَقدات اللَّوى
بالفتــيـات العيســويّاتِ	وعرّجــا يا فتــىَ عـامـر
تكنِسُ مــا بين الكنيـــساتِ	فــإنّ بى المرِّيَم رومـــيّةً
بـين صـــوامعٍ وبِيَعاتِ	أهيمُ فـــيــهـا والهَوى ضلّةٌ
بالظَّبَيـــاتِ الحَضَريّاتِ	وفى ظبـــاءِ البـــو مَن يَزْدري
بـين الأُرَيْطَى واللّوَيْحـــاتِ	أفصِحْ وَحْدى يومَ فـــصنعِ لهم
واجتــمـعــوا فــيـه لمِيقـاتِ	وقـــد أتَوْا منه إلى مَوعــدٍ
مُمْسِكِ مِصبـــاحٍ ومِنساةِ	بمَوْقِفٍ بــــين يَدَىْ أسقُفٍ
بأىِ إنصــاتٍ وإخـــبـــاتِ	وكلَّ قَسٍّ مُظهـــرٍ للتُّقَى
كـالذِّئبِ يبـــغى فَرْسَ نَعْجاتٍ	وعــينهُ تســـرَحُ فى عِينهم
وقـــد رأى تلكَ الظُّبَـــيّاتِ؟!	وأىُّ مَرءٍ ســـالـمٌ مِن هَوىً
عـــلــى قُدودٍ غُصُنــيّاتِ	فـــمِن خُدودٍ قَمَريّاتِ

rès, pp.279-83, where there is also a French translation of most of the poem, rather fferent from the one provided here. On the poet, see also Nykl, pp.194-95.

The poem, apart from providing evidence of romantic attachments between *ʼristians and Muslims, which though illegal were doubtless commonplace, also* *dicates that the Christians in the Guadix region openly practised their religion and* *d their own bishop, as indeed they were entitled to do as a protected community.*

The text is taken from Ibn Bassam, al-Dhakhira fi mahasin ahl al-jazira, I/ii (Cairo, *ʼ42), pp.213-14. In line 4, the ʻAmir were the tribe of the renowned lover Majnun, who* *ʼhausted himself in fruitless search for his beloved Laila. An arta (line 8) is a type of* *ʼe that grows in sandy soil, producing a bitter fruit. In line 7, the poet contrasts the* *ʼl gazelle of the desert with the metaphorical (human) gazelle whom he loves.*

My heart is at the place of the tamarisk trees, a hostage to desires and alarms,

So turn towards them, they are the qibla (object) of my desires, even though they treat me badly.

Take a rest from the winding sands in the folds of the mountains covered in blooms,

Stop, you two young men of ʻAmir, at the place where the Christian girls are.

I have a girl among the Christians, who bolts like a shy gazelle round the churches.

I am in raptures over her; but passion among the cloisters and the churches is a sin.

In relation to the gazelles of the desert, who would not prefer the gazelles who live in towns ?

I alone celebrate on their Easter Day, among the lofty trees and the *artas*;

They had come from there to a rendez-vous, and congregated there at the appointed time,

ʼ. To stand before a bishop holding a lantern and a staff,

. And many priests displaying piety, with signs of ostentatious quietness and humility before God,

. His eyes wandering over theirs like a wolf who longs to devour the ewes.

. What man could be safe from passion when he had seen these gazelles ?

. And from moon-like cheeks set above willowy figures ?

76

بِحُسْنِ أَلْحَانٍ وَأَصْــواتِ	وقــد تَلَوْا صُحُفَ أَناجِــيلِهِم
عَنِّى وفى ضَـــغْطِ صَبَاباتى	يَزيدُ فى نَفْرٍ يعـافــيــرِهِم
حتّ غمــامــاتِ اللّثــامـاتِ	والشمسُ شمسُ الحسنِ من بينهِم
ولمحُهــا يُضـــرِمُ لَوْعــاتى	وناظِرى مُخْــتَلسٌ لمحــهــا
عُلّقــتُهــا منذُ سُنَيّاتى	وفى الحــشــا نارٌ نُويريّةٌ
بل تلتظى فى كلّ أوْقـاتى	لا تنطفى وقتــاً رُمــتــهــا
وإنْ أَبَى رَجْعَ تحـــيّاتى	فــــحىّ عنّى رشأَ المُنحنَى

5. They recited the scriptures of their Gospels, with beautiful voices and intonations,

6. Increasing their gazelles' shunning of me, and [raising] the pressure of my passions.

7. The [only] sun is the sun of beauty, [shining] among them beneath the clouds of [her] veils;

8. My gaze snatches hers, and her glance kindles my torments.

9. My insides blaze with the fire of Nuwaira, by whom I have been captivated since my youngest years,

0. [The fire] has not gone out for a moment, though how often have I wished it; rather, it blazes ever more fiercely.

1. Wish the gazelle at the bend in the valley a long life, from me, even if it refuses to return my greetings.

89. Getting away with murder (about 1075)

If the previous selection shows how divisions between the religious communities could be broken down by tender feelings, this one demonstrates the contrary. The scene is once again Almería, in the time of al-Muʿtasim b. Sumadih (1051-91). Evidently, al-Muʿtasim employed a Jewish vizier, who has not been identified. This was far from uncommon, and we may recall the important position of Jews in the Zirid kingdom of Granada, particularly under Yusuf b. al-Naghrilla, who was accused in some Muslim sources of colluding with al-Muʿtasim against the Zirid ruler Badis, and of attempting to establish an independent Jewish state in Almería. Yusuf perished in the massacre of the Jews of Granada in 459/1066 (for which, see for instance the Memoirs of ʿAbd-Allah b.

عبدالله بن سهل بن يوسف المقرىء، إمام فى الأقراء والتجويد، فاضل. له تواليف

فى القراءات، تدل على معرفته. أخبرنى ابن عم أبى رحمه الله قال لى: كان جدك أحمد

قد مشى إلى المرية فى تجارة، وحمل معه دابتين له، كان الفقيه المقرىء أبومحمد عبدالله

بن سهل يقرىء بالمرية، وكان معظما عند أهلها، فدخل الحمام ذات يوم، فوجد فيه

اليهودى وزير صاحب المرية فى ذلك التاريخ، وبين يديه صبى اسمه محمد، وهو يناديه:

«يا محمدالـ [؟]» يردد هذا، وكان اليهودى أصلع فلم يملك الفقيه نفسه أن قام إليه

وضربه بحجر كان هناك خلف الدُابة [دفة؟] ضربة فى رأسه فقتله، وخرج كما هو فلبس

ثيابه، ولم يَستطع أحد أن يقول للفقيه شيئاً هيبة له وإعظاماً، وخرج إلى باب المدينة

وركب الطريق وخفه فى رجله، وقضى جدك حاجته وخرج بدابتيه، فوجد الفقيه على قرب

من المدينة فعرض عليه ركوب إحدى الدابتين فركبها وأعلمه بما كان فأسرع به السير،

وأوصله تلك الليلة إلى بلس وحينئذ تحقق الفقيه أنه أمن في سربه، ولم يزل يُعرفُ ذلك

لجدك ويشكره عليه.

توفى رحمه الله سنة ثمانين وأربعمائة.

Buluggin, trans. A.T.Tibi, pp.72-75). The random murder reported here may have occurred at about the same time, or probably a little later. The incident does show that there was no segregation between the major religious communities in the use of the baths (see also text 98); and that all sorts of passions could be raised there.

For the Jews in Spain, see the separate volume in this series, and E. Ashtor, The Jews in Muslim Spain (Philadelphia, 1973-79, 2 vols).

The selection is taken from the late 12th-century biographical dictionary of al-Dabbi, Bughyat al-multamis (ed. Cairo, 1967), pp.345-46. The text appears to be corrupt in a couple of places; the suggested amendment has been taken from the edition of F. Codera and J. Ribera (Madrid, 1885), p. 332.

'Abd-Allah b. Sahl b. Yusuf al-Maqqari: A distinguished master of Qur'anic reading and recitation, whose publications on the readings of Qur'anic texts demonstrate his knowledge. My father's cousin (may God have mercy on him), told me: "Your grandfather Ahmad had gone to al-Mariyya (Almería) to trade and had taken two of his mounts along with him. The faqih al-Maqqari, Abu Muhammad 'Abd-Allah b. Sahl, was reciting the Qur'an in Almería, among whose people he was greatly esteemed. He [al-Maqqari] entered the bath-house one day and found there the Jew, vizier of the ruler of Almería at that time. With him was a young [Muslim] boy called Muhammad. [The Jew] kept calling out to him, "O Muhammad, you...", doing so repeatedly. The Jew was bald. The faqih couldn't restrain himself from going up to him and hitting him with a rock that lay there behind a board. He struck him on his head and killed him. Then he went out just as he was, and got dressed. No-one was able to say anything to the faqih, because of the reverence and awe in which they held him. He left by the city gate and took to the road, with [just] his slippers on his feet. Your grandfather finished his business and left with his two mounts. He came across the faqih near the city, and offered him one of the animals to ride on. As they rode off, he told your grandfather what had happened, and made him hasten on the journey. [Your grandfather] got him to Ballis (Vélez el Rubio or el Blanco, between Lorca and Baza) that night. He then reassured the faqih that he was now safe and sound. [Al-Maqqari] never ceased to acknowledge your grandfather's role and to thank him for it."

He died (may God have mercy upon him) in 480/1087.

90. The status of property plundered from the Galera region
(late 11th century)

This excerpt is taken from al-Wansharishi's collection of legal decisions, for which see text 79. It contains a particularly full section on jihad or Holy War, covering the status of those involved in war and operating or caught on the wrong side of the borders. Abu 'Abd-Allah al-Saraqusti, whose opinions are discussed here, studied in Cordova and was qadi in Saragossa. He made the pilgrimage to Mecca and is said to have died in mid 477/November 1084. This poses some chronological difficulties, as one of the legal texts he cites, the Kitab fi nawazil al-ahkam of Ibn al-Hajj (died 529/1135) was written by a man who was barely 20 at the supposed time of al-Saraqusti's death. The other source cited in al-Saraqusti's answer, al-Mudawwana, was written by Ibn al-Qasim (died 191/806), who was responsible for spreading the Maliki legal school into North Africa. Malik himself died in 795 in Medina, having founded the most conservative school of Islamic jurisprudence.

The Ghalira (Galera) in question is the town about four km south of Huéscar in the Granada region, which had evidently been plundered during a period of truce. The question as to the legal status of this booty is raised by the people of the nearby town of Basta (Baza). Even leaving aside the chronological inconsistency noted above, which

مسألة في شراء أموال أهل غليرة من الروم

وقع البحث فيها بين الفقيه أبي يحيى بن عاصم والفقيه الخطيب أبي عبدالله السرقسطي رحمهما الله ورضى عنهما. ونص كلام أبي عبدالله السرقسطي مجاوباً لأهل بسطة:

يا أخي وسيدي وصلتني كتبكم في القضية الغليرية وعرفت منها ان مستندكم في فتياكم بحرمة شراء أموالهم من الروم أن لهم عهداً وأماناً منا مثل ما للروم، فلذلك لا نشتري أموال أهل غليرة ممن غلبهم عليها.

والجواب عن هذا أن نقول: إن اردتم بالعهد والأمان ما قضى به الشرع من حرمة مال المسلم على المسلم إلا إنْ طابت به نفسه فليزمكم عليه ان لا يشتري من الحربي ما غلب المسلم عليه من ماله، ولا نقسم في الغنائم ما عرفنا أنه لمسلم غير معين، لأنا على شك من طيب نفس مالكه المسلم، والنص بالجواز موجود، وأظنكم لم تريدوا هذا.

may reflect some error in the transmission of this judgement, the precise date of these events is uncertain; but it doubtless refers to the reign of Alfonso VI, who began to intervene actively in the affairs of Granada in 1074-75.

For some of the terminology used, see the Glossary. The word "necks" refers to slavery. Note the interesting distinction between a real Muslim and a convert, whose status remains prejudiced by his previous state of unbelief (or belief in the Trinity as opposed to the one God). The argument presented here is a slightly tortuous one, but it boils down to the fact that Muslims who are abused in the Christian realms are like Muslims abused in their own lands; they are therefore carrying on a Holy War in Christian territory as a sort of reluctant fifth column, and Christian booty captured from them is legitimate spoils of war for the Christians. It is therefore permissible for the Muslims to purchase it. A rather similar problem from a later period receives a different verdict (see text 99).

The text is taken from the Rabat edition, vol.II, pp.142-44. See also Amar, Archives Marocaines (1908), pp.216-18.

The issue of buying the property of the people of Ghalira from the Christians.

Discussion on this question occurred between the jurist Abu Yahya b. 'Asim and the jurist and preacher Abu 'Abd-Allah al-Saraqusti, may God have mercy on both of them and be pleased with them. The text of Abu 'Abd-Allah al-Saraqusti's words in reply to the people of Basta (Baza) [was]:

O brother and master, I have received your letters concerning the case of Galera, from which I have understood that your judgement, that it is illegal to buy their property from the Christians, rests its case on the fact that they [the people of Galera] enjoyed a treaty and immunity from us similar to that enjoyed by the Christians; therefore we should not purchase the property of the people of Galera from those who have plundered it from them.

We say in reply to this, if you mean by treaty and immunity what the law has determined about the inviolability of the property of a Muslim with respect to another Muslim, with the exception of what he would happily give of his own accord, then it is incumbent on you [to ensure] that one does not purchase from a Christian the property that he has seized from the Muslim. We do not divide up among the spoils of war anything that we know belonged to an unspecified Muslim, because we are doubtful whether its Muslim owner gave it up willingly. [Though] the text for such an authorization does exist, I do not think you mean this.

82

وإن أردتُم بالعهد والأمان ما عقده أمير المسلمين أيده الله للروم على الهدنة وترك الحرب وأنه شامل لأهل غليرة لكونهم تحت قهر الطاغية ففيه نظر من حيث إن الروم كانت قبل الهدنة دماؤهم ورقابهم وأموالهم مباحة لنا، ودماء أهل غليرة محترمة وبقي النظر في أموالهم هل هي محترمة لأنها لمسلم، أو مباحة لأنها في دار حرب؟ ولست أذكر فيها لمالك ولا لأحد من أصحابه نصاً، غير أن القاضي أبا عبدالله بن الحاج ذكرها في نوازله وأجراها على مسألة الحربي يسلم ويخرج إلينا، أو يبقى بداره فيدخلها المسلمون ويأخذون ماله، هل يكون له أو غنيمة؟ والقولان في المدونة. وصحيح أنه لا غنيمة له بنصوص الأحاديث الصحيحة أن مال المسلم حرام على المسلم إلا عن طيب نفس منه.

وفي هذا الاجراء نظر من حيث إنَّ الحربي مباح الدم والمال والرقبة، فإذا أسلم أحرز دمه ورقبته باتفاق، ويبقى الخلاف في ماله ما دام بدار الحرب. وأما المسلم الموحد الذي لم يسبق اسلامه كفر فلم يكن قط مباح الدم والرقبة لعدم وجود المبيح فيه وهو الكفر، وما لزم في دمه ورقبته يلزم في ماله، لأن علة الاحترام هي الإسلام، وكُلُّ الْمُسْلِمِ عَلَى الْمُسْلِمِ حَرَامٌ دَمُهُ وَعِرْضُهُ وَمَالُه، فكيف يسوى بين من كانت حرمته أصلية وبين من كانت حرمته طارئة غير أصلية، وإذا ثبتت الحرمة لمال المسلم الأصلي استصحبناها حتى تسقط بدليل صحيح، وليس كونه بدار الحرب مسقطاً لحرمته حتى يقوم الدليل عليه. ...

فإذا صح أن مال أهل غليرة كان محترماً ولم يطرأ عليه ما يبيحه لم ينزل منزلة مال الروم في كونه حصلت له حرمة بالعهد مانعة لنا من شرائه ممن غلبهم عليه. وبقي لنا النظر فيهم ولا شك أنهم كانوا تحت ذمة الرومي وعهده فنقض عهده وغدر بهم وهم

If you mean by treaty and immunity what the Amir al-Muslimin (may God upport him!) concluded with the Christians by way of truce and cessation of ostilities, and that this also applied to the people of Galera, because they are in 1e power of the tyrant, then that is a matter of opinion. This is because, before 1e truce, the blood, necks and property of the Christians were permissible for s, whereas the blood of the people of Galera was forbidden [because they are 1uslim]. The status of their property remains a matter of opinion: is their roperty protected, because it belongs to a Muslim, or is it permissible because is in enemy territory (the *dar al-harb*)? I do not recall that Malik or any of his isciples has a text on this matter. Only the qadi Abu 'Abd-Allah b. al-Hajj entioned it in his book *al-Nawazil,* and applied it to the question of a Christian ho becomes a Muslim and comes over to us; but if he remains at home [in the 1r *al-harb*], and the Muslims enter his house and take his property, is it his, or it spoils of war? Both opinions are found in *al-Mudawwana.* [Ibn al-Hajj gues that] the correct view is that it remains his and is not booty, according to e texts of the authentic traditions (*hadith*), [namely] that the property of a 1uslim is unlawful to another Muslim, except what he gladly gives of his own cord.

This formulation [by Ibn al-Hajj] is open to dispute, in as much as the blood, operty and neck of a Christian is permissible; when he becomes a Muslim, it is :reed that his blood and neck gain immunity, but there is a conflict of opinion 'er his property so long as he remains in the *dar al-harb*. As for a Muslim, ho professes the unity of God, and was not an unbeliever before being a 1slim, at no time was his blood and neck ever made permissible, due to the sence of anything that made it permissible, such as unbelief. Whatever covers s blood and neck also applies to his property, because what gives immunity is .am, and "Everything belonging to a Muslim is inviolable to another Muslim, s blood, his honour and his property". How could one equate someone who joys fundamental inviolability with one whose inviolability is recent and not ndamental? Once the inviolability of the property of the genuine Muslim is tablished, we will go along with this until it is made null and void by a real oof [to the contrary]. His being in the *dar al-harb* does not abrogate his violability until some evidence arises against him. [...]

[Thus] if it is verified that the property of the people of Galera was iolable, and nothing new occurred to make it permissible, its status is not the ne as that of the property of the Christians, which acquired its inviolability by : treaty, [and this inviolability] prevents us from purchasing it from whoever i seized it from them. [However], there remains our opinion concerning them e people of Galera]: There is no doubt that they were under the protection

بمنزلة من كانوا تحت طاعة إمام المسلمين، وعاهد الطاغية وعقد معه عقدة الهدنة إلى مدة فلم يوف وغدر وحارب واستولى على طائفة من المسلمين وأموالهم، فما أخذه بعد الغدر والنقض للعهد بمثابة ما أخذه بعد انقضاء زمانه في غير غدر، ولا نكث في جواز الشراء منه في جهاد الغنيمة.

(*dhimma*) of the Christians and had a treaty from him [Alfonso VI?]. He violated his treaty and acted treacherously towards them. Their status is [therefore] the same as one who is subject to the Imam of the Muslims, who has made a treaty with the tyrant and agreed a truce with him for a certain period. [The tyrant] does not keep his agreement and is treacherous, fights and overcomes a party of Muslims and seizes their property. What he takes as a result of treachery and the violation of a treaty is tantamount to what he takes after the [peaceful] lapse of the treaty without treachery; thus there is nothing wrong with permitting such spoils of war to be purchased from him.

91. Alfonso VI before the fall of Toledo (478/1085)

The fall of Toledo to Alfonso VI of León-Castile in May 1085 was an event of the utmost significance for the balance of forces in the Iberian Peninsula, marking a decisive and permanent shift in favour of the Christian north. Alfonso's success was the more remarkable in that only a decade earlier, for several months in 1072, he had been in exile in Toledo under the eye of the Berber ruler al-Ma'mun b. Dhi 'l-Nun, who was by that date a paria-paying client of Alfonso's elder brother, Sancho II of Castile and (briefly) of León. For the background to the fall of Toledo, the classic account is that of E. Lévi-Provençal, "Alphonse VI et la prise de Tolede (1085)", Hespéris, 13 (1931), 33-49; see also the recent book by B.F. Reilly, The Kingdom of León-Castilla under King Alfonso VI, 1065-1109 (Princeton, 1988). Alfonso cannot really be said to have conquered Toledo, which fell to him by virtue of the incompetence of its ruler, al-Ma'mun's grandson Yahya al-Qadir, who, in the face of the hostility of his own subjects, ceded Toledo to Alfonso in exchange for Valencia. None of the Ta'ifa rulers went to the assistance of Toledo, despite the opportunity given to the besieged to seek help, as mentioned in this passage, in accordance with the conventions of the period.

The Muslims relied on the assistance of the Mozarab, Sisnando Davídiz, to gain access to the king when they went to seek terms. For Sisnando's career, see R. Menéndez Pidal and E. García Gómez, "El Conde Mozárabe Sisnando Davídiz", Al-Andalus, 12 (1947), 27-41. A native of Tentugal, west of Coimbra, Sisnando had been captured by

فخرجَ من أعيانهم جُملةً إلى مَضرب أدفُونش فى بعضِ تلك الأيام، وقد ضـاقَ المجالُ، وتَلمَّظت الآجالُ، وأقبلَت الحُتوفُ تختـَالُ، فقامَ الحُجابُ دُونَه، وقالوا: «هو نائمٌ فكيفَ تُوقظونه؟» فعَدلُوا إلى مضـرب ششْنتَد، سرُّه العَتيد، وشيطانه المَريد، وهامانـه الذى أوقَدَ له على الطّين، وعلّمـه الدَّفع بالشك فى صدرِ اليَقين، أحـد أعـلاجِ ابن عبّاد كان، من رجلٍ مُتوقّد جمْرة الذكاء، بعيد المذهب بـينَ الجُرأة والنكراء، سفرَ بينَ المُعتضد الطاغية فَرْدلَنْد، فعقَّد وحلَّ، ونَهَضَ بما حَمَل من ذلك واستقَلَّ. ثم خافَ المعتضدَ على نفسِه، فنَزَع به عِرقُ اللُّوم إلى المَقَر المذمُوم. واستقرَّت قدمُه بجلّيقيّة، فاضطلَع بالدرُوب والثغور، وغلَب على سائرِ السياسة والتّدبير. وصارَ بَعْدُ قصارَى مُلوكِ الطوائفِ بالجزيرة نَظْرةً من اهتباله، وأدنَى خَطْرةٍ من بالِه.

فأدخَل على أدفُونش يومئذٍ منهم جماعةً فوجَدُوه يَمسَح الكرَى من عَينيه، ثائرَ الرأس خَبيثَ النّفس، وجـعلوا يَنظرون إليه وهو يَضفَحُ ثُغـامَة رأسِه، فمـاتَسـوا نفَرَ

he 'Abbadid ruler, al-Mu'tadid, who took him into his service. Sisnando, however, went over to the Christians and assisted Ferdinand in the capture of Coimbra (see text 86), after which he was made count of Coimbra by Ferdinand. Sisnando told 'Abd-Allah, the Zirid ruler of Granada, what were the Christian tactics for recovering their territory from the Muslims, as reported in a celebrated passage in his memoirs (see the translation by A.T. Tibi, p.90). On the fall of Toledo, Sisnando was installed as governor and attempted to encourage moderation towards the Muslims. However, his advice was quickly dispensed with (see also text 18); he died soon afterwards in 1091.

The text of this passage is taken from Ibn Bassam, al-Dhakhira fi mahasin ahl al-jazira, IV/i (ed. Cairo, 1945), pp.129-30. Unlike most of the other authors represented in these selections, Ibn Bassam (d. 1147) uses a highly florid and ornate style, that poses considerable difficulties, as will be observed from the translation, which has been kept as literal as possible.

Despite his later services to the Muslims, Ibn Bassam's portrait of Sisnando is not sympathetic. Haman was the vizier of Pharaoh, who instructed him to kindle a fire upon the clay (see Qur'an 28: 38). Predictably enough, Alfonso emerges as an entirely vicious brute, who appears to insult the Toledans by inspecting his genitals in their presence. His personal dirtiness is yet another example of the different sensibilities of the Christians and Moors in this respect (see text 83).

Some of their notables came together to the tent of Alfonso during that period, when the situation had become desperate, and death was licking its lips and the moment of fate approached with a swagger. The chamberlains were in position beside him, and said, "He is sleeping, how could you arouse him?" They turned aside to the tent of Shishnand (Sisnando), his familiar confidant and rebellious devil, his Haman who fired clay for him, and taught him how to strike doubt into the heart of certainty. One of the infidels in the service of [al-Mu'tadid] Ibn 'Abbad, he [Sisnando] was a man of blazing intellect, going a long way in both daring and reprehensible actions. He went as envoy between al-Mu'tadid and the tyrant Ferdinand (I), making and breaking agreements. He rose through his responsibilities and made himself independent. Then he feared for himself from al-Mu'tadid, and the root of censure caused him to depart to a blameworthy abode. He became firmly established in Jilliqiyya, and became well informed about the mountain passes and the borders, and mastered all other aspects of politics and administration. Thereafter the range of his scheming extended to the Party Kings of the Peninsula, and this became the closest thought to his heart.

He then caused a group of them to enter into the presence of Alfonso, and they found him rubbing the sleep from his eyes, with an angry [tousled] head and foul breath. They started to watch him while he ruffled his hoary white

أطمارَه ودَرَنَ أظفارَه. ثم أقبلَ عليهم بوجهٍ كَريهٍ، ولَحَظَ لا يَشكُّون أنّ الشرَ فيه، وقال لهم: «إلى متى تَتخادعون، وبأى شىءٍ تَطمعون؟» قالوا «بنا بغيةٌ، [ولنا] فى فلانٍ وفلانٍ أمنّيّة»، وسَمُّوا له بعضَ ملوكِ الطوائف، فصَفَّقَ بيديْه، وتَهافت حتى فَحصَ برجْليْه، ثم قال: «أينَ رُسلُ ابنِ عبّادٍ؟» فجيء بهم يَرفُلون فى ثيابِ الخَنَاعة، ويَنبِسون بألسنةِ السمعِ والطاعة. فقال لهم: «مُذْ كَمْ تحومُون علىّ، وترمونَ الوصُولَ إلىّ؟ ومتى عهدُكم بفلانٍ، وأينَ ما جئتم به لا كنتم ولا كان؟»

فجاؤا بجملةٍ ميرَة، وأحضروا بينَ يَديه كلُّ ذخيرةٍ خَطيرة. ثمّ ما زادَ على أن ركَلَ ذلك برجْليه، وأمَرَ بانتهابِه كلّه؛ ولم يَبْقَ مَلكٌ من ملوكِ الطوائف إلاَّ أحضرَ يومئذٍ رُسلَه، وكانت حالُه حالَ مَن كانَ قبلَه. وجعلَ أعلاجُه يَدفَعون فى ظهورهم، وأهلُ طُليْطَلَة يَعجبون من ذُلِّ مقامِهم ومَصيرِهم، فخرجَ مَشيخَتُها من عنده وقد سَقطَ فى أيديهم،

وطَمِعَ كلُّ شىءٍ فيهم، وخَلَّوا بينَه وبين البَلَد، لثلاثةِ أيامٍ من ذلك المشْهد. ودَخَلَ طُليطَلَة على حكْمِه وأثْبَتَ فى عَرْصَتِها قَدَمَ ظُلْمِه، حكْمٌ مِنَ الله، سَبَقَ به القَدَر، فلم يَكُنْ مِنْه وَزَرُ!

head, nor were they oblivious to the stench of his tatty garments and the filth of his fingernails. Then he advanced on them with an ugly face, and with a glance that left them in no doubt that there was evil in him, he said to them, "For how long are you going to go on deceiving yourselves, and what do you want?" They said, "We wish for something, and have reason to hope from so-and-so and so-and-so", and they named some of the Party Kings. Then he clapped his hands and fell to the floor and examined between his legs. Then he said, "Where are the messengers from Ibn 'Abbad?" They were brought in, trailing the cloaks of servility and their tongues uttering 'hearing and obeying'. He said to them, "How long have you been hovering around me and wanting to see me? When did you make your agreement with so and so, and where is what you have brought? To Hell with you and to Hell with him."

They brought a large supply of provisions and put weighty treasures in front of him. He did nothing but kick it with his feet and order it all to be carried off. That day there was not one of the Party Kings whose messengers were not summoned, and they were treated in the same way as the ones before. His infidels began pushing them in the back, and the Toledans were amazed at the humiliation of their position and at their fate. The shaikhs (elders) of the city left his presence and were aghast; he desired everything from them. For three days after that scene they passed between him and the city. He brought Toledo under his jurisdiction and planted the foot of his oppression in its courtyards. [This was] a judgement from God, decreed in advance, and there was no refuge from it.

92. The writing on the wall (478/1085)

As mentioned in the previous selection, none of the Ta'ifa rulers went to Toledo's assistance (most of them were already tributary to Alfonso); but if the attitude of the Muslim rulers to this momentous loss bordered on indifference, the reaction of their subjects reflected a very great concern. The fall of Barbastro in 1064 had caused a similar sensation, but that was quickly calmed by the Muslim recapture of the town (see text 87). The loss of Toledo brought home the real nature of the threat posed by the Christians, and also began the search for the causes of Muslim weakness. In various poems of this period, the blame falls both on the rulers, for their indolence and preoccupation with their own pleasures, and on the Muslim community, which has lost touch with the practices of its faith. For examples, see Wasserstein, pp.280-81; Pérès, p.100; and Nykl, pp.212-13. This hardening of the attitude of the Muslim population

ومن أول ما استرد الإفرنج من مدن الأندلس العظيمة مدينة طليطلة من يد ابن

ذي النون سنة ٤٧٥، وفي ذلك يقول عبدالله بن فرج اليَحْصبي المشهور بابن العسال:

فـمــا المُقــامُ بهـا إلاّ من لغلطِ	يــا أهـلَ أندلسٍ حُثُّـــوا مَطيِكـمُ
ثوبُ الجـزيرة منسـولاً مَن الوسَطِ	الثَّـــوبُ يُنسَلُ من أطرافـــه وأرى
كيفَ الحيـاة مع الحيّـاتِ في سَفَطٍ	ونـحـنُ بـينَ عَدُوٍّ لا يـفـــارقـنـا

وقال آخر:

في العُرْفِ عــاريةٌ إلاّ مـــرددّاتُ	يا أهل أندلسٍ رُدّوا المُعـــارَ فـمــا
وشــاهُنا آخـر الأبيــات شَهِــمـاتُ	ألم تَرَوْا بَيْدَقَ الكفّــــارِ فــــرزنَهُ

and their religious classes paved the way for the Almoravid intervention and its associated regeneration of pristine Islamic values (see also texts 98, 99).

The poems selected here are taken from al-Maqqari, Nafh al-tib, ed. Ihsan 'Abbas, IV, p.352. The first is by Ibn al-'Assal al-Yahsubi, who also wrote a poem on the fall of Barbastro (see text 87); the final line contains a play on the words hayat *(life) and* hayyat *(snakes). Al-Maqqari cites a couple of other variations on this poem, especially a fifth hemistich reading: "Whoever lives next door to evil cannot feel safe from its evil consequences". The second (anonymous) poem uses the imagery of chess, with the enemy queening his pawn, while the king is cornered* (shahmat: *the origin of the word* checkmate).

The city of Toledo was one of the first great cities of al-Andalus that the Franks retrieved, from the hands of Ibn Dhu 'l-Nun [i.e. al-Qadir], in 475 (1085). 'Abd-Allah b. Faraj al-Yahsubi, known as Ibn al-'Assal, has this poem on the subject:

1. O people of al-Andalus, spur on your mounts; it is nothing but a blunder to stay on here.

2. A robe [normally] unravels from its edges, but I see the robe of the Peninsula unravelled from the centre.

3. We are caught up with an enemy who will not leave us alone: How can one live in a basket together with snakes?

Another poet said:

1. O people of al-Andalus, return what you have borrowed; it is not customary to borrow without giving back.

2. Do you not see the pawn of the unbelievers has become a queen, while our king is checkmated on the last square?

93. The Battle of Zallaqa (479/1086)

The fall of Toledo lent an added weight and urgency to calls for assistance from the Almoravid ruler, Yusuf b. Tashufin, who in the previous fifteen years had made himself master of North Africa. Yusuf's seemingly reluctant involvement in the affairs of al-Andalus initiated a period of about 250 years during which the Muslim rulers of Spain were caught between the Christian Scylla to the north and the Berber Charybdis to the south. In general, the Berber dynasties, with their various brands of militant Islam, were viewed with equal if not greater alarm than the Christians. In 1085, however, the threat posed by the latter was sufficiently immediate to encourage the leading Ta'ifa rulers to set aside their mutual rivalries for the time being. The celebrated remark of al-Mu'tamid of Seville, to the effect that he would rather be a camel-herd among the Almoravids than a pig-swain among the Christians, neatly encapsulated the nature of the choices available.

The battle of Zallaqa, or Sagrajas, a little to the north of Badajoz, has recently been the subject of a detailed study by Vincent Lagardère, Le Vendredi de Zallāqa, 23 Octobre 1086 (Paris, 1989), which presents and discusses the availableArabic accounts. A. Huici Miranda, Las grandes batallas de la Reconquista durante las invasiones africanas (Madrid, 1956), pp.19-82, remains useful. For the Christian side, see Reilly, The Kingdom of Leon-Castilla, esp. pp.180-90. The victory brought a

المرابطون بالأندلس

ولما كانت سنة ٤٧٩ جاز المعتمد على الله البحـر قاصداً مدينة مـراكش الى يوسف بن تاشـفين، مستنصراً به على الروم؛ فلقيه يوسف المذكور أحسن لقاء، وأنزله أكرم نُزل، وسأله عن حاجته، فذكر أنه يريد غزو الروم، وأنه يريد امداد أمير المسلمين إياه بخيلٍ ورجُلٍ ليستعين بهم فى حربه، فأسرع أمير المسلمين المذكور اجابته الى ما دعاه إليه؛ وقال له: «أنا أوّل منتدب لنصرة هذا الدين، ولا يتولى هذا الأمر أحدٌ الا أنا بنفسى!»

فرجع المعتمد إلى الأندلس مسروراً بإسعاف أمير المسلمين إياه فى طَلبته، ولم يدر أنّ تدميره فى تدبيره؛ وسلّ سيفاً يحسبه له ولم يدر أنه عليه ...

فأخذ أمير المسلمين يوسف بن تاشفين فى أُهبة العبور الى جزيرة الأندلس؛ وذلك فى شهر جمادى الأولى من السنة المذكورة، فاستنفر مَن قدر على استنفاره من

emporary halt to the Christian advances of the 11th century and restored the initiative to the Muslims. Nevertheless, crucially, the Almoravids were unable to recapture Toledo, and Yusuf did not immediately follow up his triumph, but returned to North Africa on the news of the death of his son Abu Bakr. In the end, the main losers were the Party Kings themselves, almost all of whom were dethroned and their territories absorbed into the Almoravid empire between 1091 and 1094.

An eye-witness account of the battle of Zallaqa is given by the Zirid ruler of Granada, 'Abd-Allah; see his Memoirs, translated by Tibi, esp. pp.113-18. The text translated here is from 'Abd al-Wahid al-Marrakushi, al-Mu'jib fi talkhis akhbar al-naghrib, ed. M.S. 'Iryan (Cairo, 1383/1963), from pp.190-96. This account was written in 621/1224 and is free from the legendary and mythical elements that came to characterize the treatment of the battle in most other Arab chronicles. The author was writing in the east, probably Baghdad, thus freer from the need to flatter, but without access to other written sources. This explains the error he makes in the date of the battle, 13 Ramadan 480 (probably a misprint) instead of 12 Rajab 479, and in the information concerning Yusuf's march against Aledo, which was already in Alfonso's hands early in 1086. The Aledo campaign in fact occurred on Yusuf's second expedition, in 1088.

The Almoravids in al-Andalus

When it was 479 (1086), al-Mu'tamid 'ala-'llah crossed the sea, heading for Marrakesh, to seek help from Yusuf b. Tashufin against the Christians. The said Yusuf gave him a warm welcome and housed him in the finest style, and enquired what he wanted. [Al-Mu'tamid] mentioned that he wished to attack Christian territory and wanted the Amir al-Muslimin [Yusuf] to supply him with horses and men to help him wage war. The Commander of the Muslims hastened to grant his request, and said, "I am the first to be entrusted to come to the assistance of this faith, and none other than I myself will take charge of the matter!"

Al-Mu'tamid returned to al-Andalus happy with the assistance promised him by the Amir al-Muslimin; he did not know that his destruction lay in this arrangement. He drew a sword that he thought was for him, and did not know that it was against him [...].

Yusuf b. Tashufin, the Commander of the Muslims, began the preparations to cross to the Spanish Peninsula in the month of Jumada I this year (began 14 August). He summoned all the leaders and commanders of the army and the

القُوَّاد وأعيان الجند ووجوه قبائل البربر؛ فاجتمع له نحو من سبعة آلاف فارس فى عدد كثير من الرَّجِل؛ فعبر البحر بعسكر ضخم، وكان عبوره من مدينة سبْتة؛ فنزل المدينة المعروفة بالجزيرة الخضراء، وتلقاه المعتمد فى وجوه أهل دولته، وأظهر من بره وإكرامه فوق ما كان يظنه أميرُ المسلمين، وقدَّم إليه من الهدايا والتحف والذخائر الملوكية ما لم يظنه يوسف عند ملك؛ فكان هذا أول ما أوقع فى نفس يوسف التـشـوُّفَ الى مملكة جزيرة الأندلس.

ثم إنه فصل عن الخضراءِ بجيوشه قاصداً شرقى الأندلس، وسأله المعتمد دخولَ إشبيلية دارَ ملكه ليستريح فيها أياماً حتى تزول عنه وعثاءُ السفر ثم يقصد قصده، فأبى عليه وقال: «إنما جئت ناوياً جهاد العدوِّ، فحيثما كان العدوُّ توجهت وَجهه.»

وكـان الأدفنش – لعنه اللّه – مـحـاصـراً لحصن من حصون المسلمين يعرف بحصن اللِّيط؛ فلما بلغه عبور البربر أقلع عن الحصن راجعاً الى بلاده مستنفراً عساكره ليلقى بهم البربر.

وقعة الزُّلاُقة

ثم إنَّ يوسف المذكور استعرض جنده على حصن الرقة؛ فرأى منهم ما يسرُّه، فقال للمعتمد على اللّه: «هلُمَ ما جئنا من الجهاد وقصد العدوِّ»؛ وجعل يُظهر التأفف من الإقامة بجزيرة الأندلس، ويتشوَّق إلى مراكش، ويُصغِّر قدر الأندلس، ويقول فى أكثر أوقاته: «كان أمر هذه الجزيرة عندنا عظيماً قبل أن نراها، فلما رأيناها وقعت دون الوصف!» وهو فى ذلك كله «يُسَرُّ حَسْواً فى ارتغاء!» فـخرج المعتمد بين يديه قاصداً مدينة طليطلة.

واجتمع للمعتمد أيضاً جيش ضخم من أقطار الأندلس؛ وانتدَب الناسُ للجهاد من سائر الجهات، وأمدُّ ملوك الجزيرة يوسفَ والمعتمد بما قدروا عليه من خيل ورجال

chiefs of the Berber tribes whom he could call upon to fight. About 7,000 horsemen with a large number of infantry assembled and he crossed the sea with a vast army, embarking at the town of Sabta (Ceuta) and landing at the town called al-Jazirat al-khadra (Algeciras). Al-Mu'tamid met him with the leading men of his state, and displayed more reverence and deference towards him than the Amir al-Muslimin had expected. [Al-Mu'tamid] presented him with kingly gifts, presents and riches such as Yusuf could not imagine a king possessing. It was this that first kindled a longing for the kingdom of al-Andalus in Yusuf's heart.

He then set off from Algeciras with his troops, towards the east of al-Andalus. Al-Mu'tamid asked him to enter Seville, his capital, to rest there a few days until the rigours of his journey were soothed and then carry out his intentions. Yusuf refused, saying, "I have only come with the aim of fighting holy war against the enemy; wherever he is, I will set off to face him."

Alfonso (VI) – may God curse him! – was giving siege to one of the Muslims' castles, known as al-Lit (Aledo). When he heard that the Berbers had crossed over, he abandoned the siege and returned to his own territories, mobilizing his army to meet the Berbers [...].

The Battle of Zallaqa

The above-mentioned Yusuf then reviewed his troops at the fortress of al-Raqqa, and liked what he saw of them. He said to al-Mu'tamid 'ala-'llah, "Let's go on the Holy War that we came for, and attack the enemy." He began to grumble about staying in the Spanish Peninsula, and to long for Marrakesh, and to belittle the power of al-Andalus. He was forever saying, "We took the affairs of this Peninsula seriously until we saw it, and now that we have seen it, it has sunk beneath all description." [But] in doing so he was as one "happy to drink the froth" [i.e. pretending to want only the froth, while actually drinking all the milk]. Al-Mu'tamid left him, heading for Toledo.

A mighty army assembled round al-Mu'tamid from different regions of al-Andalus, and the people were summoned to Holy War from other districts. The kings of the Peninsula reinforced Yusuf and al-Mu'tamid with as many horses,

وسلاح، فتكامل عدد المسلمين من المتطوعة والمرتزقة زُهاءَ عشرين ألفاً؛ والتقوا هم والعدوُّ بأول بلاد الروم.

وكان الأدفنش – لعنه الله – قد استنفر الصغير والكبير، ولم يَدعْ فى أقاصى مملكته من يقدر على النهوض الا استنهضه، وجاءَ يجرُّ الشوك والشجر؛ وإنما كان مقصوده الأعظم قطع تشوُّف البرابرة عن جزيرة الأندلس والتهيُّب عليهم؛ فأما ملوك الأندلس فلم يكن منهم أحدٌ إلا يؤدّى اليه الاتاوة، وهم كانوا أحقرَ فى عينه وأقلُّ من أن يحتفل لهم.

ولما تراءَى الجمعان من المسلمين والنصارى، رأى يوسف وأصحابه أمراً عظيماً هالهم؛ من كثرة عددٍ، وجَودة سلاحٍ وخيل، وظهورِ قوة؛ فقال للمعتمد: «ما كنت أظن هذا الخنزير – لعنه الله – يبلغ هذا الحد!»

وجمع يوسف أصحابه وندَب لهم من يَعظهم ويُذكرهم؛ فظهر منهم من صدق النية والحرص على الجهاد واستسهال الشهادة ما سُرَّ به يوسف والمسلمون.

وكان ترائيهم يوم الخميس، وهو الثانى عشر من شهر رمضان؛ فاختلفت الرسلُ بينهم فى تقرير يوم الزحف ليستعدَّ الفريقان؛ فكان من قول الأدفنش لعنه الله: «الجمعة لكم، والسبت لليهود وهم وزراءنا وكُتابنا وأكثرُ خدم العسكر منهم فلا غنى بنا عنهم، والأحد لنا؛ فإذا كان يوم الاثنين كان ما نريده من الزحف». وقصد –لعنه الله– مخادعةَ المسلمين واغتيالهم، فلم يتم له ما قصد ...

فلما كان يوم الجمعة تأهب المسلمون لصلاة الجمعة ولا أمارة عندهم للقتال، وبَنى يوسفُ بن تاشفين الأمر على أن الملوكَ لا تغدِر؛ فخرج هو وأصحابه فى ثياب الزينة للصلاة؛ فأما المعتمد فإنه أخذ بالحزم، فركب هو وأصحابه شاكى السلاح، وقال لأمير المسلمين: «صلِّ فى أصحابك فهذا يومٌ ما تطيب نفسى فيه، وها أنا من ورائكم؛

men and arms as they could; the total strength of the Muslims, including
volunteers and mercenaries, was about 20,000 men. They and the enemy met
where Christian territory began.

Alfonso – may God curse him! – had already called up great and small; there
was no-one left in the furthest reaches of his territory capable of action whom he
had not stirred. He came leading a powerful army, his main intention being to
stifle the desire of the Berbers for the Spanish Peninsula and to inspire them
with fear. As for the kings of al-Andalus, every one of them was paying him
tribute; they were more than contemptible in his eyes and beneath his
contemplation.

When the two sides, Muslim and Christian, beheld each other, Yusuf and his
companions were appalled by the enormous size of the enemy numbers, the
excellence of their arms and horses and their appearance of strength. He said to
al-Mu'tamid, "I didn't realize that this pig – may God curse him – had grown to
such proportions."

Yusuf and his companions assembled, and he appointed someone to exhort
them and preach to them. A sufficient number of them affirmed their vow and
their eagerness to fight the Holy War and made light of martyrdom, to gladden
Yusuf and the Muslims.

The two sides made contact on a Thursday, 12 Ramadan (21 December, *sic*);
the envoys were unable to agree on a day for the general advance, so that they
could make their preparations. Alfonso said, "Friday is your [Holy Day].
Saturday is the Jews'; they are our ministers and scribes, and make up the
majority of the servants in the army and we cannot do without them. Sunday is
our [Holy Day]. So Monday would be the best day to begin operations." His
intention – God curse him! – was to deceive and mislead the Muslims, but it
didn't turn out as he planned...

On the Friday, the Muslims were preparing for the Friday prayers with no
sign of [preparation for] a fight. Yusuf b. Tashufin relied on the belief that kings
do not act treacherously, and he and his companions went out dressed for
prayers. Al-Mu'tamid took courage and he and his companions rode out armed
to the teeth; he said to the Amir of the Muslims, "Pray at the head of your men; I

وما أظن هذا الخنزير إلا قد أضمر الفتك بالمسلمين».

فأخذ يوسف وأصحابه فى الصلاة، فلما عقدوا الركعة الأولى ثارت فى وجوههم الخيل من جهة النصارى، وحمل الأدفنش -لعنه الله- فى أصحابه يظن أنه قد انتهز الفرصة؛ وإذا المعتمد وأصحابه من وراء الناس، فأغنى ذلك اليوم غَناءً لم يُشْهَد لأحد من قبله؛ وأخذ المرابطون سلاحهم فاستوَوْا على متون الخيل، واختلط الفريقان؛ فأظهر يوسف بن تاشفين وأصحابه من الصبر وحسن البلاء والثبات ما لم يكن يحسبه المعتمد؛ هزم الله العدوُّ، واتبعهم المسلمون يقتلونهم فى كل وجه، ونجا الأدفنش -لعنه الله- فى تسعة من أصحابه؛ فكان هذا أحد الفتوح المشهورة بالأندلس، أعزّ الله فيه دينه وأعلى كلمته وقطع طمعَ الأدفنش لعنه الله - عن الجزيرة، بعد أن كان يقدّر أنها فى ملكه وأن رؤسها خدم له؛ وذلك كله بحسن نية أمير المسلمين.

وتسمى هذه الوقعة عندهم وقعة الزُّلاقة: وكان لقاءُ المسلمين عدوهم كما ذكرنا فى يوم الجمعة الثالث عشر من شهر رمضان الكائن فى سنة ٤٨٠ ورجع يوسف بن تاشفين وأصحابه عن ذلك المشهد منصورين مفتوحاً لهم وبهم؛ فسُرّ بهم أهل الأندلس، وأظهروا التيمّن بأمير المسلمين والتبرك به، وكثر الدعاءُ له فى المساجد وعلى المنابر، وانتشر له من الثناء بجزيرة الأندلس ما زاده طمعاً فيها؛ وذلك أن الأندلس كانت قبله بصدد التّلاف من استيلاء النصارى عليها وأخذهم الإتاوة من ملوكها قاطبة؛ فلما قهر الله العدوَّ وهزمه على يد أمير المسلمين، أظهر الناسُ إعظامه ونشأ له الودّ فى الصدور.

m ill at ease today. I am here behind you, for I suspect this pig [Alfonso] has a ecret design to launch a sudden attack on the Muslims."

Yusuf and his men began to pray, and when they had performed the first ak'a the Christian cavalry burst into them. Alfonso – may God curse him! – ttacked at the head of his men, thinking that he would seize his opportunity, hile al-Mu'tamid and his men were behind the Almoravids. That day produced uch riches as no-one had ever witnessed before. The Almoravids grabbed their reapons and mounted their horses and the two sides became embroiled. Yusuf . Tashufin and his men showed a perseverance, heroism and fortitude beyond ie calculations of al-Mu'tamid, and God defeated the enemy. The Muslims ursued them, killing them on all sides, but Alfonso – God curse him! – escaped ith nine men. This was one of the most celebrated victories in al-Andalus, by hich God glorified his religion, elevated his word, and cut off Alfonso's mbitions (may God curse him!) in al-Andalus, after he had been anticipating it ɔming into his possession and believing that its kings were his servants. All ɪis came about through the pious intentions of the Amir of the Muslims.

They called this battle al-Zallaqa; the encounter between the Muslims and ieir enemy occurred, as we have mentioned, on Friday 13 Ramadan 480 [sic] 2 December 1087). Yusuf b. Tashufin and his men departed victoriously from ιe scene, conquered for them and by them, and the men of al-Andalus were ːlighted with them, and regarded the Amir al-Muslimin as a good omen and a ɪessing. Prayers for him multiplied in the mosques and from the pulpits, his ːaises spread through the Spanish Peninsula in a way that increased his ɔvetousness towards it. This was because al-Andalus, before his arrival, was ιcing annihilation by the conquests of the Christians and their exaction of ɪbute from all its kings without exception; and when God overcame the enemy ιd defeated him at the hands of the Commander of the Muslims, the people ɔclaimed his glory and love for him grew in their hearts.

94. The Cid captures Valencia (487/1094)

The career of Rodrigo Díaz, better known as El Cid, illustrates, perhaps more than anything else, the fluidity of the boundaries between Christian and Moor in the eleventh century. His complex network of alliances with other local rulers, regardless of their supposed religious affiliations, shows that the desire for immediate territorial and material gains determined the actions of the military leaders of the period, as was to be witnessed again in the crusading states of the Levant during the following century. Nevertheless, El Cid's most spectacular triumph casts him squarely in the role of villain to the Muslims and hero of the Reconquista to the Christians. There is no need to rehearse these issues here: the recent book by Richard Fletcher, The Quest for El Cid, *provides an admirable account.*

As noted by Smith (see texts 20, 22 and 23), the most important Muslim account of events in Valencia is given in the lost work of Ibn 'Alqama, which was partly preserved by later Arab authors, and also translated into Castillian. A comparison of the two versions has been made by Lévi-Provençal, "La prise de Valence par le Cid", in his Islam d'Occident. Études d'histoire médiévale *(Paris, 1948), pp.187-238, which also contains translations of other relevant Arabic texts.*

وفي سنة ٤٨٧ لما انصرف جيش الأمير أبي بكر بن ابراهيم اللمتوني بحكم لقدر السابق عن بلنسية، أيقن من فيها بالهلكة، وغلب على الناس اليأس، وضاقت النفوس؛ وزاد حقد العدو، وقسا قلبه، وهلك أكثر الناس جوعاً، وأكلت الجلود والدواب وغير ذلك، ومن فر الى المحلة فقئت عيناه، أو قطعت يداه، أو دقت ساقاه، أو قتل، رضى الناس بالموت في المدينة، وزادت هذه الأزمة على أزمة طليطلة أضعافاً لانفساح مدة الحصار، وتضاعف حقد العدو لصبرهم وطلبهم النصرة.

ذكر تغلب العدو على بلنسية في هذه السنة

لما بلغ بأهل بلنسية الماءُ الزبى، وانتهوا من الصبر إلى الغاية القصوى، ولا نصر لا غوث، ألجأتهم الحال إلى دخول العدو بحكم الاضطرار، لا بحكم الاختيار، فتجمعوا الى قاضيهم أبي المطرف ابن جحاف، وسفروا إلى الطاغية الكبيطور – لعنه الله – من توسط لهم معه أخذ الأمان، فأجاب في هذا الشأن، وعقد نيته على الختر، ونقض عهد، وإعطاء أمان مثله من الأنجاس، فخرج اليه القاضي، وعقد عليه العقود، وأخذ المواثيق والعهود، وحزم في كل ذلك، وبلغ الغاية التى ما بعدها غاية، ولا وراءها لمجتهد

The passage that follows (which does not derive from Ibn 'Alqama), concerns El Cid's capture and defence of the city in the face of two Almoravid campaigns led by Yusuf's nephews, the first in 1093 under Abu Bakr b. Ibrahim, the second under his brother Muhammad. Before its surrender, Valencia was in the hands of the qadi, Ibn Jahhaf, the latter having removed al-Qadir, who had shown himself as unfit to rule in Valencia as he had previously in Toledo (see above, p.86). This coup can again be seen as evidence of the general dissatisfaction of the Muslim religious classes with their Ta'ifa rulers. In pursuit of al-Qadir's wealth, El Cid subjected the unfortunate Ibn Jahhaf to torture and a brutal death. Earlier promises to treat his Muslim subjects with consideration (see text 23) seem to have been quickly broken, particularly after the unsuccessful attempt by Muhammad to regain the city.

The text is taken from Ibn 'Idhari, al-Bayan al-mughrib, vol. IV, ed. Ihsan 'Abbas (Beirut, 1967), from pp.33-38.

In the year 487 (began 21 January 1094), when the army of the [Almoravid] amir Abu Bakr b. Ibrahim al-Lamtuni departed from Balansiyya (Valencia) according to the preordained decree of fate, those within became certain of their destruction. Despair gripped the people and their spirits became dejected. The enemy's malice increased and his heart became harder. The majority of the people perished from hunger; [even] leather hides and pack animals were eaten. Whoever fled to the camp [of the Christians] had his eyes gouged out, or his hands cut off, or his legs broken, or was killed. The people [therefore] preferred to die in the city. The dearth became twice as bad as it had been in Toledo, due to the long duration of the siege. The enemy's hatred was compounded by the Valencians' endurance and their efforts to seek assistance [from the Almoravids].

The enemy's conquest of Valencia this year

When the Valencians could no longer keep their heads above water, and had reached the limits of their endurance, with no help or assistance [in prospect], circumstances forced them to go to the enemy, not by choice but by necessity. They gathered round their qadi, Abu'l-Mutarrif b. Jahhaf, and sent someone to the tyrant Campeador – may God curse him! – to mediate on their behalf for a safe conduct. He [the Cid] accepted this, but intended to act treacherously and to infringe the agreement. It is the dirty infidel who gives this sort of *aman*. The qadi went out to him and bound various agreements on him, and took oaths and promises, and acted firmly over everything, until the utmost limit was reached; no *mujtahid* could have done more. When this was concluded, the gates were

نهاية، فلما كمل الأمر فتحت له الأبواب، ودخل المدينة بجملته، وذلك في جمادى الأولى من هذه السنة فلم يعمل هو وأصحابه – لعنهم الله – ما يسوء المدينة وأهلها بحال من الأحوال، فانتشطت الأنفس من عقال، وانبسطت الآمال، وأمن الناس. وهو مع ذلك يراعي أمرهم ويمنعهم من الخروج من المدينة، وحصل – لعنه الله – على هذه الحضرة، ورمى [نفسه] على ما هي عليه من النعمة والنضرة والحسن والبهجة. [...]

ذكر حرق القاضي أبي أحمد ابن جحاف
ومحنة أهله وقرابته ومحنة أهل بلنسية

ولما تمهدت بلنسية للكبيطور – لعنه الله! – بدأ بثقاف قاضيها ابن جحاف وثقاف أهله وقرابته، فعمهم الثقاف، وبلغتهم المحنة، وجعل يطلبهم بمال حفيد ابن ذي النون، ولم يزل يستخرج ما عندهم حتى استصفى أموالهم واستنفد أحوالهم. فلما لم يترك لهم ظاهراً ولا باطناً، أمر بإضرام النار، وسيق القاضي أبو المطرّف، يرسف في قيوده، وأهله وبنوه حوله وقد حشر الناس من المسلمين والروم. ثم قال لملأ من المسلمين: «ما جزاء من قتل أميره عندكم في شرعكم؟» فصمتوا، فقال لهم: «جزاؤه عندنا الإحراق بالنار!» وأمر وبجملته الى ذلك الضرم، وقد لفح الوجوه على المسافة البعيدة. فضج المسلمون والروم، وتضرعوا اليه في ترك الأطفال والعيال، إذ لا ذنب لهم، ولا علم بتلك الأمور عندهم، فأسعف الرعية في رغبتهم بعد جهد ومدة، وترك النساء والصبية. وحُفر للقاضي حفرة، وأُدخل فيها الى حُجزته، وسوّي التراب حوله، وضمت النار اليه فلما دنت منه، ولفحت وجهه، قال: «بسم الله الرحمن الرحيم» ثم ضمها الى جسده، فاحترق – رحمه الله تعالى.

ولم يكف غضب الطاغية عليه إلا لشدة صبره على تلك الأزمة، واجتهاده في طلب النصرة، ودفعه إياه بالمطاولة، رجاءً في استمساك البلدة وابقاء الكلمة.

opened to him, and he entered the city with his whole army. This was in Jumada (began 19 May 1094). Neither he nor his companions – may God curse them! – acted in any way that would harm the city or its people; spirits revived, hopes were kindled and the people found security. Nevertheless he kept an eye on them, and forbade them to leave the city. May God curse him, he acquired this princely capital, and devoted himself to enjoying the favour, opulence, splendour and beauty that had been hers.

[... El Cid defeats a relieving Almoravid force under Abu 'Abd-Allah Muhammad b. Ibrahim, nephew of Yusuf b. Tashufin...]

The burning of the qadi Abu Ahmad b. Jahhaf, and the trials to which his family, relatives and the people of Valencia were subjected.

When Valencia was organized to the liking of the Campeador – may God curse him! – he began to seize her qadi, Ibn Jahhaf, his family and relations, and arrested them all. They were subjected to an inquisition, and he started questioning them about the wealth belonging to the grandson of Ibn Dhu'l-Nun [i.e. al-Qadir]. He continued to extract what they had from them, until he had confiscated all their property and exhausted their wherewithal. When he had left them nothing, whether visible or concealed, he ordered a fire to be kindled. The qadi Abu'l-Mutarrif [Ibn Jahhaf] was dragged in, bound in shackles, surrounded by his family and his sons. A crowd of Muslims and Christians had assembled. [The Cid] then said to a group of Muslims, "What is the punishment according to your law (shar') for one who has killed his ruler?"; they remained silent. Then he said to them, "With us, his punishment is to be burnt alive." He gave the order for him and his whole group to be brought to the fire, which warmed the face even at a great distance. The Christians and Muslims raised a shout, beseeching him to spare the children and members of the family, since they had committed no sin, and had no knowledge of these matters. He [only] complied with the wishes of the subjects after a prolonged struggle, and let the women and children go. A hole was dug for the qadi, who was put in it up to his waist. The ground was levelled out round him, and he was encircled by fire. When it got near him, and lit up his face, he said, "In the name of God, the Compassionate, the Merciful," and pulled it [i.e. the burning material] towards his body and was burnt to death, may God have mercy on him!

The tyrant's unjust anger towards Ibn Jahhaf was only due to the strength of his endurance in this crisis, his efforts to seek help, and for the length of time that he had resisted him, in his desire to retain his hold on the city and to preserve the [Muslim] profession of faith.

104

وعمد الطاغية - لعنه الله - بعد إحراق القاضي - رحمه الله - الى الجلة من أهل بلنسية، فثقفهم وأغرمهم حتى استأصل جميع ما عندهم وجعل الناس في المحنة أسوة، يأخذهم على طبقاتهم، حتى عمتهم المحنة، وهلك ذلك الثقاف كثير منهم - رحمهم الله وجعلها كفارة لهم.

After the burning of the qadi, the tyrant – may God curse him! – proceeded to [deal with] the notables of Valencia; he seized them and extracted fines from them until he had rooted out everything they had. Then he subjected the people to an inquisition along the same lines, seizing them according to their various categories, until the inquisition included all of them. Many of them died during this treatment – may God have mercy on them and make it a [sufficient] atonement [for their sins].

95. The recovery of Valencia (495/1102)

El Cid died in 1099, leaving his widow Jimena Díaz to defend Valencia (for some of his activities before his death, see texts 24, 25 and 26). In the late summer of 1101, Mazdali, the cousin of Yusuf b. Tashufin, moved in to besiege the city, while Jimena summoned the help of Alfonso VI of Castile. By the spring of 1102, Alfonso had arrived and Mazdali's forces retired to Cullera; but the king reluctantly decided to abandon the city, which was too far from his own now rather shrunken domains, for him to have a realistic chance of holding Valencia. In 495/April 1102 the Christians withdrew, leaving the city stripped of whatever they could carry away, and then set it on fire.

This selection is a poem written to celebrate the recovery of Valencia. The poet, Ibn Khafaja, was born in 450/1058 at Alcira, near Valencia, and died there in 533/25 June 1139. He also composed a poem on the conquest of Valencia by the Cid, which Nykl (pp.

وقال يصف حال بَلَنْسِية – حماها الله! – وقد تتاجت النفوس باسترجاعها من

يد العلو، قصمه الله!:

ألآنَ سَحَّ غَمامُ الـــنَّصرِ فَانْهَمَلا   وقَامَ صَغْوُ عَمُودِ الدّينِ فـــاعْتَدَلا

ولاحَ لِــلسَّعْدِ نَجْمٌ قَد خَوَى فَهَوَى   وكَرَّ لِلــنَّصرِ عَصرٌ قَد مَضَى فَخَلا

وثارَ يَطْلُعُ نَقْعُ الجَيْشِ مُعْتَكِـــراً   بحَيْثُ يَطْلُعُ وَجْهُ الفَتحِ مُقْتَبِـــلا

مِنْ عَسْكَرٍ رجَفَتْ أرْضُ الــعَدُوِّ بِهِ   حتّى كـــانَ بِهـــا مِنْ وَطْئِهِ وَهَلا

ما بَينَ رِيحِ طِرادٍ سُمِّيَتْ فَرَسـاً   جَوراً ولَــيـثِ شَرَى يَدعُونـهُ بَطَلا

مِنْ أدهمٍ أخضرِ الجِلْبابِ تحْسُبُهُ   قـد استعارَ رداءَ اللّيلِ فـاشتَمَلا

وأشْقرٍ قــانىءِ السِّرْبالِ مُلتَهِبٍ   قد جالَ يُوقِدُ نارَ الحَربِ فاشتَعَلا

وأشهبٍ ناصعِ القِـــرْطاسِ مُؤتَلقٍ   كأنّما خاضَ ماءَ الصُّبحِ فاغتَسَلا

تَرى بهِ مـاءَ نَصْلِ السيفِ مُنسكِباً   يَجري وجاحمَ نارِ البأسِ مُشتَعِلا

فــغادَرَ الطَّعْنُ أجفَانَ الجِراحِ بهِ   رُمــداً وصيَّرَ أطرافَ القَنى مُقَــلا

وأشرَقَ الدّمُ في خَدِّ الثَّرى خجَــلاً   وأظلمَ النقْعُ في جَفنِ الوغَى كَحَلا

وأقشَعَ الكُفرُ قسْراً عنْ بلَنسيةٍ   فانجابَ عنها حِجابٌ كانَ مُنسدِلا

227-31) describes as bearing "no special mark of originality". Another of his poems is
translated by Monroe, pp.242-45.

The text is taken from Ibn Khafaja's Diwan, ed. Sayyid Mustafa Ghazi (Alexandria,
1960), pp.208-09. Pérès, pp.107, 355-56, gives a few lines of the poem presented here,
in the context of the depiction of war in Andalusian poetry, and appears to consider that
they illustrate "heaviness in the movements of the Christians"; if anything, however, they
refer to the Muslim heroes and their performance in battle. In fact, there does not seem
to have been any major confrontation, and the battle is a figment of poetic imagination.
In line 5, Sharra is the name of a district by the Euphrates that was famous for lions: the
army was composed of horses swift as the wind and heroes like lions.

Describing the state of Valencia (may God defend it), when its recovery from
the hands of the enemy (may God shatter him!) was the subject of everyone's
conversation, the poet said:

1. The clouds of victory have now flowed over and poured down rain, the
   leaning pillars of the faith have been set up straight and are once more in
   balance.
2. A star that had set and fallen has sparkled auspiciously; an era that had
   passed and elapsed has returned to victory.
3. The dust of the army has risen up in a murky ferment, so that the face of
   triumph rises up again,
4. From an army at which the ground under the enemy has trembled, as if it
   were terrified at its tramping:
5. Consisting of a chasing wind, wrongly called a horse, and a lion of Sharra
   whom they claim to be a hero.
6. Some of them black in flowing dark green surcoats, who you would think
   had borrowed the cloak of night and enfolded themselves in it,
7. Some red, with scarlet breastplates ablaze, who [you would think] had sped
   round, kindling the fire of war until it blazed up,
8. Some white, flashing with the purity of gleaming paper, as though they had
   plunged into water in the morning and bathed.
9. Because of them, you see the water [or temper] of the swordblade poured
   out, flowing, and the burning coals of the fire of valour ablaze.
10. The spearthrust has left the eyelids of wounds, bleary, and has transformed
    the points of lances into eyes;
11. Blood has radiated in the cheeks of the earth in a modest blush, while dust
    has darkened the eyelid of the battle's uproar with *kohl*.
12. Unbelief has been forcibly dispersed from Valencia, and a veil that had
    been lowered [over her] has disappeared.

108

وطَهَّرَ السَّيفُ منهـا بلدةً جُنبـاً   لمْ يَجزهـا غيرُ ماءِ السيفِ مُغتسلَا
كـــأننـي بعلوجِ الرّومِ ســــادِرةً   وقدْ تَضعْضعَ ركنُ الكُفرِ فاستقلَا
تظلُّ تدرأُ بالإســلامِ عَنْ دمهـــا   وهبةُ السيفِ فيهـا تسبقُ العَذلَا
في مَوقفٍ يَذهـلُ الخلَّ الصفيَّ بـه   عنِ الخَليلِ وينسَى العـاشقُ الغَزلَا
ترى بني الأصفرِ البيضَ الوُجُوه به   قَدْ راعَهـا السّيفَ فاصفرّتْ لهُ وَجلَا
فكمْ هُنالكَ من ضِرغـامةٍ سـفَرَتْ   سُمرُ العوالي إلىَ أحشائِه رُسُلَا
يُربي على حمَرةِ المَريخِ ملتـهـبـاً   تَحتَ القَتـــامِ ويَعلُو همّةً زُحَـــلَا
قـدْ كَرَّ في لامةٍ خضراءَ تَحسبُهـا   بَحـراً يُلاطِمُ منْ أعطافِه جَبـــلَا
وللقنَى أعـيُنٌ قـدْ حَدَّقتْ حنقـاً   وَللظّبَى ألسنٌ قـدْ أفصَحتْ جَدلَا
فــزاحَمَ النَّقعَ حـــتَّى شَقَّ بُردَتَهُ   وناطَحَ المَوتَ حـــتَّى خَرَّ مُنجَدِلَا
مُوسَّداً فـوقَ نصلِ السَّيفِ تحسبُهُ   مُستلقياً فوقَ شاطىءٍ جَدولٍ ثَملَا
فكمْ مُمـزَّقـةٍ منْ جيــبـهَا طرَباً   قـدْ مَزّقتْ بعدهُ منْ جَيبِهـا ثُكلَا
ورقرقَ الدَّمعَ في أجفـانِهَا رَشَأً   مـثَّلَ السَّحـرُ في أجفَانِه كَحـلَا
قـدْ بلّلتْ نحرَهُ بالدّمعِ حـادثةٌ   نكراءُ تمسَحُ عنْ أعطافِه الكَسـلَا
يَفُضُّ عقـــدَ لآليـــهِ وأدمُعُهُ   في نَحرِه فـتـراهُ حـاليـاً عُطُلَا

3. The sword has purged the city of an impurity – only the water of the sword could suffice to cleanse her.

4. It is as though I see the infidel Christians in a daze; the pillar of unbelief has collapsed and broken.

5. She [Valencia] continues to defend herself with the help of Islam, and the cutting of the sword in her forestalls any rebuke.

6. In a situation where a sincere friend ignores his best friend, and the lover forgets his dalliance,

7. Where you see the yellow ones [i.e. the Franks] white-faced; the sword has startled them and turned them pale with fright,

8. How many a lion there, to whose entrails the brown lance-points have been sent as messengers!

9. Who glows brighter than the redness of Mars beneath the pall of battle, and rising higher than Saturn in his zeal,

0. Who has charged in armour of dark green that you would think a sea, crashing against a mountain on its flanks.

1. The spear has eyes that have stared angrily; the sword-edge has tongues that have expressed themselves clearly in altercation.

2. He pressed against the dust until he ripped its garment; he jostled against death until he fell, thrown down to the ground,

3. Pillowed upon the swordblades; you would think he was lying on the bank of a stream in a drunken sleep.

4. How many of those women who tore open their bodices in joy have torn their breasts in mourning after his death?

5. A gazelle's eyelids have flowed with tears; the daybreak in her eyelids has become dark as *kohl*.

6. A horrible event, which dispels languor from her flanks, has moistened her neck with tears;

7. She snaps open the clasp of her pearl necklace, and her tears roll down her neck, so you see her [both] adorned with jewels [her tears], [and] stripped of ornaments!

96. Rules for the Christians (early 12th century)

The following selections are from the hisba *manuals published by E. Lévi-Provençal,* Documents arabes inédits *(Cairo, 1955), from pp.48-49, 57, 94-95 and 122; these cover the famous treatise of Ibn 'Abdun, as well as works by Ibn 'Abd al-Ra'uf and 'Umar al-Jarsifi. The* hisba *is the function of the* muhtasib, *or market inspector, among whose duties are to ensure that traders conform to Islamic regulations, to monitor the use of weights and measures and to enforce public morality. Ibn 'Abdun lived in Seville around the turn of the 12th century, witnessing both the accession of the 'Abbadid ruler al-Mu'tamid (1068) and the fall of the city to the Almoravids (1091). The dates of the other two authors are not known; Ibn 'Abd al-Ra'uf appears to have written at a relatively early period, while 'Umar, from Guercif in Morocco, may have been active at the end of the Middle Ages. It is convenient, though doubtless inexact, to treat them together.*

A French translation of Ibn 'Abdun's treatise has been published by E. Lévi-Provençal, Séville musulmane au début du XIIe siècle *(Paris, 1947), while the others have been similarly served by R. Arié, "Traduction annotée et commentée des traités de* hisba *d'Ibn 'Abd al-Ra'uf et de 'Umar al-Garsīfī",* Hespéris Tamuda, *1 (1960), 5-38,*

(a)

يجب أن لا يحكّ مسلمٌ اليهوديَّ، ولا النصرانيَّ، ولا يرمي زبله ولا ينقي كنيفه:
اليهوديّ والنصرانيّ كانوا أولى بهذه الصنع، لأنهّا صنع الأرذلين؛ لا يخدم مسلمٌ دابّة
هوديّ، ولا نصرانيّ، ولا يستزمل له، ولا يضبط بركابه؛ وإن عرف هذا أُنكر علي فاعله.

يجب أن يُمنع النساء المسلمات دخول الكنائس المشنوعة؛ فإن القسّيسين فَسَقةٌ
ناةٌ لوطةٌ. يجب أن تمنع الإفرنجيّات من الدخول في الكنيسة، إلا في يوم فَضْلٍ أو عيدٍ؛
أنّهنّ يأكُلنَ ويشربْنَ ويزنينَ مع القسّيسيين، وما منهم واحدٌ إلا وعنده منهنّ اثنتان أو
كثر، بيبت معهنّ؛ وقد صار هذا عُرفاً عندهم، لأنّهم حرموا الحلال، واستحلوا الحرام.
جب أن يؤمر القسّيسون بالزواج كما في ديار المَشرق؛ ولو شاءوا لفعلوا.

يجب أن لا يترك في دار القسّيس امرأةً، ولا عجوزٌ، ولا غيرُها، إن تَأبّى الزواج.
جب أن يُجبروا على الختان، كما كان يفعل بهم المُعتَضدُ عبّاد؛ فإنهم متّبعون بزعمهم
سُنَن عيسى - صلعم - وعيسى قد اختتن، ولهم في يوم اختتانه عيدٌ يُعظّمونه، ويتركون
ك!

99-214, 349-86.

In the first selection, the ban on selling scientific (particularly medical) books to the Christians reveals that the Muslims became jealous of their own knowledge and wary of the use to which their rivals might put it. European interest in Islamic achievements in his field was already well developed and continued right through the Middle Ages: only medical texts were spared from the bonfire of Arabic books ordered by Francisco Jiménez de Cisneros in Granada in 1499.

Our other authors take a narrower view of their role in reforming urban morals, and restrict themselves largely to matters connected with trade and commerce. Ibn 'Abd al-Ra'uf relies heavily on the legal authority of Malik b. Anas and his principal disciples, Ibn Habib (died about 853), author of the Wadiha and mufti of Cordova, and Ibn al-Qasim (died Cairo, 806), author of the Mudawwana (see also text 90). Among the other sources cited are Mutarrif (died 835), the nephew and disciple of Malik, and Ibn al-Majishun (died about 818), who was mufti of Medina and another of Malik's pupils. Meat and drink are the main preoccupations of these jurists in so far as transactions with the Christian and Jewish populations are concerned.

(a) Ibn 'Abdun

A Muslim should not rub down a Jew, nor a Christian [in the baths], neither should he throw out their refuse nor cleanse their lavatories; the Jews and Christians are more suitable for such a job, which is a task for the meanest. A Muslim should not work with the animals of a Jew, nor of a Christian, neither should he ride in their company, nor grasp their stirrup. If [the *muhtasib*] gets to know of this, the perpetrator will be censured.

Muslim women must be prevented from entering disgusting churches, for the priests are fornicators, adulterers and pederasts. Frankish women [too] should be forbidden to enter churches except on days of particular merit or festivals, for they eat and drink and fornicate with the priests: there is not one of them who does not keep two or more of these women, spending the night with them. This has become a regular custom with them, for they have made what is lawful unlawful, and made what is unlawful lawful. The priests must be made to marry, as they do in the east; if they wanted to, they would.

No woman, old or otherwise, should be left in the house of a priest if he has refused to marry. They [the priests] should be forced into circumcision, as al-Mu'tamid 'Abbad made them do. According to their assertions, they follow the path of Jesus (God bless him and grant him salvation!), and Jesus was circumcized; with them, the day of his circumcision [1 January] is a festival which they hold in great regard, [but] they themselves abandon [this practice]!

112

يجب أن لايباع من اليهود، ولا من النصارى، كتابُ علمٍ، إلا ما كان من شريعتهم؛ فإنهم يترجمون كُتُب العلوم، وينسبونها الى أهلهم وأساقفتهم، وهي من توالیف المسلمين؛ وكان الحسن [أن] لا يترك طبيباً يهودياً، أو نصرانياً، أن يجلس ليُطبِّب المسلمين؛ فإنّهم لا يرون نصيحةً مسلم، إلاّ أن يطبِّبوا أهل ملّتهم، ومن لا يرى نصيحة مسلمٍ، كيف يوثق على المهج؟

(b)

ويُنهى المسلمون أن يتعمّدوا شراء اللحم من مَجازر أهل الذِّمّة؛ وكرهه مالكٌ. وأمر عمر – رضه – أن يُخرجوا من أسواق المسلمين. قال ابن حبيب: ولا بأس أن تكون لهم مجزرة على حدةٍ ويُنهون عن البيع من المسلمين؛ ومن اشترى من المسلمين منهم، لم يفسخ شراؤه وهو رجل سوء. «من «الواضحة»: قال مطرِّف وابن الماجشون: فإن كان ما اشتراه من اللحم منهم ممّا لا يأكلونه، مثل الطَّريف وشبهه، فيفسخ شراؤه وكذلك الشحم. قال الله تعالى: «وَمِنَ البَقَرِ والغَنَمِ حَرَّمْنَا عَلَيْهِمْ شُحُومَهُمَا»: فهي الشحوم المحملة الخالصة مثل الثُّروب، وشحم الكُلَا، وما لصق بالقَطْنة، وشبه ذلك. وقولُه تعالى: «إلاّ مَا حَمَلَتْ ظُهُورُهُمَا أو الحَوَايَا أو مَا اخْتَلَطَ بعَظْمٍ»؛ فكُل ما كان في ذلك من شحم، فهو داخلٌ في الاستثناء؛ فما كان من هذه الشحوم المحرّمة عليهم، فلا يحلُّ لنا من ذبائحهم لا آكلُهُ بعينه، ولا أصلُ ثمنه. وما لم يكن محرّماً عليهم في التنزيل من ذبائحهم، وإنّما حرّموه بفقههم مثل الطَّريف وشبهه، فهو مكروهٌ أكلُهُ وأكلُ ثمنه لأنّه ليس من طعامهم. وهو قول مالك وبعض أصحابه.

ومن «الواضحة»: وما ذبح النصارى لكنائسهم أو على اسم المسيح أو الصليب أو شبه ذلك، فإنّه يُضامي قول الله تعالى: «وَمَا أُهِلَّ بِهِ لِغَيْرِ الله»، وذلك مكروه لنا، غير محرّم لأنّ الله تعالى أحلَّ لنا ذبائحهم، وهو أعلم بما يقولون وما يدبرون بها، وما ذبحوا لاعيادهم وضلالهم، فتركُه أفضل لأنّ أكلَه من تعظيم شِركهم؛ ولم يزل قول مالك

One must not sell a scientific book to the Jews, nor to the Christians, unless it deals with their own law; for they translate books of science, and attribute them to their own people and to their bishops, when they are [really] the works of the Muslims. It would be best if no Jewish or Christian doctor were left to treat the Muslims; for they have no concern for the welfare of a Muslim, but only for the medical treatment of their co-religionists. How could one trust his lifeblood with someone who has no concern for what is best for a Muslim?

(b) Ibn 'Abd al-Ra'uf

Muslims are forbidden to buy meat intentionally from the butcheries of the *dhimmis*. Malik abhorred this and [the caliph] 'Umar [b. al-Khattab] – may God be pleased with him – ordered them to be expelled from the Muslims' markets. Ibn Habib said, "There is no objection to them having a butchery isolated from the others, and being forbidden to sell to Muslims. Any Muslim who buys from them will not have his purchase invalidated, but he will be a bad man." In the *Wadiha* [he says]: Mutarrif and Ibn al-Majishun said that if the meat [the Muslim] buys from them is the sort they do not eat themselves, such as *tarif* (non-kosher) and suchlike, the purchase is invalidated, and the same for fat. God Almighty said, "We have made unlawful for them [the Jews] the fat of cattle and sheep" (*Qur'an* 6: 147); such are the undiluted and pure fats such as the intestines, the fat of the kidneys and that which attaches to the stomach and suchlike. God says, "except what their backs carry, or the entrails, or what is mixed with the bone" (*Qur'an, l.c.*). All fat that is in this category becomes an exception. It is specifically not lawful for us either to eat or to trade in any of these fats that are forbidden to them from the animals they have slaughtered. Whatever is not forbidden to them of their slaughtered animals by Revelation, but is only forbidden by their religious law, such as *tarif* and suchlike, consumption of this trading in it are frowned on [but not illegal], because it is not their lawful meat. This is the opinion of Malik and some of his disciples.

In the *Wadiha* [it says]: Any meat the Christians slaughter for their churches, or in the name of the Messiah or the Cross or suchlike, corresponds with the word of Almighty God, "what has been consecrated for someone other than God" (*Qur'an* 2: 168), and that is frowned on for us, but not forbidden, because God Almighty has made lawful for us what they [the Christians] slaughter, for he is better informed about what they are saying and intending by this, and [also] about what they slaughter for their festivals and for their misguided purposes. Having nothing to do with it is preferable, because to eat it is to show great regard for their polytheistic ways. Malik and his disciples never ceased to

وأصحابه الكراهية في ذلك. وقد سُئل مالك – رحمه الله – عن طعام يصنعه لموتاهم يتصدّقون به عنهم؛ فـقـال: «لا ينبغي لمسلم أن يأخذه ولا يأكله لأنّهم عملوه تعظيماً لشركهم». وقال ابن القاسم في نصرانيّ أوصى أن يباع شيء من ماله للكنيسة بأنّه لا يحلّ لمسلم شراؤه، والذي يشتريه مسلمٌ سوءٌ.

وإذا اشترى مسلمٌ من نصرانيّ خمراً كُسر من وُجدت بيده منها؛ فإن كان النصرانيُّ قد قبض الثمن، تُرك له؛ وإن كان لم يقبض؛ لم يُقْضَ له به. وإن فاتت الخمر بيد المسلم، ولم يكن دفع الثمن، أخذ منه، وتُصُدِّق به، ويُعاقَبان. وإن كسر مسلم خمرَ الذَّميّ، عُوقب؛ واختلَف قول مالك في غرم قيمتها: مرّةً قال: لا غرمَ عليه، ولا يحلّ لما حرّم الله ثمنُه؛ ومرةً قال: عليه القيمة.

وكره السفر معهم في مراكبهم، لما يُخاف من نزل السخط عليهم.

(c)

ويمنع أهل الذَّمّة من الإشراف على المسلمين في مَنازلهم، والتكشيف عليهم ومن إظهار الخَمر والخنزير في أسواق المسلمين، ومن ركوب الخيل بالسروج والزيّ بما هو من زيّ المسلمين، أو بما هو من أبّهة؛ وينصب عليهم عَلَماً يمتازون به من المسلمين، كالشِكْلة في حق الرجال، والجِلْجِل في حق النساء. ويمنع المسلمين أن يُحاولوا لهم كلّ ما فيه خساسةٌ أو إذلالٌ للمسلمين، تطْرُح الكُنَاسة ونقْل آلات الخَمر، ورِعاية الخنازير، وشِبْهُ ذلك، لِمَا فيه من عُلُوّ الكُفر على الإسلام؛ ويُؤَدَّب مَنْ فعَلَ ذلك.

show their abhorrence for that. Malik (may God have mercy on him!) was asked about the food that is prepared for their funerals and which [the Christians] give as alms; he replied, "It is not appropriate for a Muslim to take it or eat it, because they prepared it to glorify their polytheism." Ibn al-Qasim said, about a Christian who willed that some of his property should be sold on behalf of a church, that it was not lawful for a Muslim to buy it, and that any Muslim who bought it would be a bad Muslim.

If a Muslim buys wine from a Christian, whatever wine is found in his possession will be destroyed. If the Christian has already received the price, this will be left to him, but if he has not received it, it will not be settled in his favour. If the wine is no longer in the Muslim's hands, and he has not paid for it, the price will be taken from him and given as alms, and both of them will be punished. If a Muslim destroys wine belonging to a *dhimmi*, he will be punished. Malik has conflicting opinions on the question of the payment of damages for its value: in one place he says, no fine is imposed on him, and none is lawful, because God has made its price unlawful; elsewhere, he says the price is incumbent on him.

He [Malik] abhorred travelling with them [*dhimmis*] in ships, because of the fear of divine wrath descending on them.

(c) 'Umar al-Jarsifi

The *dhimmis* must be prevented from having houses that overlook Muslims, and from spying on them, and from exhibiting wine and pork in the Muslims' markets, from riding horses with saddles and wearing the costumes of Muslims or anything ostentatious. They must be made to display a sign that will distinguish them from Muslims, such as the *shakla* (piece of yellow cloth) in the case of men and a bell in the case of women. Muslims must be forbidden from undertaking everything that entails baseness and humiliation for the Muslims, such as removing garbage, transporting equipment connected with wine, looking after pigs and suchlike, because this involves the elevation of unbelief above Islam; whoever does such things will be punished.

97. Pisan raids on the Balearics (508/1114)

After the fall of the 'Amirids in Cordova (see text 85), many of their Slav clients established themselves in Ta'ifa kingdoms in the east of al-Andalus. One of the most successful of these principalities became fixed in the Balearics, initially part of the Ta'ifa kingdom of Denia, but ultimately independent under Sulaiman b. Mushkiyan, al-Murtada, from around 1076. From their base in Majorca, the Muslims successfully engaged in piracy against Christian trade. This provoked a major expedition organized by Pisa, which had been granted the islands by an earlier Pope. In 1113, Pascal II

وفى سنة ثمان وخمسمائة، اجتمع أهل بيشه وجنوة، وعمّروا ثلاثمائة مركب،

وخرجوا إلى جزيرة يابسة من عمل ميورقة، فغلبوها وسبوها وانتهبوها، ثم انتقلوا إلى

جزيرة ميورقة، وكان واليها قبل حلول العدو بنواحيها، المرتضى من أهل الأندلس، ثار

فيها عند انقطاع دولة بنى أمية بالأندلس حين ثار سواه، ثم توفى وقام بالأمر من بعده

خصى من خصيانه اسمه مبشر فتقلب بناصر الدولة، وكان أصله من قلعة الحَمِير من

نظر لارده، فسباه العدو صغيراً وخصاه، فوجه المرتضى رسولا إلى الروم فى بعض

مآربه، فاستحسن الرسول عقل الفتى مبشر ونبل ذاته ففداه، وقَدِم به على المرتضى

فسر به وقربه وأدناه، فوجد عنده من حسن خدمة الملوك ما تمناه. وكان سامى الهمم،

حميد الشيم، كثير الفضائل والكرم. فلما نازله العدو، ذبّ عن حماه، ولم يُحمد رأيه فى

مقارعته إياه، إلى أن مات رحمه الله. فقام بالأمر من بعده قريبه القائد أبو الربيع

سليمان بن لبون، فحمى جهده حتى غلب عليه وتملك العدو البلد.

وفى خلال ذلك الحصار، كان ناصر الدولة (أى مبشر الخصى) كتب إلى أمير

المسلمين يستصرخه ويستنصره، ووجه كتابه مع القائد أبى عبدالله ابن ميمون، وكان إذ

ذاك عنده قائد غراب بين يديه. فلم يشعر العدو حتى خرج الغراب مَعمراً ليلاً من دار

الصناعة عليه، فانطلق فى الحين يقفو أثره، واتبعه نحو عشرة أميال والظلام قد ستره،

فلما قطع يأسه فى الظفر به، رجع خاسئاً على عقبه، فوصل ابن ميمون بالكتاب إلى

أمير المسلمين، فأمر فى الحين، بتعمير ثلاثمائة قطعة، وأن تلقى بعد شهر دفعة. فامتثل

issued a papal bull in favour of a crusade and the Pisans, with their allies from Genoa and Barcelona, were able to seize Ibiza and Majorca (see also text 29).

An Arabic account of these events is provided by Ibn Kardabus (for whom, see text 84); the passage is taken from pp.122-24. With the involvement of the Almoravids in the Balearics, the islands became effectively absorbed into the Almoravid empire, at its peak under 'Ali b. Yusuf (1106-43), and remained a last bastion of Almoravid power against the encroachments of their Almohad rivals until well into the 13th century.

In the year 508 (began 7 June 1114) the Pisans and Genoese combined, and built 300 ships and went to Yabisa (Ibiza) in the region of Mayurqa (Majorca). They overran it and took prisoners and booty. Then they went to the island of Majorca. The governor prior to the arrival of the enemy in these districts had been al-Murtada of al-Andalus, who declared himself independent there on the collapse of the Umayyads in al-Andalus, when others were doing the same. When he died [in 1094], one of his eunuchs took over, called Mubashir, with the honorific title Nasir al-Daula. He was by origin from Qal'at Hamir (Castelldasens) in the jurisdiction of Larida (Lérida). He had been captured as a youth and castrated by the enemy. Al-Murtada sent an envoy to "Rome" [probably, the Christian court at Barcelona] for various reasons, and the envoy was favourably impressed by the intelligence and the noble quality of the lad Mubashir, whom he ransomed. [The envoy] presented him to al-Murtada, who was pleased with him, and made him one of his close courtiers. [Al-Murtada] found in him the ability to serve kings that he was looking for. He was lofty in his thoughts and of a praiseworthy character, blessed with many virtues and magnanimity. When the enemy descended on him, he manned his defences until he died (God have mercy upon him!); his decision to fight the enemy was not approved of. He was succeeded by his relative, the general Abu'l-Rabi'a Sulaiman b. Labun [Burabe in the Christian sources], who fought fiercely until the enemy overcame him and took possession of the town [i.e. Palma].

During the siege, Nasir al-Daula (that is, the eunuch Mubashir) had written to the Commander of the Muslims ['Ali b. Yusuf b. Tashufin the Almoravid], calling upon his support and assistance. He despatched his letter with an officer, Abu 'Abd-Allah b. Maimun, who happened to be there as captain of a corvette. The enemy realised nothing until one night the corvette slipped out fully equipped from the shipyard. They immediately set off in pursuit and followed it for about ten miles, but it was concealed by the darkness. When the enemy gave up all hope of overtaking it, they returned on their tracks in shame. Ibn Maimum reached the Amir of the Muslims with his letter. He immediately ordered 300

أمره فى ذلك، واندفعت بجملتها من هنالك، وإذ ذاك تعين ابن ميمون عند أمير المسلمين.

فلما شعر العدو بخروج ذلك الأسطول، أخلى وصدر عن الجزيرة، وعينُه بما احتمل من السبى والأموال قريرة. فلما وصل الأسطول، وجد المدينة خاوية على عروشها محرقة سوداء مظلمة منطبقة. فعمرها قائد الأسطول ابن تاقرطاس، بمن معه من المرابطين والمجاهدين وأصناف الناس، وجلب إليها من كان فر عنها إلى الجبال فاستوطنوها وعمروها وسكنوها. وانصرف الأسطول إلى مكانه، وعاد إلى موضع مقره واستيطانه.

وفى انصراف العدو إلى أوطانه، هبت عليه ريح ببحار طامية، فحملت منه أربع قطائع إلى ناحية دانية. فعمر إليها قائد البحر أبو السداد، ففرت أمامه، وغرقت واحدة منها قدامه، وعكس الثلاث.

ships to be constructed and brought together in a month's time. These orders were put into effect. They all set sail from there in haste, and at the same time Ibn Maimun was given an appointment by the Amir al-Muslimin.

When the enemy heard of the departure of this fleet, they cleared out of the island and left, happy with the captives and riches that they carried away. When the squadron arrived, they found the city completely devastated, blackened by fires and covered in a deep gloom. Ibn Taqirtas, commander of the fleet, together with his Almoravids, fighters for the faith and all kinds of people, restored the city and brought back those who had fled to the mountains; they made it their home again, restored it and resettled it. The fleet left for its own country and returned to its home base.

As the enemy left for their own country they were hit by storm winds and heavy seas, which carried four ships to the coast at Daniyya (Denia). The admiral Abu'l-Saddad repaired there and the enemy [ships] fled before him; one of them sunk in front of him and the other three were overtaken.

98. Innovations in al-Andalus (early 12th century)

The selection that follows touches on the question of how fully Islam maintained its identity in Spain, where it was not only geographically far removed from its place of origin in Arabia, but also evolving in a society in which Christianity remained obstinately pervasive. To what extent Spanish Islam was moulded by the European environment in which it took root, or remained fundamentally indistinguishable from Islam in the Middle East, towards which it undoubtedly looked, has been a matter for debate. The behaviour of the Muslim rulers, notably in the Ta'ifa period and particularly in the face of the vigorous and reformist challenge of the North African Berber dynasties, might suggest one aspect of the question. At the popular level, too, distinctions between the two religious communities were doubtless frequently blurred. Yet if the rulers and the common folk were susceptible to the subtle influences of the Spanish milieu, the Muslim religious scholars and jurists remained generally true to the orthodox position of the predominant Maliki school.

Questions of the religious laxity of Muslim Spain were perhaps most typically aired during the Almoravid period. Ibn Abi Randaqa al-Turtushi, a native of Tortosa, was born around 1060 and died, according to most accounts, in 520/1126, having spent most of his life in Egypt, where his teaching was influential on Ibn Tumart, founder of the Almohad movement. The term bid'a *means innovation, for which there is no precedent in*

ومن البدع اجتماع الناس بارض الاندلس على ابتياع الحلوى ليلة سبع وعشرين من رمضان؛ وكذلك على اقامة ينير بابتياع الفواكه كالعجم؛ واقامة العنصرة وخميس ابريل بشراء المجبنات والاسفنج، وهى من الاطعمة المبتدعة.

وخروج الرجال جميعا، او اشتاتا، مع النساء مختلطين للتفرج، وكذلك يفعلون فى أيام العيد ويخرجون للمصلى. ويقمن فيه الخيم للتفرج، لا للصلاة.

ودخول الحمام للنساء مع الكتابيات بغير مئزر؛ والمسلمين مع الكفار فى الحمام، والحمام من البدع ومن النعيم.

ورجع الناس ينافسون فى الضحية للافتخار، لا للسنة ولا لطلب الاجر، بل لاقامة الدنيا. ...

he sunna *(or path) of Muhammad. Not all innovation (which should be distinguished from heresy) is bad and, like other matters, it can become classed as permitted, recommended or obligatory in Muslim law. The innovations listed here are practices rather than beliefs, and are implicitly or explicitly disapproved of* (makruh).

The matter of celebrating Christian festivals has already been discussed (see text 79); despite official condemnations, the practice clearly continued unabated. But even in the celebration of Muslim festivals, innovative foods were introduced: for the doughnuts and cheese fritters, see Lévi-Provençal, III, p. 419. The "Night of Power", here dated 27 Ramadan, is said to be the night on which the Qur'an was revealed to Muhammad, though it is often observed on all the odd nights in the last ten days of Ramadan. We may note, in view of other selections (see texts 83 and 89), that the baths are considered a luxurious innovation, evidently open to abuse. The Maliki school was particularly opposed to cries and lamentations at funerals, such demonstrations being severely condemned in the hisba *manual of Ibn 'Abd al-Ra'uf (for which see text 96); a good example of the literal authority given to the Qur'an is provided by the strictures on the order in which food is to be served.*

The text is taken from al-Turtushi, Kitab al-hawadith wa'l-bid'a, *ed. M. al-Talibi (Tunis, 1959), pp.140-43.*

One innovation is that all the people in the land of al-Andalus gather to buy nougat (*halwa*: turrón) on the night of 27 Ramadan, and similarly to buy fruit, like the Christians at the celebration of January (New Year's Eve); and at the celebration of *al-'Ansara* (24 June) and Maundy Thursday to purchase fried doughnuts (*isfanj*: churros) and cheese fritters (*mujabbana*), both of which are innovative foods.

[Another innovation] is that the men go out mingling with the women, separately or in groups, to enjoy spectacles, and they do the same on the days of the Muslim festivals of the *'id* [*'id al-adha* and *'id al-fitr*], when they go out to the oratories. The women set up pavilions there to watch and not to pray.

The women enter the baths without coverings, together with the "women of the book" [Christian and Jewish women]; Muslims go to the baths with the unbelievers. The hammam is both a *bid'a* and a luxury.

The people have reverted to vying with each other in the Sacrifice for the sake of their own glory, not to follow the [Prophet's] *sunna* nor to seek [God's] reward, but rather in worldly celebration.

[...]

ومن البدع اتخاذ الالوان؛ والاكل على الخوان؛ واستعمال الطيب فى آنية الفضة؛ ويرجع من الوليمة عند رؤية آنية الفضة.

ومن البدع الانذار للعرس وللجنازة للمباهاة والتفاخر لكثرة الناس؛ وكذلك الانشاد ورفع الصوت عند حمل الجنازة.

ومن البدع السؤال فى المسجد؛ والكلام ولا سيما والامام يخطب للجمعة؛ وكذلك الانذار للصلاة قبل الامام وبعده؛ وعمل التوابيت للموتى؛ وحفر القبر دون لحد؛ وكذلك الاجتماع لغير ذكر الله فى المسجد.

وكذلك تقديم اللحم على الفاكهة، والله –تعالى–! يقول: «وفاكهة مما يتخيرون ولحم طير مما يشتهون»، والأولى استعمال ادب القرآن وتقديم ما قدم الله وتاخير ما اخر الله. واكل اللحم من غير نهش؛ وشرب الماء غير مص؛ واستعمال السواك غير عرض؛ والاكل بازيد من ثلاثة اصابع، مكروه.

Another innovation is adopting various foods and eating on tables and the use of scent in silver vessels; a man should not attend a banquet when he sees silver vessels.

Another innovation is publicizing a wedding or a funeral for the sake of boasting and showing off by [attracting] many people; and similarly singing and raising the voice when carrying the corpse.

Another innovation is begging in the mosque and talking, particularly when the imam is giving the Friday sermon, and similarly announcing the prayers before and after the imam [does so]. Another is making coffins for the dead, and digging a grave without a niche for the body (*lahd*), and also gathering in the mosque for purposes other than praying to God.

Similarly, [it is an innovation] to serve meat before fruit. God Almighty has said, "And such fruits as they may choose, and the flesh of fowls such as they may desire" [*Qur'an* 56: 20, describing the meals in paradise]. It is preferable to employ the etiquette of the Qur'an and present first what God brings first, and to bring later what God brings later; and to eat meat without tearing it to pieces with the teeth, and to drink water without slurping, and to use a toothpick without showing it. It is [also] reprehensible to eat with more than three fingers.

99. The illegal trade in plundered property (about 518/1124)

*As in text 90, one of the problems created by the gradual reconquest of Spain wa[s]
that many Muslims, or their property, became trapped on the wrong side of the ever[-]
shifting frontier. The question arising here, though similar to that in text 90, illustrates [a]
slightly different situation, and the judgement offered reveals a rather harder line bein[g]
taken. Whereas before, property belonging to unknown Muslims was wrongly seized bu[t]
could therefore be regarded as legitimate spoils for the Christians, in this case th[e]
original owners are encouraged to seize their possessions back, and in addition to take
hostages against the return of captives held by the Christians.*

*The text is of interest as much for its context as for the legal theory involved. [It]
provides evidence of trade quickly resumed between the two sides on the cessation o[f]
hostilities, and suggests a remarkable entrepreneurial spirit among the Christians i[n]
attempting to get the Muslims to buy back their own captured goods. The problem
brought up here should have arisen fairly soon after the fall of Toledo, but the actua[l]*

تعرف المسلمين بقرطبة على أموالهم بأيدي نصارى طليطلة أيام الصلح

وسئل عما اعترفه المسلمون من أموالهم بأيدي النصارى الداخلين إلى قرطبة من
طليلة أعادها الله للمسلمين، باسم التجارة أيام الصلح، ونص السؤال وهو للأمير أبي
طاهر تميم بن يوسف بن تاشفين:

جوابك رضي الله عنك فيم اعترفه أهل بلدنا هذا من أموالهم بأيدي تجار أهل
طليطلة الداخلين إلى بلدنا للتجارة، بعد أن أقاموا البينة أنه مالهم ماباعوه ولاوهبوه،
لى أن ضربت سرية صح عندهم أنها من طليطلة فأخذت هذه الأموال المعترفة مع
سارى المسلمين، أن ذلك إنما كان في أيام الهدنة الكائنة بيننا وبينهم، وثبت هذا من
ول البينة. هل يحكم في ذلك أو يصرفه على معترفه فيه كما يحكم فيما يستحقه
لمسلمون بعضهم من بعض أم لا؟ وكيف ادعى أرباب هذه الأموال المعترفة أن لهم
سرى بطليطلة في دور هؤلاء التجار، وأنهم إنما أخذوا في الهدنة على ماتقدم. وهل
هم ارتهان من زعموا أن أولياءهم عندهم من التجار الذين عندنا حتى يؤدوا من عندهم
من الأسارى أم لا؟ بين ذلك مأجوراً، إن شاء الله تعالى.

فأجاب وفقه الله تعالى على ذلك بأن قال: «تصفحت سؤالك ووقفت عليه وإن كان

date at which the legal question was posed is indicated by the personalities involved. Ibn Rushd, grandfather of the famous philosopher Averroes, was an exact contemporary of al-Turtushi, and died in Dhu'l-Qa'da 520/July 1126. He served the Almoravids as chief qadi of Cordova between 511 and his resignation in 515 (1117-21), when he devoted himself to his legal writing. Abu Tahir Tamim was son of the Almoravid ruler, Yusuf b. Tashufin, and among other posts in al-Andalus, he was governor of Cordova between 517 and 519 (1123-25); it was doubtless during this period that he consulted Ibn Rushd on the question presented here. For further events involving both Ibn Rushd and Abu Tahir, see text 100.

The text is taken from al-Wansharishi, IX, pp.598-99. See also Amar, Archives Marocaines, *13 (1909), pp.210-12, and Lagardère,* Le Vendredi de Zallaqa, *pp.137-53, for a selection of Ibn Rushd's other legal opinions.*

> The Muslims of Cordova identify their property in the hands of the Christians of Toledo during peacetime.

[The jurist] was asked about the property which the Muslims recognized as theirs, in the hands of Christians entering Cordova from Toledo (may God return it to the Muslims!) by way of trade during peacetime. The text of the question, which was put by the amir Abu Tahir Tamim b. Yusuf b. Tashufin, [is]:

[We seek] your response, may God be pleased with you, concerning the property which the people of this city of ours recognize as theirs, in the hands of merchants coming from Toledo to our city to trade. They have indisputable evidence that it is theirs, and they did not sell it nor give it away, before a detachment which they were sure came from Toledo attacked, and seized these belongings which they have recognized, together with Muslim prisoners. This occurred during a period of truce that existed between them and us, as has been confirmed by clear oral proof. Should one judge in this as one judges cases of litigation between Muslims, or not; or should one [simply] hand back [the goods] to the persons who recognized them [as theirs]?   And what if the owners of these identified possessions claim that they [also] have prisoners held in the houses of these merchants in Toledo, who were only taken captive during the truce, as has already been mentioned?   Are [the Muslims] who assert that they have friends [trapped] with the Christians allowed to take hostages from the merchants who are now with us, until they release the prisoners who are with them, or not? Clarify this for us, may God reward you, if God Almighty is willing.

He [Ibn Rushd] replied (may Almighty God give him success) by saying, "I have examined your question and have understood it. If the merchants of Toledo

التجار من أهل طليطلة أعادها الله للإسلام خرجوا عنها بعد أن غارت سريتهم على بلاد المسلمين فأسرت الرجال وأخذت الأموال، فلا عهد لهم لأن العهد في الدخول إلى بلاد المسلمين في التجارة إنما أعطوه على يكفوا عن المسلمين ولايغيرون عليهم فيأسروهم ويأخذوا أموالهم. فالجواب أن يرتهونهم وما معهم من الأموال فيما أخذت السرية حتى يصرفوا ذلك إليهم، فإن أجابوا إلى ذلك وفعلوه بقيت الهدنة على ما كانت عليه، وإن أبوا ذلك انتقضت وعادوا حرباً. وكانت التجار المرتهنين أسارى المسلمين وأموالهم فيئاً ومن أثبت من الناس شيئاً مما وجد بأيديهم أنه ماله وملكه أخذته السرية المذكورة الخارجة من طليطلة بعد المهادنة قضي له به، وبالله التوفيق».

may God restore it to Islam) left the city after their detachment attacked Muslim territory and took them prisoner and plundered their goods, then they are not covered by any agreement. This is because the agreement [allowing them] to enter Muslim territory to trade was only given to them on condition that they desist from [attacking] the Muslims, and do not carry out raids against them, taking prisoners and seizing their possessions. The reply is that [the people of Cordova] may take them hostage and take [back] whatever goods are with them, which the detachment had seized, until they give it [all] back. If they agree to this and carry it out, then the truce continues as it was before. If they refuse to do so, then the treaty is violated and they return to a state of war. The merchants taken as hostages become prisoners of the Muslims, and their goods become *fay'* (booty). Anyone who can establish that anything found in their possession is his property and belongings, which was taken by the above-mentioned detachment that made a sortie from Toledo after the truce had been agreed, shall be judged to be its owner. Success is granted by God."

100. Christian treachery in Andalusia (519/1125)

*The presence, numbers and organization of the Christians in southern Spain i
attested by their role in encouraging the king of Aragon, Alfonso I "the Battler",
invade Andalusia in the winter of 1125-26. Their part in this episode is made explicit b
the Arabic sources, which rely particularly on the lost history of the Almoravids by Ib
Sairafi (the "Kitab al-anwar al-jalila"). The account followed here is taken from al
Hulal al-maushiyya, ed. I.S. Allouche (Rabat, 1936), from pp.75-80, by an anonymou
author of the late 14th century. A detailed study of these uprisings has been made b
Vincent Lagardère, "Communautés mozarabes et pouvoir almoravide en 519 H/1125 e
Andalus", Studia Islamica, 67 (1988), 99-119.*

*The Christians are referred to in this account as tributaries (mu'ahadun). Since the
had submitted to the Muslims on terms (see text 81a) they enjoyed legal protectio
(dhimma) and freedom of worship. One upshot of the revolt was that many of them, o
the advice of Ibn Rushd, were deported to North Africa. Here, as discussed b
Lagardère, similar legal questions arose over the statutory position of their remainin
property in Spain, to those arising among Muslims over their possessions in Christia
territory (see text 99). This incidentally reveals that a well-developed system o
endowments existed for the upkeep of the Christian religious communities in Islami
territory.*

وفي هذه السنة ٥١٩ه خرج الطاغية ابن ردمير إلى بلاد المسلمين بلاد الأندلس،
تحركت له ريح الظهور وذلك أن النصارى المعاهدين بكورة غرناطة وغيرها خاطبوه من
لك الأقطار وتوالت عليه كتبهم وتواترت رسلهم ملحّة في الإستعداد مطمعة بدخول
غرناطة. وإنه لما أبطأ عنهم وجهوا إليه تفسيراً يشتمل على اثني عشر ألفاً من أنجاد
مقاتلتهم وأخبروه مع هذا أن من سموه هو ممن شهدت أعينهم لقرب مواضعهم وأن
بالبعد منهم من يخفى أثره ويظهر عند ورود شخصه عليهم. فاستثاروا طمعه وابتعثوا
جشعه واستفزوه بأوصاف غرناطة وما لها من الفضائل عن سائر البلاد وكثرة فوائدها
من القمح والشعير والكتان وكثرة المرافق من الحرير والكروم والزيتون وأنواع الفواكه
وكثرة العيون والأنهار ومنعة قصبتها، وانطباع رعيتها، وتأتي أهل حاضرتها المباركة
التي يملك منها غيرها وأنها سنام الأندلس عند الملوك في تواريخها.

فرموا حتى أصابوا غرضه فانتخب واحتشد وتهيّأ في أربعة آلاف فارس
اختارها من بلاد رغونة بتوابعهم وتعاقدوا وتحالفوا بالإنجيل أنه لا يفر أحد منهم عن
صاحبه. فخرج عن سرقطة في منسلخ شعبان من هذه السنة ...

In addition to this forced expulsion of Christians from Andalusia, Alfonso I took
~ny of them north when he returned to his own kingdom; the number is sometimes put
high as 10,000. Any such influx of Christians to Aragon would have been welcome,
Alfonso had significantly extended his territory in the north by capturing the great
ifa kingdom of Saragossa (1118), and he was seeking further expansion. Despite
se movements of population, both voluntary and enforced, there remained significant
ristian communities in Andalusia, who played a part in the struggle between Ibn
rdanish and the Almohads forty years later.
Alfonso I of Aragon (1104-34) was the son of Sancho Ramírez, not "Rudmir". For a
ent account of the expansion of Aragon during his reign, see Reilly, The contest, esp.
157-73. Because of his incompetence in handling Alfonso's destructive expedition, the
ιslim leader in Spain, Abu Tahir Tamim, was removed from the governorship and he
d shortly afterwards in 520/1126. The battle of Aranzuel, which appears to have been
most significant encounter in the field between the opposing armies, occurred on 13
'ar 520/10 March 1126. For the Prayer of Fear (salat al-khauf), see Qur'an 4: 102-

In this year 519 (began 7 February 1125) the tyrant Ibn Rudmir [Alfonso I
ᴇ Battler] set out for al-Andalus and the territories of the Muslims. The scent
victory got him going, in that the Christians who had surrendered by
reement [or tributaries] in the district of Gharnata (Granada) and elsewhere
d turned to him and sent repeated letters and continuous messengers from
ᴇse parts, importuning him to make ready and enticing him to enter Granada.
hen he kept them waiting, they sent him by way of elaboration a document
ntaining [details of] 12,000 of their brave warriors, and in addition informed
n that those whom they had named were those who had been seen personally
cause they were close by. Behind them were others who were hiding their
ιcks but would appear when he arrived in person among them. They aroused
s desire and provoked his greed, exciting him with descriptions of Granada
d the superiority it had over other lands, its many advantages [in terms] of
ain, barley and flax, its numerous resources in silk, vines, olives and different
pes of fruit, its large number of springs and rivers and the strength of its
tadel. [They mentioned] the docility of its subjects and the easy-going
ιpulation of its auspicious capital. Other places could [easily] be subdued from
ere. The kings of all ages considered it the camel's hump of al-Andalus.

They aimed until they hit the target of [arousing] his interest. He selected,
ιustered and prepared 4,000 knights whom he had chosen from the land of
ιghuna (Aragon), together with their followers. They swore and pledged on
ᴇ Gospels that no-one would abandon his colleague. He set off from Saragossa
the end of Sha'ban this year (30 September 1125).

ونزل بقرية غيانة وقاتلها من غربها أقام عليها نحو شهر. قال مصنف كتاب نوار الجليلة فبدا نجيث النصارى المعاهدين بغرناطة في استدعائه فافتضح تدبيرهم في اجتلابه. وهم أميرهم بثقافهم فأعياه ذلك وجعلوا يتسللون إلى محلته على كل طريق. كان يومئذ على الأندلس أبوطاهر تميم بن يوسف وحاضرة سكناه قاعدة غرناطة أحدقت به جيوش المسلمين وأمده أخوه أمير المسلمين من العدوة بجيش وافر. وصارت جيوش كالدائرة على غرناطة وهي في وسطها كالنقطة. وتحرك ابن ردمير من وادي فنزل بقرية دجمة، وصلى الناس بغرناطة صلاة الخوف يوم عيد النحر من هذه سنة في الأسلحة والأهبة. ولم يصل ابن ردمير إلى غرناطة حتى كان معه خمسون ألفاً، ثم نزل بوادي فردش في يوم عيد الأضحى وأقلع منها إلى المزوقة (؟) ومنها نزل إلى غرناطة ونزل بقرية النبيل وأقام بمحلته بضع عشرة ليلة لم تسرح له سارحة بتوالي الأمطار وكثرة الجليد إلا أن المعاهدة كانت تجلب إليه الأقوات فأقلع وقد ارتفع طمعه من المدينة. ... فتبعه الأمير أبوطاهر إلى أن اجتمعا على مقربة من اليسانة بارنيسول طمعوا فيه وانتدبوا لقتاله أول النهار، وكبسوه وأخذوا له جملة من الأخبية. ولما كان في وقت الظهر تدرع وتعبى بناسه للقتال وعقد عليهم أربعة ألوية وساروا فرقاً أربعاً وحملوا على المسلمين بعد فشلهم وافتراقهم وسوء الرأي في نزولهم، فألفوهم على لمأنينة وحكم الله بأحكامه فكانت الوقيعة الشنيعة على المسلمين، واستولى على محلتهم وانتقل منها إلى جهة الساحل. ...

والعساكر في كل ذلك تطأ أذياله والتناوش يتخطر به والوباء يسرع إليه حتى وصل إلى بلاده. وهو يفخر بما ناله في سفره من هزيمة المسلمين وفتكه في بلادهم وكثرة مآسر وغنم مع أنه لم يفتح مكاناً مسوراً صغيراً ولا كبيراً إلا أنه أخلى ديار

... Alfonso progressed via Valencia, Denia, Játiva, Murcia, Baza and
ιdix...] On Wednesday 6 Dhu 'l-Qa'da (4 December) he descended on the
ιge of Ghiyana, and attacked [Guadix] from its western side. He stayed there
ιt a month. The author of the "Kitab al-anwar al-jalila" says that the secret
ιgement of the tributary Christians in Granada to summon him came to
ι, and their plan to attract him was discovered. Their leader was intending to
ι up with them, but was thwarted from doing so. They began to slip through
ιs [Alfonso's] camp using every route. Abu Tahir Tamim b. Yusuf was
ιmor of al-Andalus at that time, and the place which he used as his capital
ιGranada. The Muslim armies surrounded him and his brother, the Amir al-
ιlimin ['Ali b. Yusuf], supplied him with a large army from North Africa.
ιarmy was like a ring round Granada and she was in the middle like the key
ιt. Alfonso left Guadix and descended on the village of Dajama (Diezma).
ιinhabitants of Granada prayed the Prayer of Fear on the feast of the
ιifice (10 Dhu 'l-Hijja/7 January 1126) fully armed and equipped. Alfonso
ιot reach Granada until he had 50,000 men; he stopped at Wadi Fardash the
ιday, then moved to al-Mazuqa (?) and from there descended on Granada.
ιtopped at the village of Nibal (Nivar) and stayed encamped there for more
ιten nights, not sending out any of his forces because of the continuous rain
ιgreat cold, but the Mu'ahadun brought in provisions. Then he departed,
ιng lost his appetite for the city. [...Alfonso withdrew towards Cordova,
ιing the territory through which he passed, harried by Muslim forces...]. The
ιAbu Tahir followed him until they met near al-Yanasa at Arnisul (Aranzuel
ιnzul). They [the Muslims] were eager to get at him, and stood ready to fight
ιat first light. They made a surprise attack and took many tents. Around noon
ιlfonso] donned his armour and set his men in battle order. He raised four
ιers over them and they marched in four divisions to attack the Muslims,
ιwing their failure and disunity, and the poor judgement [that had been
ιn] over their positioning. The Christians came upon them while they were
ιst, and God decreed his judgement; the battle was a disaster for the Muslims
ι[the enemy] seized their camp. [Alfonso] then left for the coast. [...Alfonso
ιns through Muslim territory, passing through Guadix to Murcia...].
ιhroughout all that, the [Muslim] armies were treading on his heels and
ιng repeated attacks on him, with sickness in hot pursuit until he reached his
ιterritory. He was boasting of the achievements of his expedition, among
ιh were the defeat of the Muslims, the slaughter he had carried out in their
ιtry, and the large number of captives and booty he had taken, even though
ιd not conquered a single walled town, small or large. But he had emptied

132

دية الأندلس، وعفا آثارها. وكان مقامه في بلاد الإندلس وارداً وصادراً سنة كاملة
لائة أشهر.

ولما بان للمسلمين من مكيدة جيرانها النصارى المعاهدين ما أجلت عنه هذه
نضية أخذهم الإرجاف وتوغرت لهم الصدور وتوجه إلى مكانهم الحزم. فاحتسب
ناضي أبوالوليد بن رشد الأجر وتجشم المجاز ولحق بعلي بن يوسف بن تاشفين
ناضرة مراكش، فبيّن له الأمر بالأندلس وما منيت به من النصارى المعاهدين وما جنوه
يها من استدعاء الروم وما في ذلك من نقض العهد، والخروج عن الذمة. وأفتى
غريبهم وإجلائهم عن أوطانهم، فأخذ بقوله ونفذ بذلك عهده وأزعج إلى العدوة منهم
ـدجم.

he country districts of al-Andalus and wiped out all trace of them. His stay in
he territories of al-Andalus, between his coming and going, was a whole year
nd three months.

When the extent of the treachery of their Christian tributary neighbours
ecame clear to the Muslims, through what had resulted from it, they were
eized by disquieting rumour, and bitter feelings were aroused in them. They
iewed the position of the tributaries with resolution. The qadi Abu 'l-Walid ibn
ushd anticipated a reward in the hereafter and took it upon himself to cross [to
orth Africa]. He came before 'Ali b. Yusuf b. Tashufin in his capital at
arrakesh and explained the situation in al-Andalus to him, what it had
xperienced because of the tributary Christians and the offences they had
ommitted against it by calling in the Aragonese. [He also explained] how this
iolated their agreement and went beyond their rights to protection (*dhimma*).
e then delivered a *fatwa* on [the permissibility of] removing and expelling
hem from their homeland. [The sultan] accepted his word, and put a decree to
his effect into operation. A great number of them were banished to North
frica.

101. The Battle of Alarcos (591/1195)

Unlike the dramatic arrival of the Almoravids (see text 93), their successors took
several decades to commit themselves to an all-out effort in Spain, and their greates
success came towards the end of their involvement, rather than at the beginning. Just as
Almohad activities in North Africa precipitated the collapse of the Almoravic
government in al-Andalus, particularly after the fall of Marrakesh in 1147, so their own
continuing preoccupations there restricted the scale of their operations in Spain. In the
meanwhile, the Christians took advantage of a second period of Ta'ifa states to make
further inroads into Muslim territory (see for example texts 35 and 36).

After the death of Alfonso VII of Castile in 1157, the initiative passed to the
Almohads, who made several important gains, particularly under Yusuf I (1163-84,
who was assisted in recapturing Badajoz by an alliance with Ferdinand II of León
against the Portuguese. Yusuf died while failing to take Santarém, but his son and
successor Ya'qub (1184-99) was more fortunate, regaining Silves in 1191 on his first
expedition. Alfonso VIII of Castile (1158-1214) retaliated with a bold raid into th
region round Seville, the Almohad capital in Spain. This provoked Ya'qub's second
campaign, in which he achieved the spectacular victory of Alarcos (Santa María d

الأرَك: هو حـصنٌ منيـع من قلْعـة رِبَاح أوّل حـصـونِ إذْفُونْش بالأندلس، وهناك
كانت وقعةُ الأرَك على صـاحب قَشْتالة وجمـوع النصارى على يد المنصور يعقوب بن
يوسف بن عبدالمؤمن بن علىّ ملك المغرب في سنة ٥٩١؛ وكان بلغَ المنصورَ يعقوبَ أنّ
صاحب قشتالة شَنّ الغارات على بلاد المسلمين بالأندلس شرقاً وغرباً فى يومٍ واحدٍ،
وعمّ ذلك جهة إشبيلية ونواحيها، فامتعض من ذلك ثمّ تحرّك من حضرته مرّاكش إلى
الأندلس واستقرّ بإشبيلية فأعْرَض الجُنْدَ وأعطى البَرَكات، ثم نَهَضَ فى الحادى عشر
من جمادى الأخرى ووصل قرطبة فروّحَ بها فالتقى الجمعان بجِسْرِ الأرَك والتحم القتال،
فانهزم العدوُّ وركبهم بالسيف من ضُحَى يوم الأربعاء تاسع شعبان إلى الزوال. وانتهب
محلَّه الروم وقتل منهم زهاء ثلاثين ألفاً، واستشهد من المسلمين دون الخمسمائة، وأفلتَ
إذْفُونْش واجتاز على طليطلة لا يُعَرِّج على شىء فى عشرين فارساً، وحصر المسلمون
فَلَهّم بحصن الأرَك وكانوا خمسة آلاف فصالحوا بقدرهم من أسارى المسلمين.

وسمعتُ مِنْ يُحدثُ أنّ هذا الفتح كان اتفاقيّاً بسَبب إحرازِ الروم بعض رايات
المسلمين وذهابهم بها قائمةً منتصبةً. وانبعاث حفائظ بعض القبائل لما عاينُوا رايةً

Alarcos, near Calatrava), on 19 July 1195 (see also text 37). Like the victory at Zallaqa in 479/1086, Alarcos heralded a new phase of Muslim aggression, but one that was to be even more ephemeral than the first.

Various descriptions of the battle are available in North African sources of the 13th and 14th centuries. These differ slightly in the dates given for Ya'qub's campaign; Ibn 'Idhari and Ibn Abi Zar', for example, state that he did not arrive in Spain until Rajab 591/June 1195. The figures given for the scale of the Christian defeat also vary, Ibn Abi Zar' reporting that the Christian army was at least 300,000 strong, of whom 24,000 were taken prisoner! Al-Marrakushi says Alfonso VIII escaped with only 30 men, but also notes that many leading Almohads were killed, including the vizier, Abu Yahya. For a full account of the battle, see Huici Miranda, Las grandes batallas, pp.137-216.

Al-Himyari, a 15th-century author, nevertheless had access to much original information for this period (see also text 103). The text is taken from his al-Raud al-mi'tar, pp.12-13. See Lévi-Provençal's note to his French translation, p.19, concerning the identification of Balansiyya in the text as Plasencia.

Al-Arak (Alarcos): an impregnable fortress near Qal'at Rabah (Calatrava), the first of Alfonso's strongholds in al-Andalus. It is here that the disaster of Alarcos was suffered by the ruler of Castile and the Christian forces, at the hands of al-Mansur Ya'qub b. Yusuf b. 'Abd al-Mu'min b. 'Ali, ruler of the Maghreb, in 591 (1195). Al-Mansur Ya'qub had heard that the ruler of Castile had launched raids on the Muslim territories of al-Andalus, both to the east and west, on the same day, extending as far as Seville and its surrounding districts. He was angered by that, and left his capital at Marrakesh for al-Andalus. He established himself in Seville, where he reviewed the troops and distributed bonuses. On 11 Jumada II (23 May 1195) he set off, and reached Cordova, where he rested. The two sides met at the bridge of Alarcos and battle was joined. The enemy fled and were put to the sword, from early morning to midday on Wednesday 9 Sha'ban (19 July). The camp of the Christians was plundered and about 30,000 of them were killed. Fewer than 500 Muslims found martyrdom. Alfonso escaped and got through to Toledo with twenty knights, stopping for nothing. The Muslims besieged the remnants of their army, 5,000 men, in the fortress of Alarcos; terms were arranged [for the release of] the same number of Muslim prisoners.

I heard someone relate that this victory happened by chance, because the Christians had captured some of the standards of the Muslims and were marching with them held up high. This aroused the zeal of some of the tribes, when they saw the standards of their brothers raised ahead of the enemy, as they

إخوانهم مُقدَّمةً على العدوّ، وإذ ظنّوا أنّ أصحابَهُمْ حملوا على العدوّ فأوغلوا وهُمْ لا يعلمون الحال، وكيفما كان فهو فتحٌ مبينٌ ونصرٌ مُؤزَّرٌ.

ثمّ رجع المنصورُ إلى إشبيلية ظافراً فأقام مُدةً ثمّ غزَا بلاد الجوف فحاصرَ ترْجَالُه ونزل على بلنسية ففتحها عنوةً، وقَبَضَ على قائدها يومئذ مع مائة وخمسين من أعيان كفّارها، ووجَّهم إلى خِدْمة بناء الجامع الكبير بسَلا مع أسَارى الأرَك. ثمّ انتقل إلى طَلَبِيرة ومكّادة فخرّبَهُما، ثم برز على طُلَيْطِلَة فَشَنَّ عليها الغارات، ثم نَازلَ مجْريط وشرع في القفول، فأخذ على جيَّان إلى قرطبة إلى إستِجَّة إلى قَرْمُونةَ، ووصل إلى إشبيلية فى رمضان.

situation, they rushed to attack them. However it came about, it was a clear victory and a triumph assisted by God.

Al-Mansur [Ya'qub] then returned in triumph to Seville and stayed there for a while. Then he launched an expedition to the north; he besieged Tarjalah (Trujillo) and descended on Balansiyya (Plasencia, *sic.*), which he took by storm, capturing its governor along with 150 of its leading infidels. He sent them to work on the construction of the Friday Mosque at Sala (Salé) with the prisoners taken at Alarcos. He then turned on Talabira (Talavera) and Makkada (Maqueda) and destroyed them; then advanced against Toledo, against which he launched several assaults. Then he fell on Majrit (Madrid) and began the return home, starting with Jayyan (Jaén) and on to Cordova, Ecija and Qarmuna (Carmona), arriving in Seville in Ramadan (592)/August 1196.

102. The Muslim disaster at Las Navas de Tolosa (609/1212)

Despite some successful raids in the aftermath of Alarcos, the Muslims did not make full use of their victory, largely because of the death of al-Mansur Ya'qub in 595/January 1199. The Christians, on the other hand, worked hard to reconcile their differences and forge a powerful alliance against the Almohads. The Christian response was given the status of a crusade by Pope Innocent III (1198-1216), thanks to the efforts of Alfonso VIII of Castile and the archbishop of Toledo, Rodrigo Jiménez de Rada. But though the crusade started as an international venture, the foreigners deserted, for reasons that were perfectly well understood by the Muslims as well as the Spaniards (see also text 40). The battle that crowned this campaign, at Las Navas de Tolosa, was a triumph for the combined forces of León, Castile, Navarre and Aragon; its result was to reverse completely the Almohad success at Alarcos eighteen years earlier, and put a short term on the Almohad's presence in the Peninsula.

Abu 'Abd-Allah Muhammad (al-Nasir) had succeeded his father Yaq'ub on the latter's death in 1199. His reign is generally regarded as disastrous by Muslim

وبعد رجوع أمير المؤمنين أبى عبدالله من هذا الفتح المتقدم الذكر إلى إشبيلية،

استنفر الناس من أقاصى البلاد، فاجتمعت له جموع كثيفة، وخرج من إشبيلية فى أول

سنة ٦٠٩، فسار حتى نزل مدينة جيّان؛ فأقام بها ينظر فى أمره ويعبّى عساكره،

وخرج الأدفنش -لعنه الله- من مدينة طليطلة فى جموع ضخمة، حتى نزل على قلعة

رباح -وهى كانت للمسلمين، افتتحها المنصور أبويوسف فى الوقعة الكبرى- فسلمها

إليه المسلمون الذين بها بعد أن أمنهم على أنفسهم؛ فرجع عن الأدفنش -لعنه الله-

بهذا السبب من الروم جموعٌ كثيرة، حين منعهم من قتل المسلمين الذين كانوا بالقلعة

المذكورة، وقالوا: «إنما جئتَ بنا لتفتح بنا البلاد وتمنعنا من الغزو وقتل المسلمين؛ ما لنا

فى صحبتك من حاجة على هذا الوجه!»

وقعة العقاب وهزيمة المسلمين

وخرج أمير المؤمنين من مدينة جيّان، فالتقى هو والأدفنش بموضع يعرف

بالعقاب، بالقرب من حصن يدعى حصن سالم؛ فعبأ الأدفنش جيوشه ورتب أصحابه،

ودَهَم المسلمين وهم على غير أُهبة؛ فانهزموا، وقُتل من الموحدين خلقٌ كثير.

chroniclers, one of whom notes that he was so proud of the huge size of his army that he considered himself invincible. In 608/1211 he spent nearly two months reducing the castle of Salvatierra, and was still in a confident mood when he marched to face Alfonso's forces the following summer. However, unlike the Christian army, his troops were of doubtful loyalty, as mentioned in our selection.

The text is taken from al-Marrakushi, al-Mu'jib, pp.401-03, which was written in 621/1224 (see text 93 for details). Other sources confirm that the pay of the Almohad troops was in arrears, and further grievances are cited; the fact that the Christians attacked when the Muslims were not ready is also mentioned to help explain the defeat. For a detailed study of the battle, see Huici Miranda, Las grandes batallas, pp.219-327. Abu 'Abd-Allah barely escaped with his life, having been offered a faster horse by a loyal Arab soldier; he returned to Marrakesh, where he died the following year, either from a brain tumour or poison, or, according to some accounts, from a dog bite.

After returning to Seville from this victory [at Salvatierra], the Amir al-Mu'minin Abu 'Abd-Allah called up the people from the furthest reaches of the country, and they assembled in great numbers. He left Seville at the beginning of 609 (June 1212) and marched to Jaén. He stayed there to make his arrangements and organize his troops. Alfonso – may God curse him – left Toledo with a vast army and proceeded to Calatrava, which he besieged. The castle had been in Muslim hands since al-Mansur Abu Yusuf (Ya'qub) conquered it following the great victory [of Alarcos]. The Muslims surrendered it to Alfonso after he had given them a safe conduct. Thereupon, a large number of the Christians withdrew from Alfonso (may God curse him!), when he prevented them from killing the Muslims who were in the castle. They said, "You have only brought us along to help you conquer the country, and forbid us to plunder and kill the Muslims. We don't have any need of your company [if we're only going to act] in this way."

The battle of al-'Iqab and the defeat of the Muslims

The Commander of the Faithful left Jaén and encountered Alfonso at a place called al-'Iqab, near the castle called Hisn Salim. Alfonso drew up his army, arranged his men and launched a surprise attack on the Muslims, who were not prepared for battle. They were defeated, and a great number of the Almohads were killed.

140

وأكبر أسباب هذه الهزيمة اختلافُ قلوب الموحدين؛ وذلك أنهم كانوا على عهد أبى يوسف يعقوب يأخنون العطاءَ فى كل أربعة أشهر، لا يخلّ ذلك من أمرهم؛ فأبطأ فى مدة أبى عبدالله هذا عنهم العطاء، وخصوصاً فى هذه السُّفرة، فنسبوا ذلك إلى الوزراء؛ وخرجوا وهم كارهون؛ فبلغنى عن جماعة منهم أنهم لم يَسُلّوا سيفاً ولا شرعوا رمحاً ولا أخنوا فى شيء من أهبة القتال؛ بل انهزموا لأول حملة الإفرنج عليهم قاصدين لذلك.

وثبت أبوعبدالله هذا فى ذلك اليـوم ثبـاتاً لم يُرَ لملك قـبله، ولولا ثبـاته هذا لاستُؤصلت تلك الجموع كُلّها قتلا وأسراً! ثم رجع من هذا الوجه إلى إشبيلية، وأقام بها إلى شهر رمضان من هذه السنة، ثم عبر البحر قاصداً مدينة مراكش ... وكانت هذه الهزيمة الكبرى على المسلمين، يوم الاثنين منتصف صفر الكائن فى سنة ٦٠٩.

وفصل الأدفنش –لعنه الله– عن هذا الموضع بعد أن امتلأت يداه وأيدى أصحابه أموالاً وأمتعة من متاع المسلمين؛ فقصد مدينتَى بيّاسة وأبذَة؛ فـأما بياسة فوجدها أو أكثرها خالية، فحُرق أنوُرها وخرّب مسجدها الأعظم؛ ونزل على أبذة وقد اجتمع فيها من المسلمين عدد كثير من المنهزمة وأهل بياسة وأهل البلد نفسه؛ فـأقام عليها ثلاثة عشر يوماً، ثم دخلها عَنوةً فقتل وسبى وغنم؛ وفصل هو وأصحابه من السّبى من النساء والصبيان بما ملئوا به بلادَ الروم قاطبة؛ فكانت هذه أشدُّ على المسلمين من الهزيمة!

The main reason for this defeat was the divisions in the hearts of the Almohads. In the time of Abu Yusuf Ya'qub they drew their pay every four months without fail. But in the time of this Abu 'Abd-Allah, and especially during this particular campaign, their payment was in arrears. They attributed this to the viziers, and rebelled in disgust. I have heard from several of them that they did not draw their swords nor train their spears, nor did they take any part in the preparations for battle. With this in mind, they fled at the first assault of the Franks.

This Abu 'Abd-Allah stood firm on that day like no king before him; were it not for his steadfastness, the whole of that army would have be been exterminated, either killed or captured. He then returned to Seville and remained there till Ramadan (January 1213), when he crossed over to Marrakesh... This great defeat of the Muslims took place on the Monday in mid Safar 609 (14 Safar = 16 July).

Alfonso – God curse him! – pulled out of this place after he and his men had taken their fill of the chattels and possessions of the Muslims, and set off towards the towns of Bayyasa (Baeza) and Ubbadha (Ubeda). He found Baeza, or most of it, empty. He burnt its houses and destroyed its largest mosque. He then descended on Ubeda, where many of the defeated Muslims, and the people of Baeza, as well as the town's own population, had collected. He invested it for thirteen days, and then took it by force, killing and capturing and plundering. He and his men set aside as prisoners enough women and children to fill all the Christian territories. This was a greater blow to the Muslims than the defeat in battle.

142

103. Tit for tat (614/1217)

After Las Navas, Almohad power in Spain was effectively ended, and among those who strove to fill the vacuum was Muhammad b. Yusuf b. Hud al-Judhami, who claimed descent from the former Hudid rulers of Saragossa. The exploit recounted here is his first appearance on the scene. In due course, following an open proclamation of "revolt" in 625/1228 in Murcia, he was able to claim at least nominal control over most of al-Andalus, with the exception of Valencia, but he enjoyed few successes against the Christians, who inflicted a heavy defeat on him near Jerez in the southwest (see text 42). With the rise of his namesake, Muhammad b. Yusuf b. Nasr, in the region round

شنفيرُه: حصنٌ على أربع مراحل من مُرْسِية بالأندلس فى شرقيها، مشهورٌ بالمنعة، ظفر به فى الصُّلح محمدُ بن هود سنة ٦١٤، ومعه خمسمائة من أجناد الرجال، غدر به؛ لأنّ أبا سعيد بن الشيخ أبى حَفْص الهنتاتىّ، لما طاف على حصون الأندلس يتفقّدُها فى أيام الهدنة، نظر إلى هذا المَعْقِل وهو بارزٌ إلى السماء مع وثاقة بنائه أعجبه وقال: «كَيْفَ أخذ الرومُ هذا الحصن من المسلمين؟» فقيل: «غدروا به فى زمان الصلح!» فقال: «أمّا فى أجناد المسلمين مَنْ يجازيهم بفعلهم؟»

فسمعه ابن هود فأسَرَّها فى نفسه، إلى أن تَمَّت له الحيلة، فطلع فى سلّم من حبال فذبح السامِرَ الذى يحرس بالليل، ولم يزل يُطْلِع رجاله واحداً واحداً إلى أن حصلوا بجملتهم فى الحصن، وفَرَّ الروم الذين خلصوا من القتل إلى بُرْج مانع. فقال بن هود: «إن أصبح هؤلاء فى هذا البرج جاءهم المددُ من كل مكان! فالرأى أن نطلق النيران فى بابه!» فلما رأوا الدخان، وأبصروا اشتعال النار طلبوا الصلح على أن يخرجوا بأنفسهم، فكان ذلك واستولى المسلمون على الحصن؛ وكان الروم قد أرسلوا فى الليل شَخْصاً دَلُّوهُ من البرج، فأصبحَت الخيل والرجال على الحصن، وقد أحكم المسلمون أمره، فانصرفوا فى خجلةٍ وخيبة.

وترددَّت فى شأنه المخاطبات إلى مراكش، فقال الوزير ابن جامع لابن الفخار: أخذناه فى الصلح، كما أُخِذ عنا فى الصلح! ومن هذه الوقيعة اشتهر ابن هود عند أهل شَرْق الأندلس، وصاروا يقولون: «هو الذى استرجع شنفيرُه!»

ranada, Ibn Hud lost further ground, and was eventually assassinated in Almería in 35/December 1237. For a brief outline of his career, see R. Arié, L'Espagne usulmane, pp.52-57.

The selection is from the work of al-Himyari, already frequently cited; the same uthor also has details of Ibn Hud's revolt against the Almohads. The Arabic text is from 'e edition of Lévi-Provençal, La Péninsule Ibérique, p. 116. The identification of hanfiro has not been established.

Shanfiro – a stronghold four stages to the east of Murcia in al-Andalus, amous for its impregnability. Muhammad b. Hud captured it in a period of truce n 614 (1217), with a troop of 500 men. He took it by treachery, because Abu a'id b. al-Shaikh Abu Hafs al-Hantati made a tour of the castles of al-Andalus o inspect them during a period of truce, and when he saw this fortress, its solid onstruction standing out against the sky, he was amazed and said, "How did the Christians take this castle from the Muslims?" He was told that they took it by reachery in a time of truce. He said, "Is there no-one among the soldiers of slam who can outdo what they have done?"

Ibn Hud heard him, and kept it to himself until he had devised a plan. He limbed up on a rope ladder and cut the throat of the night watch. Then his men limbed up, one by one, until they all got into the castle. The Christians who scaped being killed fled to an impregnable tower. Ibn Hud said, "If those men re still in the tower in the morning, help will reach them from every quarter. he best plan is to set fire to the door!" When [the defenders] saw the smoke nd noticed the burning flames, they sued for peace on condition that they be llowed to go free, which is what happened, and the Muslims took possession of he castle. During the night, the Christians had sent someone whom they owered from the tower [to get help], and in the morning horses and men were in osition round the castle; but the Muslims consolidated their position, and [the Christians] retired in shame and frustration.

Word of this affair was frequently repeated in Marrakesh, where the vizier bn Jami' said to Ibn al-Fakhkhar, "We took it during a ceasefire, just as they ook it from us!" Ibn Hud became famous for this exploit among the people of astern Andalusia, who used to say, "He is the one who got back Shanfiro."

104. A lament for the loss of Seville (646/1248)

Ferdinand III of Castile was quick to take advantage of the weakness of the Muslim on the break-up of the Almohad power in Spain, particularly once he had effected the permanent union of the kingdoms of León and Castile in 1230. By 1236 he had acquired Cordova; Jaén followed in 1245. With the latter, he reduced Muhammad, the first Nasrid ruler, to submission and agreed a treaty to last twenty years (see text 105). As proof of his fidelity, Muhammad assisted Ferdinand at the siege of Seville, the former Almohad capital and the final prize in this phase of the reconquest (see also text 47).

The following account of the siege is taken from the chronicle of Ibn 'Idhari (early 14th century). He states that the siege lasted about a year and a half, in contrast with the accounts in some Christian sources. Other Arab accounts date the fall of Seville Sha'ban 646/December 1248, which is more accurate. The poem, by Abu Musa Harun b. Harun, is 65 lines long and only a flavour of it is given here. It was designed to move the heart of the Almohad caliph in Marrakesh, 'Ali al-Sa'id b. Idris, but in vain. Al-Sa'id was killed in Safar 646/June 1248 and his successor was more concerned with the

وفي سنة خمس وأربعين وستمائة أحدقت النصارى بمدينة إشبيلية وحاصروهم

براً وبحراً وأذاقوا أهلها شراً وكان نزولهم عليها ووصول جموعهم إليها في شهر

جمادى الأولى من العام المذكور، فاشتد في هذه السنة حصارها وتملأت منهم أنظارها

وأقطارها وأخنوا خلقاً كثيراً من أهلها واختطفوا في الأجفان بعض أطفالها وضيقوا

بها غاية التضييق، ورموا الحجارة بالمنجنيق، وعدموا المرافق كلها قليلها وجليلها إلا

ماكان في بعض ديار الأغنياء فإنهم كانوا يحتاطون في تلك الأمور مثل الفقيه القاضي

ابن منظور فإنه كان يطمع في إقلاع النصارى عن المدينة فيأمر الناس بالقتال والرمي

بالنبال، والناس مع ذلك حيارى، يمشون سكارى وما هم بسكارى، ومات بالجوع خلق

كثير، وعدمت الأطعمة من القمح والشعير، وأكل الناس الجلود، وفنيت المقاتلة من العامة

وأصناف الجنود.

ولما انتهى بإشبيلية شدة الحصار، وعدموا الأنصار من الأمصار، وصاروا قبضة

في يد أعداء الله الكفار خاطبوا أمير المؤمنين المعتضد بالله السعيد وكافة المسلمين من

أهل عدوة الغرب يستصرخونهم ويعرفونهم بما نالهم من الجهد العظيم والكرب الشديد

الأليم، ويرغبونهم في نصرتهم ويحضونهم على جهاد أعداء الله الكافرين، فمن ذلك

قصيدة يرق لها القلب القاسي وتأتمر لها الجبال الرواسي:

disintegration of Almohad power in North Africa.

Monroe, pp.332-37, translates another poem "inspired by the capture of Seville", by Abu'l-Baqa Salih b. Sharif al-Rundi (from Ronda), which was also designed to stimulate the North Africans to Holy War. In fact, it was written in 665/1267, after Muhammad b. al-Ahmar the Nasrid had handed over Jerez, Alcalá and other territories to Alfonso X, to win his support in the struggle against the Banu Ashqilula (see below, texts 105-106). Al-Rundi's poem is preserved in al-Dhakhira al-saniyya, ed. Ben Cheneb, pp.127-29.

This selection is taken from Ibn 'Idhari, al-Bayan al-mughrib, ed. A. Huici Miranda (Tetuan, 1963), pp.381-85. It will be noted that the author describes Ferdinand III as Alfonso, which was used indiscriminately by the Muslim chroniclers for the Christian kings. In the first line of the poem, Seville is called Hims, because it was Arabs from Hims in Syria who settled there after the conquest of Spain. The Arabic text has been altered in one or two places, as indicated, the original wording appearing in square brackets.

In the year 645 (1247) the Christians encircled the city of Seville and laid siege to it by land and sea. They gave its inhabitants a taste of disaster. Their descent on the city and the arrival of their hosts there was in Jumada I (September); the siege intensified during the year and the surrounding regions and districts became full of [their forces]. They captured a large number of the inhabitants [of these districts] and seized some of their children in ships, with which they maintained a very tight blockade. They kept up a bombardment from mangonels and destroyed all amenities, both small and great, except what was in the houses of a few rich people, who kept on their guard over these things. One such was the jurist and qadi, Ibn Manzur, who was striving for the Christians to withdraw from the city and would order the people to fight and to shoot their arrows. Nevertheless, the people became dismayed, and staggered around like drunkards even though they weren't drunk; a great many died of starvation. Resigning any hope of corn or barley, the people began to chew skins; the fighting men among the general populace and the ranks of the army perished.

When the siege at Seville reached extremes of severity, and support from other towns was non-existent, and [the Sevillians] became squeezed in the grip of the enemies of God, the infidels, they turned to the Amir of the Believers al-Mu'tadid bi'llah al-Sa'id [the Almohad ruler], and all the Muslims of western North Africa, beseeching their help and letting them know of the terrible struggle and the severe and excruciating distress that had overtaken them. [The people of Seville tried] to waken their desire to come to their help and incited them to wage Holy War against the infidels, enemies of God. Among their words was an ode which would delight the hard of heart and which the unmoveable mountains would respond to:

ياحمص أقصدك المقدور حين رمى   لم يرع فـيـك الردى إلا ولا ندماً

حزت [جرت؟] عليك يد للدهر ظالمة   لايعـدل الدهر في شيء إذا حكمـا

ولاتوهمت ذاك الحـسـن يطمـسـه   ريب الزمـان ويكسو نوره الظلمـا

قد كان حسنك فتـان الشبـاب فمذ   أصبت عوضت منها القبح والهرمـا

يا جنة زحـزتنا عن زخـارفـهـا   ذنوبنا فلزمنا البث والندمـا

يا سائلي عن مـصـاب المسلمين بها   أصخ لتسمع أمراً يورث الصممـا

ثارت حـفـائظ للتثليث فـابتدروا   وأيقظوا من سنات الغفلة الهممـا

فكم أسارى غدت في القيد موثقة   تشكو من الذل أقداماً لها حطمـا

وكم صـريع ظل مـخـتطفـاً   عن أمـه فـهـو بالأمـواج قـد فطمـا

ياأهل وادي الحما بالعدوة انتعشوا   هذا الذماء فـقـد أشفى بها سقمـا

فـتح الجـزيرة مما سن أولكم   فلتثبتوا للهدى في أرضنا [رأضنا] قدماً

لا عـذر في تركهـا للكفر مسلمة   إن الزمـان وأنتم فـيـه مـاعـقـمـا

هل من مجيب لداعينا فـيركبنا   ملك النجاة فبـحـر الحادثات طمـا

لم يبق فينا سـوى الأنفاس خافتة   فكنا في وجـود يشبـه العـدمـا

ياحسـرة الدين والدنيا لأندلس   مـهما استطال بها التثليث واجترمـا

لم يبق للحق في شـتى مطالعهـا   نور فـأصبح ليل الكفر مـرتكمـا

1. O Hims (Seville), was it your predestined fate when it shot at you, that destruction observed neither pact nor [claims to] protection?
2. The tyrannical hand of Time has pointed at you; Time never acts justly when it makes a decision.
4. I did not imagine that the disasters of Time would blot out that beauty, clothing its splendour with darkness;
5. Your beauty had the charm of youth, but after being stricken it has exchanged for this ugliness and senility.
6. O Paradise, from whose flowing streams our sins have snatched us, while sorrow and regret attend us.
7. O you who ask me about the disaster suffered by the Muslims there, listen that you might hear of something that will leave a legacy of deafness.
10. The guardians of the Trinity have risen up; forestall them and rouse your thoughts from heedless slumber.
15. How many captives have come to have their feet bound in fetters, shattered, complaining of abasement ?
16. And how many a suckling babe continues to be cast down, snatched away from his mother, and has been weaned in the waves [i.e., thrown in the river].
38. O you of Wadi al-Hima in al-'Udwa, revive this last gasp of life, which is near the end of its days through disease.
44. Conquering the Peninsula is one of the customs of your forefathers; so plant your feet in our land to spread guidance.
46. There is no excuse for leaving it and abandoning it to the unbelievers. Time, and you within in, are not sterile.
48. Is there anyone who will answer our call, and give us a lifeboat in the swelling sea of disasters?
49. Nothing remains in us but dying breaths; all of us, [though] in existence, are like the non-existent.
52. Alas for the faith and for this world in al-Andalus, as the Trinity-worshippers have seized power over it and wronged it.
53. Truth no longer has a radiance in the various rising-places [of the sun], while the night of unbelief is thick.

المؤمنين وحسبي في النجـاء ممـا	فـالمفـزع الله والذخـر العتـاد أمـيـر
فـريما ضن قطر السـحب ثم ممـا	فـلا مـبـالاة بالأيام إن مطلت
فـرب دهـر غيـور عـاد مبـتـسـمـا	فـاصـدع بحـقك إن الدهر ممتـثل

وفي سنة ست وأربعين وستماية كان استيلاء الطاغية أذفونش اللعين على مدينة إشبيلية أعادها الله للإسلام، بعد ماجرعوا أهلها كأس الحمام، من كثرة المجاعة وعدم الطعـام، فكل منهم في بحـر المنايا غاص وعـام، مما حل بهـم من الأوجـال والآلام، مما يطول في وصفه وشرحه الكلام، ويستنفد فيه القراطيس والأقلام، فسلموا لهم في المدينة وخرج منها الخاص من أهلها والعام، كان ذلك في يوم سبع وعشرين من شهر رمضان المعظم من هذا العام، وكان نزول الطاغية عليها في شهر جمادى الأولى من العام الفارط فكان حصارهم عليها مدة عام وخمسة أشهر.

56. Fearfully we seek refuge in God, and the ready treasure – the Amir al-Mu'minin: these two are sufficient for salvation.

64. There is no need to worry about the days if they put off [their promise]; sometimes the clouds withhold their raindrops, and then pour them down.

65. Come out openly with your truth. Time has become submissive: many a jealous age has turned out smiling again.

In the year 646 (1248) the accursed tyrant Alfonso (Ferdinand III) gained control of the city of Seville – may God restore it to Islam! – after its inhabitants, from the prevalence of famine and the dearth of food, had drained the cup of death. All the population was immersed and floating in a sea of death, because of the terrors and agonies that had befallen them, the description and explanation of which would be protracted and would exhaust both pen and paper. They surrendered to them in the city and then the populace left, nobles and commoners alike. This was on 27 Ramadan 646 (13 January 1249), after a siege of one year and five months.

105. The Muslims revolt in southern Spain (662/1264)

The so-called revolt of the Mudejars was not a Peninsula-wide rebellion of Muslim who had long been living in Christian territory, but rather a concerted effort by the firs Nasrid ruler, Muhammad I Ibn al-Ahmar (1237-73), to reverse the recent trend o Christian expansion in the south, which had dramatically reduced the territory i Muslim hands. The revolt was joined by the Muslims who had fallen under Christia control in the regions to the west and east of the kingdom of Granada. The episode which initially achieved considerable success, demonstrates to what extent Muhammad regarded himself as a true vassal of the King of Castile (Alfonso X, 1252-84). The fina defeat of the revolt led to the dispossession of the Mudejars of Andalusia and thei replacement by Christian settlers. For a recent discussion, see Harvey, Islamic Spain *pp.51-54.*

Two accounts are presented below, both by authors writing in North Africa, wh naturally highlight the participation of Marinid forces. The Banu Marin, under thei sultan Abu Yusuf Ya'qub (1258-86), were in the final stages of eliminating Almoha power in the Maghreb. This was the first of their many interventions in Spanish affairs and was led by two of Abu Yusuf's nephews. For background, see Abun-Nasr, pp.122-23

The first text is taken from al-Dhakhira al-saniyya fi tarikh al-daulat al-mariniyya *ed. M. Ben Cheneb (Algiers, 1339/1920), from pp.108-12. It is not a coherent narrative but rather a string of unconnected incidents, some of which have been extracted here*

(a)

فيها جاز المجاهدون من بنى مرين والمتطوّعة من بني مرين والمتطوّعة من أهل

المغرب إلى الأندلس برسم الجهاد وقائدهم الأنجد أبو معرّف محمد بن إدريس بن

عبدالحق واخوه الفارس المجاهد أبوثابت عامر بن إدريس والحاج المجاهد التاهرتي.

. زوا في جيش عظيم من بني مرين وقبائل المغرب خيلاً ورجالاً يزيدون على ثلاثة

آلاف بين فارس وراجل فعقد لهم أمير المسلمين أبويوسف رايته المنصورة وجهزهم

بالخيل والعدد ابتغاء ثواب الله عز وجل.

وكتب إلى الفقيه أبي القاسم العزفي صاحب سبتة في تجويزهم، وودعهم ودعا

لهم وانصرفوا من حضرته فجازوا إلى الأندلس وهو أول جيش جاز إلى الأندلس من

بني مرين والسبب في جوازهم أن النصارى دمرهم الله تعالى كانت قد تكالبت على

بلاد المسلمين بالغارات والسبي فأبادوا أكثرها وأهلكوا قواعدها فتفجع أهل العدوة

The main action is the fall of Jerez to the Muslims, and the capture of its commander (García Gómez Carillo). According to our source, Jerez had been seized by Alfonso X on 17 Dhu'l-Qa'da 659/13 October 1261, so his calculation of the time it was held by the Christians is not quite accurate.

The second selection provides a more connected account of the revolt, though it does not contain many of the details reported by the first. The text is from Ibn 'Idhari, al-Bayan al-mughrib, ed. A. Huici Miranda (Tetuan, 1963), pp.436-39. The siege and fall of Niebla is put by Christian sources on 16 February 1262; Ibn Mahfuz had been master of the town since the fall of his native Seville in 1248. He sought refuge in North Africa with the Almohad caliph, 'Umar b. Ibrahim al-Murtada (d. 665/January 1267). For the Banu Ashqilula, see Harvey, esp. p. 31 ff., and Arié, pp.55-76. Abu Muhammad, who disgraced himself at Murcia, was a nephew of Ibn al-Ahmar. One reason advanced for disenchantment of the Banu Ashqilula with their Nasrid kinsman is that they feared their favoured position in the kingdom would be undermined by the arrival of the Marinids. In fact, as the situation became more complicated, the Banu Ashqilula sought assistance from the Marinids, who ultimately offered them a refuge in North Africa (see p.160). Murcia was quickly recaptured by James I of Aragon (1213-76), and thereafter remained in Christian hands. The ill-treatment of the Murcians in 673/1275 coincides with the period shortly before a full-scale Marinid invasion under their sultan Abu Yusuf.

(a)

This year [662/began 4 November 1263], Marinid Fighters for the Faith and Volunteers from the people of the Maghreb crossed over to al-Andalus to promote the Holy War. Their bravest leader was Abu Mu'arrif Muhammd b. Idris b. 'Abd al-Haqq, with his brother, al-Faris al-Mujahid Abu Thabit 'Amir b. Idris, and al-Hajj al-Mujahid al-Tahirti. They crossed at the head of a large army composed of Marinids and [other] Maghrebi tribesmen, both horse and foot, between them exceeding 3,000 men. The Commander of the Muslims Abu Yusuf (Ya'qub) put them under his own victorious banner and fitted them out with horses and equipment, aspiring to a good reward from Almighty and Glorious God.

He [the Marinid sultan] wrote to the faqih Abu 'l-Qasim al-'Azafi, governor of Ceuta, with orders to assist their passage. He bid them farewell and prayed for them. They left his presence and crossed to al-Andalus; this was the first Marinid army to do so. The reason for their expedition was that the Christians (may God Almighty annihilate them!) had ravaged the lands of the Muslims with raids and taken many captives; the Christians exterminated most of [al-Andalus] and destroyed its main bases. The people of North Africa were

152

لحالهم فصنع الفقيه الأديب المكنى بأبي الحكم بن المرحّل رحمه الله قصيدة يحرض فيها بني مرين وسائر المسلمين على جهاد الكافرين ونصرة بلاد الأندلس من المسلمين المستضعفين. فإنه رحمه الله كان في تلك السنة بمدينة فاس يكتب للأمير أبي مالك ابن أمير المسلمين أبي يوسف فقرئت تلك القصيدة بصحن جامع القرويين من فاس يوم الجمعة بعد الصلاة فبكى الناس عند سماعها وانتدب كثير منهم للجهاد. ...

وفي هذه السنة نزل الفنش لعنه الله مدينة غرناطة فأقام عليها أياماً وأقلع عنها خائباً خاسراً.

وفيها نزل عامر بن إدريس بن عبدالحق مدينة شريش فدخل ربضها بالسيف هو ومن كان معه من المطوعين من قبائل المغرب. ... وفي يوم الجمعة الثالث عاشر من شوال منها أخرج عامر بن إدريس النصارى من قصبة شريش وكان مدة ملكهم لها ثلاث سنين تنقص إثنان وعشرون يوماً. ...

وفيها قام المسلمون الدُّجن بالاريولة على الروم فغلبهم الروم فقتلوا من الروم [كذا] خلقاً كثيراً. ...

وفيها أعطى ابن يونس مدينة اسجة إلى دن جيل الرومي وأدخله المدينة فأخرج عنها المسلمين، ثم قتلهم وسبى حريمهم وأموالهم إلا قليلاً منهم تداركهم دون نونه فأطلقهم من يده ونفاهم للاسنة [كذا] وقائدها يومئذ ابن ربيبه، وعذل دن جيل على غدره بالمسلمين ولامه على ذلك.

(b)

وفي هذه السنة دخل الروم أبادهم الله مدينة لبلة بعد حصار عظيم وأمر جسيم وكان صاحبها ابن محفوظ لم يدخل في الصلح المنعقد بين ابن الأحمر والروم، بل قاطع

tormented by the situation of the Spanish Muslims and the learned faqih called Abu'l-Hukm Malik b. al-Marahhal (may God have mercy on him!) composed an ode to encourage the Marinids and other Muslims to join a Holy War against the infidels and go to the assistance of the oppressed Muslims of al-Andalus. This year, he (may God have mercy on him!) was in Fez, where he wrote to the amir Abu Malik son of the Commander of the Muslims, Abu Yusuf. The ode was read in the Qarawin mosque in Fez on Friday, after the prayers. The people wept when they heard it and many applied to take part in the Holy War. [There follows a poem of 51 verses.]

This year, Alfonso [X] (may God curse him!) descended on the city of Granada and remained there for several days, but then abandoned it, having achieved nothing but losses.

'Amir b. Idris b. 'Abd al-Haqq descended on the town of Shirish (Jerez) and entered the suburbs by the sword, together with the Volunteers from the Maghrebi tribes. [...] On Friday 13 Shawwal (8 August 1264) 'Amir b. Idris expelled the Christians from the citadel of Jerez: it had been in their hands for 22 days under three years.

The same year the Mudejars rose in Orihuela against the Christians, but the Christians overcame them. Many of the Christians (*sic.*) were killed. [...]

Ibn Yunus gave the city of Ecija to Don Gil the Christian and let him enter the city. He threw out the Muslims and then killed them, took their women captive and their possessions, except for a few of them whom Don Nuno (Nuño González de Lara) provided with an indemnity and released. He banished them to al-Asina (al-Lisana, or Lucena), whose commander at that time was Ibn Rabiba, and censured Don Gil for his treachery towards the Muslims and reproached him for it.

(b)

In this year [661/began 15 November 1262], the Christians – may God wipe them out – entered the town of Labla (Niebla) after a great siege and a momentous struggle. Its ruler, Ibn Mahfuz, had not joined in the treaty that was arranged between Ibn al-Ahmar and the Christians, but had fixed on his own

على نفسه في العام بمال معلوم، يعطيه في بعض السنين، وفي بعضها يجاهد في سبيل رب العالمين مع جماعته بزعامته وشهامته إلى أن حاصره الروم فيها في هذا العام فلما اشتد حاله، وانقطعت آماله أعطى البلد النصارى وأخرج منها المسلمين أهلها ودخلت الروم إليها وقيل بل كان ذلك في آخر السنة التي قبل هذه المؤرخة. ووصل ابن محفوظ إلى المرتضى مع جماعته، فكان بمراكش يركب معهم فيها في جملة الأجناد، كأحد رؤساء القواد، إلى أن مات رحمه الله تعالى.

وفي سنة اثنين وستين وستمائة جاز الأمير أبوعبدالله محمد بن إدريس مع أخيه عامر وجملة من بني مرين الأكابر في نحو ثلاثمائة من الفرسان، الأنجاد برسم الغزو والجهاد، وكان قد بقي من أمد الصلح المنعقد بين ابن الأحمر والروم بقيه هذه السنة فقد كان عقده معهم في سنة ثلاث وأربعين إلى عشرين سنة. وكان السبب في هذا النفاق قبل تمام أمد الصلح إن الأمير أبا عبدالله بن الأحمر توجه إلى إشبيلية برسم الإجتماع مع اذفونش ليجدد معه الصلح على مايقع الإتفاق عليه، فلما وصل ابن الأحمر إلى إشبيلية نزل بخارجها بالصهريج الأحمر وكان معه خمسمائة فارس من الفرسان الأنجاد والرؤساء والقواد، فخرج اذفونش إليه وحلف عليه أن يدخل إليه فدخل ونزل بالعبادية منها ودخل معه الرئيسان الزعيمان ابنا اشقيلولة أبومحمد وأبوإسحق ونزلا معه في ذلك الزقاق مع من كان معهم من الرجال والفرسان إلى ذلك المكان، وبقى سائرهم حيث نزولهم الأول.

وحين دخول ابن الأحمر ونزوله عمل النصارى على الزقاق الذي نزل فيه خشباً مسمرة على الدروب تمنع جواز الخيل فلما اتصل بالأمير المذكور ذلك الحال خاف أن يتوغل في الأوحال، فدبر على نفسه في الخروج والإرتحال، حين عاين أسباب الحيلة عليه والغدر إليه، فخرج بجماعته، بما علم من زعامته، وأمر رجاله أن يكسروا ذلك الخشب المعمولة وخرج فحصل بمحلته مع جماعته وبني اشقيلولة، وأمر في الحين

account to pay a certain amount of money every year. Some years he would pay
it, and others he would gallantly wage Holy War with the men under his
leadership, on the path of the Lord of the Worlds. So this year the Christians
besieged him there. When his situation became desperate and he gave up hope,
he gave the town to the Christians and brought out its Muslim population, and
the Christians entered it. It is [sometimes] said that this occurred at the end of
the previous year [660/1261-62]. Ibn Mahfuz came with his men to al-Murtada.
He used to ride with his men in Marrakesh, at the head of the troops, as one of
the leading generals, until he died (may God have mercy on him).

In the year 662 (began 4 November 1263), the amir Abu 'Abd-Allah
Muhammad b. Idris crossed over [from North Africa] with his brother 'Amir
and a number of the chiefs of the Banu Marin, at the head of about 300 intrepid
horsemen, to raid and wage Holy War. Of the period of truce arranged between
Ibn al-Ahmar and the Christians, there still remained the rest of this year [to
run], for a truce lasting 20 years had been agreed with them in the year
(6)43/1245. The reason for this double-dealing before the expiry of the period
of the truce, was that the amir Abu 'Abd-Allah b. al-Ahmar went to Seville to
meet with Alfonso [X] to renew the treaty, as had been agreed. When Ibn al-
Ahmar arrived in Seville, he camped outside the city at al-Sahrij al-Ahmar (the
Red Cistern). He was accompanied by 500 of his boldest horsemen, leaders and
generals. Alfonso went out to him and swore to him [that it was safe] to come
in. He entered the city and lodged in the 'Abbadiyya district. Two of the leading
commanders of the Banu Ashqilula, Abu Muhammad and Abu Ishaq, went with
him and lodged with him in the same narrow alley where those men and knights
were who had entered the place with him. The remainder stayed in their first
quarters [outside the city].

On Ibn al-Ahmar's entry and taking lodgings, the Christians boarded up the
alley where he was staying, using planks fastened by nails; they did it at night,
after he had come and settled in there. In the morning, the alley was nailed up,
preventing horsemen from passing through. When news of this reached Ibn al-
Ahmar, he feared that he was advancing further and further into the mire, and
planned in his mind to get out and leave. Then he inspected the means by which
this trick and treachery against him had been effected, and left with his party,
showing the leadership for which he was known, and ordered his men to break
down the planks that had been put up. So he left and regained his camp, together
with his party and the Banu Ashqilula. He gave the orders for leaving and

بالرحيل منصرفاً إلى بلاده مع قواده وأجناده، ثم خرج اذفونش وحلف إليه أنه ما عاملت تلك الاطرنكات إلا احتياطاً من النصارى السراق عليه، فأظهر له أنه صدقه، وقد علم الأمر وحققه، وحصل ما حاصل في النفوس فما نفعت أيمان الغموس، فانصرف عنه دون اتفاق ولا ارتباط وبسبب ذلك وقع في الأندلس ما وقع من النفاق. وأخبرني من حضر ذلك الوقت بإشبيلية المذكورة أنه ما كان فيها مع اذفونش من الفرسان إلا أقل مما كان مع ابن الأحمر هناك أو قريباً من ذلك، وحلف ابن الأحمر بأيمانه حين ذلك أنه لا يراه أبداً ولا يلقاه إلا في قتال أو جلاد فكان الأمر كذلك.

ولما وصل إلى مدينة ابن السليم، بقلب منشرح وصدر سليم، فإنه كان عاين هلاكه ثم خلصه الله وسلم فأوصى أهلها وأهل تلك الجهات بالتحصن والإحاطة، وانصرف مجتازاً عليهم إلى غرناطة، فعلم المسلمون إنه انفصل من اذفونش من غير اتفاق ولا ارتباط، فأخذوا في التحصن على أنفسهم والإحتياط، وأخرج أهل شريش من كان معهم في القصبة ساكنين فقد كانوا سكنوا بها نحواً من أربع سنين، وضبطوا مدينتهم وقصبتهم بقية هذه السنة فكانوا بها هادنين، لأنهم كانوا بايعوا ابن الأحمر ودخلوا تحت طاعته وكان اشترط اذفونش اللعين أنه مَن يدخل تحت طاعته من بلاد المسلمين يدخل في صلحه، فكان بقيه هذه السنة انصرامه وتمامه.

وكان أيضاً أهل شرق الأندلس صالحوا الروم بمال معلوم يدفعونه لهم في كل عام وأعطى أهل مرسية قصبتهم للروم الذي هو قصرهم، إلى أن وصلهم الروم الساكنون فيه بأذاهم وضرهم فأخرجوهم في هذه السنة منه بالقتال لهم والحصر، وسموه عندهم قيمة القصر، فقاموا على النصارى وضيقوا بالحصار عليهم، وحينئذ أخرجوهم بعد ما ألقوا السلاح إليهم وكتب أهل مرسية إلى الأمير ابن الأحمر ببيعتهم فبعث الرئيس أبا محمد بن اشقيلولة إليهم والياً عليهم فزحف النصارى إليها، ونزلوا عليها فبقى الرئيس فيها محصورا، وفي نفسه مقهوراً، فخرج منها بخيله ورجله فراراً.

eturning to his own country with his generals and troops. Then Alfonso came ut and swore to him that he had only set up the timbers [lit: tree-trunks] as a recaution against Christian thieves. He pretended to believe him, but had ealized what was afoot and verified it. In their minds, what had happened had appened, and there was no use swearing false oaths. Ibn al-Ahmar left him with o agreement or commitment, and it was because of this that the double-dealing ccurred in al-Andalus as it did. Someone who was present in Seville at that me told me that Alfonso only had with him fewer knights than there were with on al-Ahmar, or nearly as many. Ibn al-Ahmar then swore an oath that he vould never see him again, or meet with him, except in battle or combat, and so turned out.

When he reached Madinat Ibn al-Salim (Medina Sidonia ?), with a cheerful eart and sound mind, because he had seen his own destruction and God had escued and saved him, he advised the inhabitants of those districts to defend hemselves and be on the alert. He passed through them and returned to iranada. The Muslims realized that he had parted from Alfonso without greement or commitment, and they began to take defensive measures and recautions. The people of Jerez expelled the [Christians] who had been living 1 the castle with them for about four years, and took over their town and castle, maining in a state of truce for the rest of the year, because they had sworn an ath of allegiance to Ibn al-Ahmar and given him their obedience. It had been greed with the accursed Alfonso that anyone from Muslim territory who gave on al-Ahmar his obedience would come under the terms of his treaty, which xpired and terminated at the end of this year.

The people in the east of al-Andalus, too, had undertaken with the Christians) pay them a specified amount every year. The inhabitants of Mursiyya Murcia) handed over their citadel, which was their castle, to the Christians, ntil the Christians who were living there began to cause them damage and arm. The Muslims expelled them this year by fighting and besieging them. his was known among them as "the revolt of the Alcázar". They rose up gainst the Christians and besieged them closely, and then expelled them after ney had thrown down their arms. The Murcians wrote to Ibn al-Ahmar with eir allegiance, and he sent them the chief Abu Muhammad b. Ashqilula to be eir governor. The Christians advanced against the town and descended on it. he chief remained there under siege, already defeated in his mind, and he left 1 flight with his cavalry and infantry. After this, the people of Murcia found no

فلم يجد أهل مرسية بعده حماة ولا أنصاراً، فضاقت عليهم أحوالهم، بما أصابهم من العدو ونالهم، وطال عليهم حصارهم وعدموا حماتهم وأنصارهم، فأعطوا مرسية للنصارى وخرجوا منها بأمان إلى الرشاقة. فسكنوا بها مدة من عشرة أعوام إلى أن كان من أمرهم ما كان حين أخرجوهم في سنة ثلاث وسبعين، وغدروهم في الطريق أجمعين وذلك بموضع يعرف بوركال، فسبوا النساء والأطفال، وقتلوا جميع الرجال، وقد كانوا أخرجوهم بالأمان دون سلاح، فتحكموا فيها كيف شاءوا بالسيوف والرماح، ولاحول ولاقوة إلا بالله العلي العظيم.

ولما جاز الأمير أبوعبدالله محمد بن إدريس وأخوه عامر ومن كان معهم من الفرسان الأنجاد برسم الغزو كما ذكرنا والجهاد كان الأمير أبوعبدالله بن الأحمر استصرخهم يرغبهم في ذلك، فوصلوا إليه فاستعد لهم بطريف ضيافات وكرامات حين جوازهم، وأمر لهم بكل مايحتاجون لجهازهم، ثم استقروا بعد ذلك بمالقة بقية هذه السنة وانتقلوا إلى شريش في السنة التي بعدها، حين اشتعلت نيران الحروب بعد خمودها واقتدح زندها فنالت الغزاة المذكورين في غزوها وجهادها مناها وقصدها. ودامت الحروب مدة من ثلاث أعوام من هذا العام، إلى أن عقد الصلح ولد الأمير ابن الأحمر بعد ذلك على مايأتي ذكره إن شاء الله تعالى.

other protection or help. Their situation became desperate because of what happened and befallen them on account of their enemy; the siege was prolonged and they had no protection nor assistance. They handed Murcia over to the Christians and left with a safe-conduct to al-Rushaqa (Arreixaca, a suburb of Murcia), where they lived for ten years until there occurred what happened to them in the year (6)73/1274-75, when the Christians evacuated them and betrayed them altogether on the road. This was at a place called Urkal (Huercal-Overa). They took the women and children captive, and killed most of the men, having sent them out with a safe-conduct, unarmed. They dealt with them as they wished with their swords and spears. There is no power or might but with God, the Most High, the Mighty.

When the amir Abu 'Abd-Allah Muhammad b. Idris crossed over [to Spain] with his brother 'Amir and those valiant knights who were with them, to raid, as we have mentioned, and for Holy War, it was the amir Abu 'Abd-Allah [Muhammad] b. al-Ahmar who had called them and incited them to do so. They came to him and he prepared entertainments marks of honour for them in Tarif (Tarifa) while they passed through [his territory]. He then ensured that they had all the equipment they needed. They remained in Malaqa (Málaga) for the rest of the year, and in the following year went to Jerez, while the fires of war, which had been extinguished, flared up and the flints of war struck fire. These invaders achieved their wishes and objectives in their raids and Holy War. The wars lasted three more years after this, until the son of the amir Ibn al-Ahmar made peace, as will be mentioned, if God wishes.

160

106. Black and white (684/1285)

If the account presented here paints a striking contrast between the white-robed Marinids and the black-clad Castilians, the diplomatic scene was actually nothing like so clear-cut. At the end of his reign, Alfonso X of Castile had called the Marinids over to assist him against his own son, Sancho, who thereupon became an ally of Nasrid Granada. A further shade of grey is provided by the Banu Ashqilula, kinsmen and former allies of the Nasrids of Granada, but now their bitter opponents (see previous text). On his succession, Sancho IV (1284-95) maintained his ties with Muhammad II al-Faqih, ruler of Granada (1273-1302), who was trying to eject the Banu Ashqilula from their base at Guadix. It was the Banu Ashqilula who now invited the Marinid army to intervene. For fuller details, see Arié, pp.74-76 and Harvey, pp.158-60.

This was the fourth full-scale Marinid expedition to Spain under their sultan, Abu Yusuf Ya'qub (1258-86), see Khaneboubi, pp.84-91. He and his son and heir, Abu Ya'qub Yusuf, engaged the forces of Sancho IV in a series of devastating raids in the Guadalquivir basin between mid-April and the end of July 1285, as a result of which Sancho sued for peace. His first overtures were rebuffed; Sancho was also fearful of

فلما سمع شانجة هذه المقالة التى قصد بها ابو محمد عبدالحقّ تعطيل مرامه من دخول الامير ابى يعقوب فى شريش، استنكفّ عن مقالته الاولى ورجع عنها وقال: «وانا ايضا اخرج الى لقائه فالقاه خارج المدينة»، فسار ابو محمد عبدالحقّ الى الامير ابى يعقوب فعرّفه بخبر شانجة واستجارته به وميله الى جانبه واعلمه برضاه بعهده وانه راغب ان يكون فى ذمّته حتى يصل معه الى امير المسلمين، فاجابه الامير ابويعقوب الى ذلك واسعفه به فسار مع ابى محمد عبدالحق الى لقاء شانجة فى جيش عظيم من انجاد بنى مرين وشجعانها واهل الباس والفتك منها. فتلقاه شانجة على مسيرة أميال من شريش فسلّم عليه وأظهر له السرور والفرح والبشاشة كثيراً واخرج له الضيافة لجميع المحلّة فامر الامير ابويعقوب رحمه الله بالنزول بخارج البلد، فضربت قبابه ومضاربه ونزل فيها ونزل شانجة فدخل معه فى خبائه.

فقال له: «اعلم ايها الامير الاسعد والسلطان المبارك الاصعد انى اردت ان اكون دخيلك وفى وفاء ذمّتك ومتفيّاً بظل حرمتك حتى اجتمع مع امير المسلمين والدك». فاعطاه الامير ابويعقوب امانه والتزم له ما يرضيه من والده وتكفل له بجميع قضاء اغراضه وشؤنه عنده. فقال له شانجة: «الان طابت نفسى ورجعت الى حسبى».

oing to the Marinid camp, and wanted Abu Ya'qub to come to him. 'Abd al-Haqq, the
nvoy, managed to talk him out of this, and at this point our selection begins.
   The text is taken from Ibn Abi Zar', Raud al-qirtas, ed. C.J. Tornberg (Uppsala,
843), pp.246-48. The author was writing in about 1326. Among the conditions imposed
·y Abu Yusuf Ya'qub on Sancho was that Muslims should be free to travel and trade,
'ay or night, without hindrance or fear, and that Sancho should dissociate himself from
·is alliance to Muhammad II the Nasrid, and no longer intervene in the affairs of
;ranada.
   It is notable, at the end of this passage, how Arabic books were saved from al-
\ndalus, and came to swell the libraries of North Africa. Among those specifically
nentioned, Ibn 'Atiyya of Granada (d. 546/5 January 1152) was author of a
ommentary on the Qur'an called Kitab al-jami' al-muharrar, and al-Tha'alabi of
:nother called al-'Ara'is. The Istidhkar was written by Yusuf b. 'Abd-Allah b. 'Abd al-
·irr of Cordova (d. 463/February 1071), and was an abridgement of the same author's
'amhid. Finally, al-Tadhhib fi ikhtisar al-mudawwana was written by a scholar called
·l-Baradha'i in Syracuse, about 372/982.

When Sancho heard these words, by which Abu Muhammad 'Abd al-Haqq
ntended to put a stop to Sancho's wish that the amir Abu Ya'qub should come
o Jerez, he found his earlier words repugnant, and went back on them. "Very
vell", he said, "I will go to him, and will meet him outside the city". Abu
Muhammad 'Abd al-Haqq went to the amir Abu Ya'qub and informed him
·bout Sancho, and how he sought his protection and wished to come before him,
·nd told him that [Sancho] was satisfied with the terms and wanted to be under
·is safe-conduct until he came to the Amir al-Muslimin (Abu Yusuf). Abu
/a'qub gave a favourable answer and granted his request, and, together with
·Abd al-Haqq, went to meet Sancho, at the head of a large force consisting of
ome of the bravest, most powerful and murderous of the Marinid troops.
·ancho met him a few miles from Jerez, greeted him with a demonstration of
;reat joy and many smiles, and provided him with hospitality for the whole
·amp. Abu Ya'qub (God have mercy upon him) gave orders for a halt to be
nade outside the town, pitched his pavilions and tents, and alighted. Sancho,
oo, halted and went into his tent with him.
   "Most fortunate Amir, most sublime and blessed Sultan," he said, you should
:now that I have sought to become your protégé and to enjoy the trust of your
·rotection and the refuge of the shadow of your inviolability, until I meet your
·ather, the Amir al-Muslimin." Abu Ya'qub granted him his safe-conduct, and
·ledged him what he wanted from his father and vouched for the attainment of
·ll his objectives and of the business he had with him. Sancho said, "Now I feel
·appy, and my equanimity has returned".

162

فلما كان فى عشى النهار وركب الامير ابو يعقوب الى خارج محلّته فوقف بها،
وخرج جميع من بشريش ينظرون اليه فركبت ابطال بنى مرين تلعب بين يديه وركب
شانجة ووقف بازائه وبنوا مرين فى لعبها، وقال شانجة: «وانا ايضا العب سروراً بما
منّ الله عز وجلّ به على من اقبالكم الىّ واسعافكم لى بالصلح والمهادنة، فانا اولى
الناس بالسرور». ثم اخذ الترس والرمح بيده فلعب بهما مع زعمائه بين يدى الامير ابى
يعقوب حتى غربت الشمس.

فلما كان من الغد ارتحل الامير ابو يعقوب وشانجة الى لقاء امير المسلمين
فاجتمع له بحصن الصخراة على مقربة من وادى لكّ واستعدّ امير المسلمين رحمه الله
الى لقائه فى ذلك اليوم. وامر رحمه الله جميع جيوشه وجنوده بلباس البيض والعدد
الكاملة فابيضت الأرض من بياض المسلمين. واقبل شانجة فى عقدة من المشركين
مسودة فكان ذلك «عبرة للمعتبرين». فسلّم على امير المسلمين وقعد بين يديه تادّبا منه،
ثم قال: «يا امير المسلمين انّ الله عزّ وجلّ اسعدنى بلقائك وشرفّنى فى هذا اليوم
برويتك وانى لارجوا ان انال طرفا مما اعطيت من السعادة حتى اقهر به ملوك
النصرانية. ولا تظنّ انى جيتك رضى منّى وطوعا من نفسى بل والله ما قدمت لحضرتك
الا رغما على انفى فانك نسفت بلادنا وسبيت حريمنا واولادنا وقتلت حماتنا ولا طاقة
لنا بحربك ولا مقدرة على معاندتك فكّل ما تامرنى به امتثلته وكلّما شرطته علىّ الزمتُه
واحمله ويدك الباسطة على جميع بلادى ورعيتى تحكم فى الكلية بما شئت.»

ثم قدّم له هدايا نفيسة وتحفا عظيمة وكذلك لولده الامير ابى يعقوب استجلابا
لمرضاتهما فكافأه امير المسلمين عنها باضعافها ليخرج عن ايادیه وتمّ الصلح بينهما
وذلك يوم الاحد الموفى عشرين لشعبان من سنة اربع وثمانين وستّ مائة.

ولما صرفه الى بلده امره رحمه الله تعالى ان يبعث اليه بما يجده فى بلاده بايدى
النصارى واليهود من كتب المسلمين ومصاحفهم فبعث اليه منها ثلاثة عشر حملا فيها

In the evening, Abu Ya'qub rode out of the camp and remained there. Everyone in Jerez went out to watch him. The Marinid warriors rode and played games before him. Sancho mounted and rode up to him, while the Marinids were going through their exercises, and said, "I too feel playful, enjoying the favour that Almighty and Glorious God has bestowed on me, through your responsiveness to me and your granting me a peaceful truce. I am the happiest of men." He then took a shield and spear, and joined in the games with his chiefs, in front of the amir Abu Ya'qub, until the sun set.

The next day, Abu Ya'qub and Sancho went to meet the Amir al-Muslimin. They joined up with him at Hisn al-Sakhra, near Wadi Lago, and he prepared to receive him that same day. The Amir al-Muslimin (God have mercy upon him) ordered all his armies and troops to wear white and to be fully equipped, and the ground was carpeted with the white of Muslims. Sancho arrived with a group of polytheists in black – "which is surely a lesson to men possessed of minds" (Qur'an 12: 111). Sancho greeted the Amir al-Muslimin and sat down in front of him, showing him proper courtesy, then said, "Prince of the Muslims, God Almighty has made me happy to meet you, and has ennobled me through seeing you today. I hope that I may donate a part of the felicity that I have been given towards defeating the kings of the Christians. Do not think that I have come to you at my own pleasure, or of my own free will. No, by God, I have only come into your presence in spite of myself, for you have razed my country to the ground, taken our women and children captive, and killed our defenders. We have no power to fight you, and no strength to resist you. I submit to everything you command of me, and adhere to all the conditions that you impose on me, and will carry them out. Your hand is stretched out over my whole country and my subjects; rule over it as you wish."

Then he presented him with great and precious gifts, and likewise his son, the Amir Abu Ya'qub, seeing the desirability of pleasing them both. The Amir al-Muslimin repaid him two-fold, not to come under his obligation, and peace was concluded between them, on 20 Shawwal 684 (19 December 1285).

When he sent him back to his territory, he ordered Sancho to send him any of the Muslims' books or copies of the Qur'an that he could find there in the hands of Christians or Jews. Sancho sent him thirteen loads of books, consisting of

جملة من الكتاب العزيز وتفسيره كابن عطية والثعالبى ومنها كتب الحديث وشروحاتها كالتهذيب والاستذكار وكتب الفروع وكتب الاصول واللغة والعربية والادب وغيرها، فامر رحمه الله بها فحملت الى مدينة فاس فحبسها على طلبة العلم بالمدرسة التى بناها، نفعنا الله تعالى بقصده.

Qur'ans, Commentaries (like those of Ibn 'Atiyya and al-Tha'alabi), books of Traditions and their interpretation (such as the *Tahdhib* and the *Istidhkar*); works on the branches and roots [of Law]; on philology, Arabic, *adab* literature and others. The Amir of the Muslims (God have mercy upon him) gave the order for them to be transported to Fez and set aside for the religious students in the madrasa which he had built there, through which endeavour God Almighty has benefitted us.

107. A diplomatic request (724/1324)

Among the documents preserved in the archives of the court of Aragon is one containing an unusual letter from the vizier of Nasrid Granada. His disingenuous request for the return of a missing despatch box was perhaps a way of letting James II of Aragon (1291-1327) know the contents of the diplomatic correspondence passing between Granada and the ruler of Egypt. The Mamluk regime in Cairo was currently the strongest power in the Middle East, at its peak under al-Nasir Muhammad b. Qalawun (3rd reign, 1310-41). Al-Nasir's letters are unlikely to have held out any great hope of assistance from Egypt, but the possibility of collaboration remained a worthwhile diplomatic position at this period. On the other hand, James II was also in communication with al-Nasir, as a series of letters preserved in the same collection shows: these have been discussed by A.S. Atiya, "Egypt and Aragon, embassies and diplomatic correspondence between 1300 and 1330 A.D.", Abhandlungen fur die Kunde des Morgenlandes, 23/vii (Leipzig, 1938). Letters from James dated 1318 and 1322 were

السلطان الاجل الاعز المكرم المبرور المشكور الشهير الاوفى نون جيمى ملك
ارغون، اسعده الله برضاه واكرمه بتقواه، شاكر عهده ووفائه بعلو منصبه بين
امثاله من ملوك النصرى ونظرائه ،عثمن بن ادريس بن عبدالله بن عبدالحق.

اما بعد فانى كتبته اليكم من حضرة غرناطة حرسها الله تعلى عن الخير الاكمل
واليسر الاشمل والحمدلله وعن الشكر لجانبكم والعلم لمقاصدكم ومذاهبكم والى هذا،
فان كتابكم المكرم وصل مع راجلكم احمد بن الحاج سلمه الله تعلى وما قصر فى
خدمتكم ونصيحتكم فى هذه المرة وفى كل مرة توجهونه فلا تسمعوا فيه قول احد ولا
تشكوا فى خلوصه فى خدمتكم.

ولى عندكم ايها الملك المعظم حاجة وذلك انه لما وصل اليكم الحاج راجلى احمد
بن عبدالسلام من اسكندرية وعملتم معه من الكرامة ما شكرتكم عليه، نسى خريطة فى
الدار التى نزل فيها هنالكم بكتب من صاحب مصر لمولانا السلطان ايده الله ويعرف
الدار سيون راجلكم وكانت الخريطة من كنانة من الخشب. فعسى ان تتفضلوا بالبحث
عنها وتجهوها الى محبكم وهذه اكبر حاجة لى قبلكم والله يسعدكم برضاه ويعزكم
بتقواه والسلام يراجع سلامكم كثيرا اثيرا. كتب فى التاسع عشر لشعبن المكرم من عام
اربعة وعشرين وسبعمائة .

ot answered by al-Nasir until 1323, and the envoys from the courts of both Granada nd Aragon evidently returned from Cairo together. It seems from the name of this nvoy that Aragon was using Muslim ambassadors to the court of Granada. In the 15th entury, when the position in Granada became more desperate, further but equally ruitless efforts were made to secure help from Egypt, by which time, however, the Mamluks were in their decline and a new Muslim power, the Ottoman empire, was on he rise. For a review of Spanish relations with Egypt, see A. Zequi (Zeki), "Mémoire sur es relations entre l'Egypte et l'Espagne pendant l'occupation musulmane", in Homenaje . Don Francisco Codera, *ed. D. Eduardo Saavedra (Saragossa, 1904), pp.455-81.*

The text is taken from Los documentos árabes diplomáticos del Archivo de la Corona le Aragón, *ed. Alarcón y Santón and García de Linares (Madrid, 1940), p.41. The Nasrid ruler at this time was Isma'il I (1314-25); see also Harvey, pp.182-83.*

[To] The Most Exalted, Powerful, Noble, Revered, Praiseworthy, Renowned, and Accomplished Monarch, Don Jaime King of Aragon (may God cause him to prosper in His approval and confer on him His piety!), in gratitude for his good faith and the fulfilment of his pledges, and knowing his high rank among his fellow Christian Kings and his peers, [from] 'Uthman b. Idris b. 'Abd-Allah b. Abd al-Haqq.

To proceed I wrote you this from the court of Granada (may God Almighty protect it!), about the most perfect welfare and most complete prosperity [that prevail here] (praise be to God), out of gratitude to you and in the knowledge of your [friendly] intentions and policies, for this reason: your respected letter has arrived with your envoy, Ahmad b. al-Hajj (may God Almighty preserve him!), who has not fallen short in your service and your counsel, either on this occasion or on all the [previous] occasions on which he has been despatched. No-one hears anything [bad] about him, nor criticizes his sincerity in your service.

I need a favour from you, Great King, which is that when my envoy, al-Hajj Ahmad b. 'Abd al-Salam reached you from Alexandria, and you treated him with the honour for which I am in your gratitude, he forgot a leather bag in the house in which he was lodged, containing letters from the ruler of Egypt to our master, the Sultan [Isma'il II] – may God support him! Your man, Zaidun, knows the house: the bag was in a wooden case. Could you possibly be so kind as to enquire after it and send it to your friend? This is the greatest favour that I ask of you. May God bless you through His pleasure and empower you with His piety. Many choice greetings in reply to your own greetings. Written on 19 Sha'ban 724 (12 August 1324).

168

108. The defeat at Tarifa (741/1340)

If Christian accounts of the major battle of Tarifa or Salado tend to be lengthy (se text 58), Muslim ones are predictably rather briefer. Two are presented here, the first b the Granadan historian and statesman Ibn al-Khatib (d. 1374), who lost his brother an father in the battle, the second by the famous historian Ibn Khaldun (d. 1406).

The battle of Tarifa was part of a long-running contest for control of the Strait o Gibraltar. This was a three-cornered struggle between Castile, Granada and th Marinids in North Africa, the latter anxious to retain a firm bridgehead on the Peninsula, the Castilians equally anxious to deny them, and the Granadans caught in the middle, sometimes willing to facilitate Marinid landings and sometimes preferring not to encourage them. Tarifa fell to the Castilians in 1292 and was bravely defended by them the following year. Despite various negotiations, it then remained in Christian hands Algeciras had been in Marinid hands since 1309; the date of its surrender to Alfonso X. (1312-50) is given by Christian and Muslim sources as 26-27 March 1344, i.e. a yea later than the date given here. It was regained by Muhammad V of Granada in 1369, by which time relations between the Nasrids and the Marinids, which had remained generally fairly close, were beginning to deteriorate. For accounts of the relation: between North Africa and Spain during the fourteenth century, see the papers by M

(a)

وأولا بفاس –دار الملك بالمغرب– :السلطان المتناهي الجلالة أبوالحسن علي بن عثمان بن يعقوب بن عبدالحق، وجاز على عهده الى الاندلس إثر صلاة يوم الجمعة تاسع شهر صفر من عام أحد وأربعين وسبعمائة، بعد أن أوقع بأسطول الروم المستدعَى من أقطارهم وقيعة كبيرة شهيرة استولى فيها من المتاع والسلاح والاجفان على ما بَعُد به العهد واستقرّ بالخضراء في جيش وافر، وكان جوازه في مائة وأربعين جَفناً غزوياً. وبادر الى لقائه في وجوه الاندلسيين وأعيان طبقاتهم بظاهر الجزيرة الخضراء في اليوم الموفي عشرين من الشهر ونازل إثر انقضاء المولد النبوي مدينةَ طريف ونصب عليها المجانيق وأخذ بمجنتها واستحث من بها من المحصورين طاغيةَ الروم بمصرهم، فبادر يقود جيشاً يشوق الشجر والمدّر، وكانت المناجزة يوم الاثنين السابع لجمادى الأولى من العام، ومحّص الله المسلمين بالوقيعة الشهيرة وأسرع اللحاقَ بالمغرب مفلولا في سبيل الله صابراً محتسباً يروم الكرّة ويرتقب الطائلة.

García Fernández and R. Arié in Relaciones de la Península Ibérica con el Magreb siglos XIII-XVI, *ed. M. García-Arenal and María J. Viguera (Madrid, 1988), 249-73 and 21-40 respectively. The first text is taken from Ibn al-Khatib,* al-Lamhat al-badriyya fi 'l-daulat al-Nasriyya, *ed. Muhibb al-Din al-Khatib (Cairo, 1347/1928), pp.92-93. The battle occurred during the reign of the Nasrid Yusuf I (1333-54), and this extract comes at the beginning of an account of his contemporaries. The Marinid sultan Abu'l-Hasan 'Ali reigned from 1331 to 1351. The naval victory referred to is the defeat of the Castilian fleet under Alfonso Jofre Tenorio in Algeciras bay in April 1340, which provided the Marinids with a splendid opportunity to launch their attack on Tarifa.*

The second text is from Ibn Khaldun, Kitab al-'ibar, *ed. J.A. Dagher (Beirut, 1958), IV, pp.374-75, which reports a raid in 1339, in which Abu Malik, son of the Marinid sultan, was killed. Huici Miranda includes this raid and the naval battle of Algeciras in his lengthy treatment of Salado, in* Las grandes batallas, *pp.331-77. For a detailed account of the sieges of Qal'at Bani Sa'id (Alcalá) and of Algeciras that followed, see Harvey, pp.194-204, and the briefer treatment by Arié, pp.102-03. Chaucer's knight took part in the lengthy siege of Algeciras, along with many of England's chivalry.*

(a)

First, in Fez, capital of the Maghreb, was the sultan in the highest degree of majesty, Abu'l-Hasan 'Ali b. 'Uthman b. Ya'qub b. 'Abd al-Haqq, who crossed to al-Andalus during his reign, immediately after the prayers on Friday 9 Safar in the year 741 (4 August 1340). After attacking a Christian fleet that had been summoned from their territories in a great and celebrated battle, he gained possession of supplies, arms and ships; it was a long time since such [spoils] had been [acquired]. He established himself at Algeciras with a large army. He had crossed in 140 warships. He [Yusuf I] set out to meet him with the Andalusian nobility and the leaders of their people outside Algeciras on the 20th of the same month (15 August). Immediately after the end of the Feast of the Birth of the Prophet (12 Rabi' I = 5 September), they descended on the city of Tarifa and set up the siege engines and began to bombard it. Those who were being besieged urged the Christian tyrant to [come to] their city. He set out leading a huge army; the battle took place on Monday 7 Jumada I (29 October 1340, a Sunday) and God put the Muslims to the test in a celebrated encounter. He [Abu'l-Hasan] hastened to return to the Maghreb, defeated in the path of God, persevering and earning reward in the hereafter, longing for a comeback and watching out for the chance of revenge.

(b)

واستدعى السلطان أبو الحجاج السلطان أبا الحسن صاحب المغرب فأجاز ابنه عندما تم له الفتح بتلمسان، وعقد له على عساكر جمة من زناته والمتطوعة فغزاهم، وغنم وقفل راجعاً. وتلاحقت به جموع النصارى وبيته على حدود أرضهم فاستشهد كثير من الغزاة.

وأجــاز السلطان أبو الحـسن سنة احدى وأربعين بكافـة أهل المغرب من زناته ومغراوة والمرتزقة والمتطوعة فنازل طريف، وزحف اليه الطاغية فلقيه بظاهرها فانكشف المسلمون، واستشهد الكثير منهم، وهلك فيها نساء السلطان وحريمه وفسطاطه من معسكره وكان يوم ابتلاء وتمحيص. وتغلب الطاغية اثرها على القلعة ثغر غرناطة، ونازل الجزيرة الخضراء وأخذها صلحاً سنة ثلاث وأربعين.

(b)

Sultan Abu'l-Hajjaj (Yusuf I) invoked the help of Sultan Abu'l-Hasan, ruler of the Maghreb; the latter authorized his son to go, once he had completed his conquest of Tlemcen, and entrusted him with numerous troops of Zanata [Berbers] and Volunteers. He led them on a raid, took much booty and set off for home. The Christian forces caught up with him and attacked him by night on the borders of their territory; many of the fighters for the faith found martyrdom.

In 741 (began 27 June 1340), Sultan Abu'l-Hasan crossed over [to Spain] with all the people of the Maghreb, Zanata and Maghrawa [tribesmen], professional soldiers and Volunteers, and descended on Tarifa. The tyrant (Alfonso XI) advanced on him and met him outside [the town]. The Muslims were put to flight and many of them were martyred. In this [rout] the wives and harem of the sultan were killed and the [royal] pavilion was destroyed in his camp. It was a day of affliction and severe examination. Afterwards, the tyrant seized al-Qal'a (Alcalá la Real) on the borders of Granada, and descended on Algeciras, which he took by capitulation in 743 (began 6 June 1342).

109. The fall of Gibraltar and its aftermath (869/1464)

Although Tarifa and Algeciras were no longer in the firing line by the end of the 14th century, the Muslims had retained Gibraltar, except for a brief period between 1309 and 1333, when it was held by Castile. Since 1374, it had been in the hands of the Nasrids, reducing the likelihood of further interventions from North Africa. On the accession of Henry IV of Castile (1454-74), fighting was resumed against Granada where Abu Nasr Sa'd (1453-64), formerly a Castilian protégé, had renounced this link and by 1455 had emerged as the sole Nasrid ruler. The campaign against Gibraltar began after the expiry of a four-year truce (1457-61).

The Egyptian historian 'Abd al-Basit (1440-1514) visited Muslim Spain as part of a protracted voyage in the Maghreb, leaving Alexandria in July 1462 and returning in May 1467. His journey is recorded within a general chronicle, from which Professor Levi della Vida extracted the passages relevant to Spain. The passages concerning North Africa, which are also of interest, have been published by R. Brunschvig, Deux récits de voyages inédits en Afrique du nord au XVe siècle (Paris, 1936), with a French translation.

'Abd al-Basit's account of the fall of Gibraltar is thus exactly contemporary, for he says he was in Tlemcen at the time (August-December 1464). Inexplicably, his date is two or three years after the date given by the Christian sources, cited by Arié (p. 144) and Harvey (pp.262-64), namely August 1462, i.e. before 'Abd al-Basit had even arrived in Tunis from Rhodes. Some Arabic evidence for the earlier date is provided by a letter

وفيه اعنى هذا الشهر [صفر سنة ٨٦٩] اخذ الفرنج البرطقال البلد المعظم احد
اعز حصون الاسلام وبلدانه بالاندلس المسمى بجبل الفتح، وذلك فى هذه الفتنة الكائنة
بين الاب والابن اعنى ابا النصر سعد بن الاحمر وولده ابا الحسن الماضى خبرهما وانا
لله وانا اليه راجعون. فان ذلك من اعظم المصائب فى الاسلام لان من هذا الحصن
كانت بداية اخذ بلاد الاندلس من الكفار فى الزمن الاول وهو اعظم معاقل الاسلام
بالاندلس وخرج اهلها منها بالامان وبالله المستعان. ولما بلغ هذا الخبر تلمسان وغيرها
من بلاد الاسلام بهذه الجهة عظم ذلك عليهم وكثر التأسف على ضعف الاسلام
بالاندلس واشتغالهم عن حفظ الحصون الاسلامية لما هم فيه من الفتن وطلب العز
والسلطان المقصى الى الذل والهوان. وبلغنا ان الكفار احتالوا بعض حيلة على اهل
جبل الفتح ثم امنوهم فخرجوا ولم يتعرضوا لهم البتة بل اعانوهم على نقل الكثير من
امتعتهم وانساتهم الى حيث مأمنهم.

ated Jumada I, 868/January 1464, written by Sa'd to the sultan of Egypt, which refers
▸ the loss of Gibraltar; see G.S. Colin, "Contribution à l'étude des relations
'plomatiques entre les Musulmans d'Occident et l'Egypte au XVe siècle", Mémoires de
Institut français d'archéologie orientale, 68 (1935), 197-206. 'Abd al-Basit's lapse of
emory must have been more serious than he himself allows for. He says the fall of
ibraltar occurred at the same time as discord between Sa'd and his son Abu'l-Hasan,
hereas in fact Sa'd was at this period turning on the powerful clan of the Banu Sarraj
Abencerrajes). The latter fled to Málaga where they set up Yusuf V (a cousin of Sa'd) as
ultan for a brief period in September-December 1462.

Our author is more accurate over dating the events that followed, for the discord
etween Sa'd and his son Abu'l-Hasan did occur in 1464, culminating in Sa'd's
verthrow in August. He was imprisoned in either Salobreña or Moclín. The Egyptian
storian Ibn Iyas (II, pp.424-25) also mentions their fluctuating struggle. 'Abd al-
asit's statement that Sa'd ended his days in Almería would seem to be entirely
ceptable. His notice of the serious revolt of the Castilian nobility against Henry IV is
so correctly dated, but he must be wrong about Loja, which remained in Muslim hands
util 1486.

The text is taken from G. Levi della Vida, "Il regno di Granata nel 1465-1466 nei
cordi di un viaggiatore egiziano", Al-Andalus, 1 (1933), pp.325-26.

In this month [Safar 869 = October 1464] the Franks of Portugal took the
reat city known as Jabal al-Fath (Gibraltar), one of the finest strongholds
elonging to Islam and of its towns in al-Andalus. That occurred during the
scord that existed between father and son, I mean Abu Nasr Sa'd b. al-Ahmar
id his son Abu'l-Hasan (both of whom have already been mentioned) – Indeed
e are God's, and to Him we return! This was one of the greatest disasters for
lam, because the original conquest of al-Andalus from the infidels began from
is stronghold, which is the greatest bulwark of Islam in al-Andalus. Its people
ft with a safe-conduct – help lies in God! When this news reached Tlemcen
id other places in this part of the Muslim lands, it greatly affected them, and
ere were bitter regrets at the weakness of Islam in al-Andalus and at [the
luslims'] distraction from defending Muslim strongholds by the disorders in
eir ranks, and the pursuit of power and dominion ended up in disgrace and
nominy. We heard that the infidels had used a trick against the people of Jabal
-Fath, and then given them a safe-conduct. They came out of the city and not
ily did [the Christians] not molest them at all, but they even assisted them to
ansport the bulk of their chattels and women to a safe place.

وفيه [يعنى ٢٧ صفر سنة ٨٦٨] ورد الخبر الى تلمسان من الاندلس بان الفنس صاحب قشتالة واشبيلة وقرطبة وما والى ذلك من بلاد الفرنج وممالكها قد عزم على الزحف على الاندلس لغزوها واخذها لما علمه من الخلاف الكائن بين الاب والابن اعنى ملك الاندلس سعدا وولده ابا الحسن وما وقع لهما. وارجف بذلك فى تلك البلاد ولما بلغ ابو الحسن ذلك بعث باستقدام ابيه من الحصن الذى كان به ولما خرج الاب توجه الى مدينة المرية فاقام بها ولم يعارضه ولده فى ذلك بل بعث اليه يطلب رضاه والاعتذار اليه وانه الملك وهو فى معنى وزيره ونحو ذلك من الكلمات وكان بالمرية القائد محمد بن سيدهم فقام بالامر المستعين بالله سعد هذا اتم القيام وخدمه. ولم يزل بالمرية كالمتصافى مع ولده حتى مات بها فى اخر السنة هذه على ما بلغنى.

وفيه اعنى هذا الشهر [جمادى الاولى من سنة ٨٦٩] ثار بعض ملوك الفرنج بصاحب قشتالة فاشغله الله تعالى عن المسلمين وما كان قصده ورد الله تعالى كبره فى نحره، حتى بعث يلتمس الصلح بينه وبين المسلمين من اهل الاندلس. واتفق الحال على عقد الصلح بينه وبينهم فى هذه السنة الى مدة خمس سنين وحصل لبعض الناس بل لعامة اهل الاندلس بعض الطمأنية وامنوا شر صاحب قشتالة. وفيه اخذ الفرنج فى اثناء التكلم فى الصلح قبل ان يقيد حصنا للمسلمين بالاندلس، وكنت اعرف اسمه وانما نسيته الآن واظنه حصن لوشا وما حررت ذلك الى الآن لبعد العهد بذلك البلاد.

On 27 Safar (29 September) news came to Tilimsan (Tlemcen) from al-
ndalus that Alfonso (i.e. Henry IV), ruler of Castile, Seville and Cordova and
he Frankish towns and districts dependent on them, had decided to march
gainst al-Andalus to raid it and take it, because he was aware of the discord
xisting between father and son, that is, the king of al-Andalus, Sa'da [sic.] and
is son, Abu'l-Hasan, and of what had befallen them. Alfonso caused rumours of
is intentions to be spread in that country. When Abu'l-Hasan heard this he
ummoned his father from the castle where he was [imprisoned], and when the
ather came out he went to the city of Almería and established himself there. His
on [Abu'l-Hasan] did not offer resistance to this, but rather sent seeking his
avour and making his excuses to him, saying that he [Sa'd] was the king and he
imself was, as it were, his vizier, and making other such remarks. At Almería
he governor (qa'id) was Muhammad, son of their master (sayyid ?), who
trongly supported the cause of this Sa'd al-Musta'in bi-llah and was completely
t his service. Sa'd remained in Almería as though reconciled with his son, until
e died there at the end of this year [i.e. mid 1465], according to the information
received.

In this month [Jumada I = January 1465] some of the Frankish kings rebelled
gainst the ruler of Castile (may God distract him from the Muslims and from
is hostile intentions!), and God Almighty rammed his pride back down his
hroat, so that he sent requesting a truce between himself and the Muslims of al-
Andalus. An agreement was reached to sign a truce between him and them this
ear, for a duration of five years. Many people in al-Andalus – or rather,
veryone – enjoyed a respite and were secure from the evil of the king of
Castile. While the talks were in progress but before the truce had been signed,
he Franks took a castle belonging to the Muslims in al-Andalus. I used to know
ts name but now I have forgotten it – I think it was the castle of Lusha (Loja) –
ut I haven't written it down before, and it is a long time since I was in that
ountry.

110. The capture of Alhama (887/1482)

Among the places visited by 'Abd al-Basit during his visit to Spain in 1465-66 was
Alhama, situated between Málaga and Granada (see previous text, ed. della Vida, p.
313). Like many earlier travellers, he admired the baths which gave the town its name.
These same baths, when noticed by Fernando del Pulgar during the struggle for Alhama
in 1482, provided him with the moral explanation he sought for the destruction he had
witnessed: the baths were the cause of sinfulness and sloth.

The capture of Alhama marks the beginning of a sustained Christian attempt to
capture key Muslim positions, culminating in the fall of Granada itself. This final
assault follows the succession of Ferdinand to the throne of Aragon in 1479, and
Isabella's consolidation of her position as ruler of Castile the same year. The Alhama
episode is treated by Arié, pp.153-55, and Harvey, pp.269-74, where Christian sources
(including the musing of Pulgar), are quoted at length. Our text is provided by an
anonymous author, who gives a contemporary account of the last decade of Muslim rule
in Spain. The extract starts with his strictures on the amir Abu'l-Hasan 'Ali (1464-82),
whose internecine fights with his son Abu 'Abd-Allah Muhammad XII (Boabdil)

انقضاء معاهدة الصلح، واستئناف الحرب
بين النصارى والمسلمين [محرم عام ٨٨٧]

ولم يزل الأمير مستمراً على حاله، والجيش في نقص، والملك في ضعف إلى أن

انقضى الصلح الذي كان بينه وبين النصارى، فلم يشعر بهم أحد حتى دخلوا مدينة

الحَمَّة، وذلك أنهم طرقوها ليلاً على حين غفلة من أهلها، فدخلوا قصبتها – وكانت خالية

– فلم يكن بها إلا عيال قائدها، فملكوا القصبة والناس نيام مطمئنون، فلم يشعر أحد

إلا والنصارى قد هبطوا من القصبة على البلد بالسيف والقتل والسبي الشديد حتى قتل

من نفد أجله، وفر من قدر على الفرار. واستولى النصارى على البلد، وجميع ما كان فيه

من الرجال والنساء والصبيان والأموال.

وكان ذلك في التاسع عشر من شهر الحرام فاتح سبعة وثمانين وثمان مائة. فلما

بلغ أهل غرناطة ما فعلت النصارى بإخوانهم المسلمين هاجت الرعية وقالوا: «لا صبر

لنا على هذه المصيبة العظمى، ولا خير لنا في عيش بعد هذه النكبة الكبرى: إما أن نفك

إخواننا أو نموت دونهم!» فاجتمعوا مع الأمير أبي الحسن ووزيره، فجعل الأمير والوزير

presented the Christians with an unexpectedly easy task. Despite the evident bias of the author, the passage is interesting not only because it reveals the fatal tensions within Muslim Granada, but also because it suggests that the Christians had originally planned the attack on Alhama only as a raid, rather than a permanent occupation. The hostility of the people of Granada towards their rulers is hardly surprizing, in view of their disastrous divisions and fecklessness.

The text is taken from Nubdhat al-'asr fi inqida daulat Bani Nasr, *ed. Muhammad Ridwan al-Daya (Damascus 1404/1984), pp.50-57. We may note that al-Maqqari, Nafh al-tib, ed. Ihsan 'Abbas (Beirut, 1968), IV, pp.512-13, has a parallel account, though couched in different language, which he derived from a work by Abu 'Abd-Allah Muhammad b. al-Haddad al-Wadi Ashi (from Guadix); this is included in the translation by Gayangos, II, pp.370-72. The account of Wadi Ashi appears to have been written after the final expulsions of 1017/1610, but he was very probably aware of the* Nubdhat, *judging by the similarity of their contents.*

The expiry of the period of truce and the resumption of war between the Christians and the Muslims (Muharram 887/began 20 February 1482)

The amir [Abu'l-Hasan] did not cease to carry on in the same way, with the army in decline and the kingdom growing weaker, until the truce between him and the Christians elapsed. No one was aware of them until they entered the town of al-Hama (Alhama). They came upon it by night, while the inhabitants were unawares, and entered the citadel, which was empty: there was no-one there but the family of the governor. They took the citadel while the people were sleeping peacefully. No-one knew anything until the Christians came down from the citadel into the town, sword in hand, with fierce slaughter and the taking of captives; those whose time was up were killed, and those who were able to do so fled. The Christians took over the town, with all the men, women, children and belongings that were in it.

That was on 19 Muharram at the start of 887 (10 March 1482). When the Granadans heard what the Christians had done to their Muslim brothers, the citizens were in uproar and said, "We cannot stand this terrible disaster, and life is no good for us after this great calamity. Either we redeem our brothers or we perish alongside them!" They gathered round the amir Abu'l-Hasan and his vizier, who began to try to put them off going and sought to delay them, saying,

يُعجزانهم عن المسير ويتربصان بهم، ويقولان لهم: «اصبروا حتى نأخذ أهبتنا، ونعمل على حال الحرب». فلم تزل بهم العامة حتى أخرجوهما.

فتقدم صدر الجيش، فوجدوا النصارى قد أخرجوا من البلد ما سبوا من الرجال والنساء والصبيان والأموال، وقد أوقروا الدواب بذلك، وهم عازمون على المسير إلى بلادهم. فلما رأوا خيل المسلمين قد أقبلت عليهم حطوا الأحمال ودخلوا البلد وتحصنوا بالأسوار.

ثم أقبل المسلمون بمحلتهم، واقتربوا منهم، فقاتلوهم قتالا شديداً بجد وعزم وقلوب محترقة، وحزم، حتى دخلوا بعض أبواب المدينة، وكسروه، وحرقوه، وتعلقوا بأسوار البلد، وطمعوا في الدخول إليه. فبينما هم كذلك إذ وصل لهم أمر من الأمير أبي الحسن والوزير، يأمرانهم فيه بالرجوع عن القتال فأبى الناس عن الرجوع، فقالا لهم: «إذا كان غداً ندخل عليهم أول النهار، لأن الليل قد أقبل، ودخل علينا!». فترك الناس القتال، ورجعوا إلى محلاتهم.

أما النصارى فباتوا يصلحون شأنهم، ويمنعون أسوارهم ويغلقون نقابهم. فلما أصبح الصباح ونظر المسلمون إلى البلد فإذا هو على صفة أخرى من المنعة والتحصين والاستعداد، فصعب عند ذلك على المسلمين الدخول إليه بل والدنو منه.

عزم المسلمون على حصار البلد والإقامة عليه؛ فأقبلت وفود المسلمين من كل أرض من بلاد الأندلس، واجتمع في ذلك المحل محلة عظيمة، وفتحوا الأسواق للبيع والشراء، وجلبوا لأسواقهم كل ما يحتاجون إليه من الأطعمة والعلف والزاد وغير ذلك، وحاصروا العدو حصاراً شديداً، ومنعوا عليه الماء والحطب والداخل والخارج، والعامة في ذلك بحزم وعزم وجد واجتهاد، ونية صادقة، وقلوب محترقة.

"Wait until we have made our preparations, and are ready to act on a war footing." But the common people didn't leave them alone until they got them to set out.

The front of the army approached and found that the Christians had brought the men, women and children out of the town with booty that they had captured, and had already loaded it onto pack animals, with the intention of returning to their own territory. When they saw the Muslim cavalry approaching them, they took down the loads and went into the town, where they took up defensive positions on the walls.

Then the Muslims came up to their camp, and closed with [the Christians]. They fought hard, with determination and resolution, with energy and with ardour in their hearts, until they entered one of the gates of the town, which they smashed and burned. They hung onto the walls of the town, and strove to enter it. And even while they were so placed, an order reached them from the amir Abu 'l-Hasan and his vizier, in which he commanded them to desist from fighting. The people refused to do so, and the pair then told them, "First thing in the morning we shall overcome them, because now night has arrived and overcome us!" So the people stopped fighting, and returned to their camp.

The Christians spent the night improving their position, making the walls stronger and blocking up the breaches. In the morning, when the Muslims looked at the town, they saw it was transformed in its defensive strength and state of preparation, whereupon it was much harder for the Muslims to enter, or even to approach.

The Muslims determined to besiege the town and to stay there; new arrivals came from all over al-Andalus, and congregated in a great camp in that place. They opened markets for buying and selling, and brought in all the food, forage, provisions and other things that they needed. They besieged the enemy closely, denying him water and firewood and preventing all coming and going. The common people were imbued with resoluteness, determination, fortitude and energy, with sincere intentions and ardent hearts.

والوزير يعد الناس بالدخول والقتال وعداً بعد وعد، ويقول: «عن قريب نأخذهم عطشاً! وها نحن نعمل الحيلة في الدخول عليهم». والتقصير والتفريط [والغش] يبدو منه شيئاً بعد شيء حتى تبين لعامة الناس وخاصتهم، ولاح لهم كالشمس، وظنوا بالملك والوزير ظنون السوء، وكثر الكلام القبيح بينهم. فعند ذلك هاج شيطان الفتنة بينهم. وتحدث الناس بعضهم مع بعض في مسائل غشهما للمسلمين.

فبينما الناس كذلك في إساءة ظنهم بأميرهم ووزيرهم إذا بهما قد استعملا حيلة وكتبا كتباً مزورة كأنهما أتتهما من بعض من نصحهم من ناحية المسلمين المجاهدين المجاورين لبلاد الكفرة -دمرهم الله! - يُعلمونهم بها أن الطاغية ملك النصارى جمع جمعاً عظيماً، وحشد حشوداً كثيرة، وعزم على نصرة النصارى المحصورين في بلد الحَمة، وهو قادم عن قريب، ولا طاقة لكم بملاقاته.

فحين أعلمهم الوزير بما ذُكر، وخوّفهم بذلك سقط في أيدي الناس، فأمرهم حينئذ بالرحيل والإقلاع عن دار الحرب، فرحل الناس كرهاً باكين متأسفين بحسرة وفجعة، يا لها من حسرة، وانصرف الناس كل واحد إلى وطنه.

ثم إنه بعد ذلك بشهور قلائل أمر الأمير أبو الحسن بالمسير إلى بلد الحمة مرة أخرى، فذهبوا ثانية، وحاصروها، فلم يقدروا منها على شيء، وانصرفوا عنها وتركوها. فلما رأى العدو - دمره الله! - أن المسلمين قد عجزوا عن أخذ الحمة، ونُصرة من فيها من الأسارى، وقع له الطمع في بلاد الأندلس، فأخذ في الاستعداد، والخروج إليها.

The vizier piled promise upon promise to the people that they would [soon] enter [the town] and fight; he would say, "we're nearly getting them through thirst. We're devising a trick to enter the town." [But] he displayed his shortcomings, negligence and perfidy, one after another, until they became obvious to the common people and their leaders and shone like the sun. They began to think ill of the king and the vizier, and many ugly words were spoken among them, whereupon Satan stirred up discord among the people, who told each other about the problems caused by their treachery towards the Muslims.

While the people were in this state, mistrusting their amir and vizier, these two devised a stratagem and forged a letter purporting to have reached them from some of their advisers in the territory of the Muslims who were fighting in districts adjoining the unbelievers (may God destroy them !), in which they informed them that, "the tyrant king of the Christians has assembled a great host and mustered numerous auxiliaries. He intends to come to support the Christians besieged in the town of Alhama and he is nearly there; you will not be able to withstand him."

When the vizier informed them of what had been reported, and aroused their fear, the people were aghast. He ordered them to leave and depart from the scene of battle, and they did so reluctantly, weeping and saddened by pain and distress – O what grief! – and each one of them returned to his own home.

Then after a few months, the amir Abu'l-Hasan ordered another expedition to the town of Alhama and they went there a second time and besieged it, but they could do nothing against it, so they returned and left it. When the enemy – may God annihilate him – saw that the Muslims were incapable of taking Alhama and aiding the prisoners who were [held] there, he was overcome with desire to possess the whole of al-Andalus, and began to prepare to go out and get it.

111. A lament on the fall of Granada (897/1492)

Within ten years of the fall of Alhama, the Christians finally reduced Granada itself (see also text 65). The anonymous poem that follows is part of a lament, 144 lines long, which reflects on the fate of the cities of the kingdom of Granada. The poet starts by enquiring whether the news of the fall of Ronda (in 1485) is true, and upon learning that it is, he weeps for the humiliation inflicted on the Muslims. He then reviews the fate of Málaga, al-Gharbiyya (the district round Málaga), and Vélez (all fell in 1487), Almuñécar (1489), al-Iqlim (Lecrín); Granada (1492), and Guadix, Baza and Almería (all fell in 1489). The author then reflects that these disasters occurred because the people had neglected their duties to God – a common theme (see also texts 87b, 104).

مَحَــلُّ قَرَارِ المُلْكِ غَرْنــاطــةَ الـتــي   هي الحَضْرَةُ العُلْيــا زِهَتْـهــا زُهُورُهــا

فَــمَا فِي العِراقَيْنِ العَتيــقيْنِ مِثْلُهــا   ولا فــي بِلادِ اللهِ طُرًّا نَظيـــرُهـــا

تَرى الأسى أعـــلامَـــهــا وهيَ خُشَّعُ   وَمِنْبَرُهـا مُسْـــتَعَـــبِــرٌ وسَريرُهـا

وَمَأمُومُهـــا ساهي الحِجى وإمـامُهـا   وَزائِـــرُهـــا فـــي مَأتَمٍ وَمَزُورُهـا

لَمــا حَالُ نَفْسٍ قـــد أُصيبَ فُؤادُها   وَبُثَّتْ لَهــــا اليُمْنَى وَحُمَّ ثُبُورُهـا

فَأنفُسُهَا فِي الصَّعْقِ دُونَ إفـــاقَةٍ   كَنَفْسٍ كَلـــيمٍ اللــهِ إذ دُكَّ طُورُهـا

وَقَـــد ذُعِرتْ تِلْكَ البُنَيَّاتُ حَوْلَهــا   فَهُنَّ بَواكي الأعْيُنِ الرُّمْدِ صُورُهـا

وَقَـــد رَجَفَتْ وادي الأشى فَبِقــاعُهـا   سُكارى وَمــا اسْتـاكَتْ بِخَمْرٍ ثُغُورُهـا

لَقَـــدْ أظْلَمَتْ حَـــتَّى لِفَـــرطِ حِدادِها   سَواءٌ بِهَا نُجْـــلُ الـــعُيُونِ وعُورُهـا

وَبَسْـــطَةُ ذاتُ البَسْـــطِ مَا شَعُرتْ بِمَا   دَهاهَا وأنَّى يَسْـــتَقيمُ شُعُورهـا

عَلى عُظْمِ بَلْواهَا وطولِ وَبـالِهــا   وَمَا كَابَـــدتْ مِنْ ذا المُصابِ نُحُورهـا

وَمَــا أنْسَ لَا أنسَ المَرِيَّةَ إنهــا   قَتيـــلَــةُ أوجالٍ أذيـــلَ عَذيـــرُهـا

فَلوْ أحَـــرَقَ الثُّكْلُ المُصـــابِينَ أصـــبَحَتْ   تَـأجَّجُ مِنْ حَرِّ الوَجــــيفِ بُحُورُهـا

The only remedy is repentance, a sincere return to godliness, and the vigorous pursuit of holy war.

The text is taken from the edition by Soualah Mohammed, Une élégie andalouse sur la guerre de Grenade (Algiers, 1914-19), from pp.60-65. The editor gives a detailed commentary on the poem, and reviews the evidence for the identity of the poet, who might have come from either Ronda or Almería. For another ode written after the fall of Granada, see the anonymous poem addressed to the Ottoman sultan, in al-Maqqari, Azhar al-riyad, reproduced with an English translation by Monroe, pp.376-89.

For the reference to Moses at Sinai, see Qur'an 7: 139.

75. [...Halt at] the seat of kingship, Granada, the exalted capital, whose flowers bedeck her;

76. There is nothing like her in the two noble Iraqs, nothing at all similar in all God's lands.

77. Sadness contemplates her landmarks, which are cast down; her minbar and her throne shed tears.

78. Both the imam and those who are guided have become deranged; both those who visit her and those who are visited are attending a funeral.

79. What a situation for one whose souls have been stricken, whose right hand has been cut off and whose destruction has been decreed.

80. Her spirits are thunderstruck, beyond recovery; like the spirit of Moses (kalim Allah) when mount Sinai was flattened.

81. These buildings [i.e. castles] all around her have been terrified [by bombardments], and her bleary-eyed walls are weeping.

82. Wadi al-Ash (Guadix) has been shaken and her territories are drunken, though she has not even rinsed her teeth with wine;

83. She has been plunged in such darkness that, because of her excessive mourning, those with eyes wide open can see no better than the blind [lit: one-eyed].

84. Baza (Basta) the joyous (*bast*) has not worked out what has befallen her; how could her perceptions be working properly

85. After the magnitude of her misfortunes and the long duration of the mischief done there, and the disasters that her bosoms have endured?

86. Whatever I forget, I will not forget Almería, the victim of terrors it would be despicable to excuse;

87. If bereavement burnt up those who had suffered, [even] the waves [of her harbour] would have been ignited by the heat of the commotion.

أو اسـتَودِعـوهـا مَن إليـهِ أُمُورُهـا	فـيَا أصـدِقـائي ودّعـوهـا كَريمةً
وفُضّتْ عُرى الإسـلام إلاّ يَسيرُها	أضَعنا حُقـوقَ الّرب حـتّى أضـاعنا
مِنَ النُّكْرِ فـانظُرْ كَيْفَ [كان] نَكيرُها	وَملّتُنـا لَمْ نَعْرِف الدَّهْرَ عُرْفَهـا
كَذا السّيـرةُ السّوأى لَدَى مَنْ يَسيرُها	بِمـا قَدْ كَسَبْنـا نـالَنا مـا أنالَنا
وَبُؤنـا بـأحْوالٍ ذَميمٍ حُضُورُهـا	بِشَقْوَتِنا الْخِذْلانُ صـاحَبَ جَـمْعَنا
وَعـاثت بِنا أُسْدُ العِدى ونُمُورُها	بعِصْيـانِنا استَوْلَى علَيْنـا عَدُوُّنـا
وأمـوَالَنا فَيـنـا أُبيـحت وفُورُها	نعـمْ سلَبُوا أوطـانَنا ونُفـوسَنا
قَناةً ولاَ غَارتْ عَليـهِـمْ ذُكـورُها	عَلوهـا بلاَ مـهـرٍ ومـا غُمِرتْ لهـم
عَلـيـنا فَوقَتْ لِـلـصـليـب نُثُورُها	وقَـدْ عَوتِ الإفْرَنْجُ مِنْ كُلّ شـاهِقٍ

88. My friends, say farewell to her as a noble place, or else entrust her to whomever her affairs [will] belong to [i.e. God].

92. We have neglected the rights of the Lord so he has allowed us to perish, all but a few of the bonds of Islam have been broken.

93. Our [Muslim] community has never distinguished what it is right to do from what is forbidden; see how this disapproval is now [turned on us].

94. We have obtained what [God] has given us through what we have deserved; such is the evil life for those who lead it.

95. In our misery, splitting up [disunity] accompanies our unity; we have been brought to circumstances that are blameworthy.

96. Our enemy has gained power over us because of our sinfulness; the lions and leopards of the enemy have wreaked havoc on us.

97. Yes, they have pillaged our homelands, our lives and our possessions; its abundance has been allowed [them] as legitimate spoils;

98. They have seized [ravished] her [Andalusia] without providing a bride-price; no spears have been watered [whetted] for them, nor have her menfolk fought them for her;

99. The Franks have howled down at us from every hilltop and their vows to the Cross have been completely achieved.

186

112. The final agonies (1492-1501)

Numerous accounts of the fall of Granada are available, most recently in Harvey pp.307-23, who translates several passages from the Nubdhat al-'asr *(for which see text 110), including the surrender terms that were agreed between Ferdinand and Isabella and Muhammad XII (Boabdil). These included free passage to North Africa for three years, and thereafter on the payment of "one ducat", and guaranteed freedom of worship for the remaining Mudejar community. The selection given here concerns what happened after the capitulation, and the Christian violation of these terms, and is taken from the same text, pp.127-32. The comparable text preserved in al-Maqqari, IV, pp*

فـما اطمـأن في البلد سرّح لهم الجواز، وأتاهم بالمراكب إلى السـاحل؛ فصار كل
من أراد الجواز يبيـع مالـه ورباعـه ودوره، فكان الواحد منهم يبيع الدار الكبيرة الواسعة
المعتبرة بالثمن القليل. وكذلك يبيـع جنانه وأرض حرثه، وكَرْمـه، وفدّانـه، بأقل من ثمن
الغلة التى كانت فيه. فمنهم من اشتراه من المسلمين الذين عزموا على الدّجن، ومنهم
من اشتراه من النصارى. وكذلك جميع الحوائج والأمتعة. وأمرهم بالمسير إلى الساحل
بما معهم فيرفعهم النصارى في البحر محترمين مكرمين. ويجوزونهم إلى عدوة الغرب
آمنين مطمئنين.

وكـان ملك الروم قـد أظهر للمسلمين في هذه المدة العناية والإحترام، حتى كـان
النصارى يغيرون منهم ويحسدونهم ويقولون لهم: «أنتم الآن عند ملكنا أعز وأكرم منا!»
ووضـع عنهم المغارم وأظهر لهم العدل، حيلة منه وكيـداً ليغرّهم بذلك، وليـثبطهم عن
الجواز، فوقع الطمع لكثير من الناس وظنوا أن ذلك يدوم لهم. فاشتروا أموالاً رخيصة
وأمتعة أنيقة وعزموا على الجلوس مع النصارى.

ثم إن ملك الروم أمر الأمـير محمـد بن علي بالانصراف من غرنـاطة إلى قرية
اندرش من قرى البشرة، فارتحل الأمير محمد بعياله وحشمه وأمواله وأتباعه فنزل قرية
أندرش وأقام بها ينتظر ما يؤمر به. [...]

عند ذلك عزمـوا على الاقـامـة والدّجن؛ ولم يجوز النصارى أحداً بعد ذلك إلا

526-28, *is translated by Gayangos, II, pp.389-92. The revolt of the Muslims in the
Alpujarras is also referred to in the anonymous poem published by Monroe, cf. text 111.
For an interesting study of the question of emigrations from Granada, see J. E.
López de Coca Castañer, "Granada y el Magreb: la emigración andalusí (1485-1516)",
in the collection of papers edited by García-Arenal and María J. Viguera (see text 108),
409-51. The Islamic legal position on Mudejar status is also discussed by Harvey,
pp.55-64, with particular reference to the opinions of al-Wansharishi (d. 1508); cf.
Amar (1908), pp.192 ff.*

When he [Ferdinand V] felt secure in the city, he granted [the Muslims]
permission [to leave], and brought ships for them to the coast. Everyone who
wanted to leave began to sell his property, residence and dwelling. One would
sell a large, spacious and valuable house for a small price, likewise his gardens,
cultivation, vineyards and land [*fiddan* also means oxen] for less than the value
of the standing crops. Another would buy from him, either one of the Muslims
who intended to remain as Mudejars, or one of the Christians. So it was with all
everyday objects and household goods. He ordered them to travel with their
[remaining] possessions to the coast, where the Christians took them to sea with
every respect and courtesy, and ferried them across to North Africa safe and
sound.

The Christian king during this period displayed favour and honour towards
the Muslims, to the extent that the Christians were jealous and envious of them,
and said, "You are now more honoured and respected by our king than we are!"
He rid them of the burden of financial liabilities and treated them justly, thereby
deceitfully plotting to delude them and to prevent them from departing. Many
people desired [to stay] and thought that this [favourable state of affairs] would
last. They bought property cheaply as well as elegant household furnishings, and
decided to remain with the Christians.

Then the Christian king ordered the amir Muhammd b. 'Ali (Boabdil) to
leave Granada for Andrash (Andarax), one of the villages of al-Bashra (?). Amir
Muhammad travelled to Andarax with his family, retinue, possessions and
followers, and established himself there while he waited for further orders.

[...Boabdil was then sent to North Africa, together with many others who
wished to leave. However, severe shortages, famine and plague affected Fez,
encouraging many to return to Spain and discouraging others from leaving...]

At this, they determined to stay on as Mudejars, and thereafter the Christians
would only allow them to leave on the payment of a heavy fine and a tithe on

188

بالكِراء والمغرم الثقيل، وعُشر المال؛ فلما رأى ملك الروم أن الناس قد تركوا الجواز وعزمـوا على الدجن والاستيطان والمقام في الأوطان، أخذ في نقض الشروط، التى شرطوا عليه أول مرة، ولم يزل ينقضها شرطاً شرطاً، ويحلها فصلاً فصلاً؛ إلى أن نقض جميعها. وزالت حرمة الاسلام عن المسلمين وأدركـهم الهوان والذلة. واستطال النصارى عليهم وفُرضت عليهم الفروضات، وثقلت عليهم المغارم؛ وقطع لهم الأذان من الصوامع، وأمرهم بالخروج من مدينة غرناطة إلى الأرباض والقرى؛ وأن لا يبقى بها إلا أولاد السراج خاصة. فخرجوا أذلة صاغرين.

ثم بعد ذلك دعاهم إلى التنصر وأكرههم عليه. وذلك سنة أربع وتسع مئة فدخلوا في دينه كرهاً، وصارت الأندلس كلها نصرانية. ولم يبق من يقول فيها: «لا إله إلا الله محمد رسول الله (صلى الله عليه وسلم) جهراً، إلا من يقولها في نفسه وفي قلبه، أو خفية من الناس، وجُعلت النواقيس في صوامها بعد الأذان، وفي مساجدها الصور، والصلبان بعد ذكر الله تعالى وتلاوة القرآن. فكم فيها من عين باكية وكم فيها من قلب حزين وكم فيها من الضعفاء والمعدومين لم يقدروا على الهجرة واللحوق باخوانهم المسلمين. قلوبهم تشتعل ناراً ودموعهم تسيل سيلاً عزيزاً مدراراً. وينظرون أولادهم وبناتهم يعبدون الصلبان، ويسجدون للأوثان، ويأكلون الخنزير والميتات ويشربون الخمر التى هي أم الخبائث والمنكرات. فلا يقدرون على منعهم ولا على نهيهم ولا على زجرهم. ومن فعل ذلك، عُوقب أشد العقاب. فيا لها من فجعة ما أمرّها، ومصيبة ما أعظمها وأضرها، وطامّة ما أكبرها. عسى الله أن يجعل لهم من أمرهم فرجاً، ومخرجاً، إنه على كل شيء قدير.

وقد كان بعض أهل الأندلس قد امتنعوا من التنصر وأرادوا أن يدافعوا عن أنفسهم كأهل قرى ونجر والبشرة وأندراش وبِلّفيق. فجمع ملك الروم عليهم جموعه، وأحاط بهم من كل مكان حتى أخذهم عنوة بعد قتال شديد؛ فقتل رجالهم، وسبى نساءهم وصبيانهم وأموالهم ونصّرهم، واستعبدهم. إلا أن أناساً في غربية الأندلس

their property. When the Christian king saw that the people had abandoned emigrating and decided to remain as subject people, wishing to stay put in their native homeland, he began to default on the conditions that they had first made with him, and he continued to default on one after another, and to revoke one clause after another, until he had gone back on the whole thing. Respect for Islam ceased and he treated the Muslims with scorn and contempt. The Christians became overbearing towards them, imposed various injunctions and heavy fines on them, and stopped the call to prayer from the minarets. He (Ferdinand) ordered them to leave Granada for the suburbs and the villages, only giving the Banu Sarraj [Abencerrajes] special permission to stay. They [the others] left, submissive and abject.

After that, he summoned them to become Christians and compelled them to do so. This was in 904 (began 19 August 1498); they entered his faith under duress, and the whole of al-Andalus became Christian. There remained no-one to proclaim openly, "There is no God but God, Muhammad is the Messenger of God", only those who said it to themselves in their hearts, or clandestinely among the people. Bells replaced the call to prayer in the minarets, images went up in the mosques, crosses appeared in place of the name of God Almighty and the recitation of the Qur'an. How many there were with weeping eyes and grieving hearts, how many destitute and impoverished, who were unable to emigrate and join their Muslim brothers! Their hearts were consumed by fire, their eyes were flooded with torrents of copious tears. They saw their sons and their daughters worshipping crosses and bowing down before idols, eating pigs and carrion and drinking wine, which is the mother of all indecencies and abominations, and they were powerless to prevent them or to restrain and rebuke them. Whoever did such things, will be punished with a painful punishment. O what a calamity it was – nothing could be more bitter; no misfortune could be greater or more hurtful, no disaster could be worse. Maybe God will give them freedom and release from their position, for He has power over everything.

Some of the Andalusians had refused to become Christian and wished to defend themselves like the villagers of Najar (? Nerja), al-Bashra (?), Andarax and Ballafiq (Belefique, near Almería). The Christian king gathered an army against them and surrounded them everywhere, until he took them by force after a desperate fight; he killed the men, captured their women and children and possessions, converted them to Christianity and enslaved them. But some people in the west of al-Andalus refused to convert and withdrew to a rugged and

امتنعوا من التنصر وانحازوا إلى جبل منيع وعر فاجتمعوا فيه بعيالهم وآموالهم وتحصنوا فيه. فجمع عليهم ملك الروم جموعه وطمع في الوصول إليهم كما فعل بغيرهم، فلما دنا منهم وأراد قتالهم خيّب الله سعيه ورده على عقبه ونصرهم عليه بعد أكثر من ثلاثة وعشرين معركة. فقتلوا من جنده خلقاً كثيراً من رجال وفرسان وأقناد. فلما رأى أنه لا يقدر عليهم طلب منهم أن يعطيهم الأمان ويجوزهم لعدوة الغرب مؤمّنين فأنعموا له بذلك إلا أنه لم يُسَرّح لهم شيئاً من متاعهم غير الثياب التي كانت عليهم. وجوّزهم لعدوة الغرب كما شرطوا عليه.

ولم يطمع أحد بعد ذلك أن يقوم بدعوة الاسلام. وعم الكفر جميع القرى والبلدان وانطفأ من الاندلس نور الاسلام والايمان. فعلى هذا فليبك الباكون ولينتحب المنتحبون. فانا لله وإنا إليه راجعون. كان ذلك في الكتاب مسطوراً. وكان أمر الله قدراً مقدوراً.

mpregnable mountain range, where they collected their families and possessions and defended themselves. The Christian king amassed his troops against them and hoped to deal with them as he had with the others. When he approached them and sought battle, God foiled his efforts and threw him back on his heels, giving them victory over him after more than twenty-three battles. They killed many of his men, knights and counts. When he saw that he could do nothing with them, he suggested to them that they should have a safe-conduct to go to North Africa in peace, to which they assented, except that he did not allow them to take anything except the clothes they were wearing. He let them go as agreed between them.

Thereafter, no-one strove to proclaim Islam. Unbelief spread through all the towns and villages and the light of Islam and the true faith in al-Andalus were extinguished, at which the weepers cry and the wailers lament. We are God's and to Him we return. All this was inscribed in the book [of fate]; God's will was ordained and predestined.

Glossary

Adab: etiquette, norms of conduct; works of adab deal with the knowledge required for different offices, social behaviour and suchlike.

Adl (pl. *'udul*): irreproachable witness, person of good reputation. Such people formed a branch of the legal profession and acted as notaries assigned to the *qadi* (q.v.).

Ahl al-Kitab: Jews and Christians, who possessed scriptures before the revelation of Islam (see also *dhimmi*).

Aman: safe-conduct, or quarter in battle.

Amir: commander, prince. Both a military title and one used by independent rulers, such as the Umayyad amirs. The title Amir al-mu'minin (Prince of the Believers) is equivalent to Caliph; other rulers, such as the Almoravids, styled themselves Amir al-Muslimin, or Commander of the Muslims.

Ansar: the people of Medina who helped and supported Muhammad when he fled from Mecca.

Bid'a: innovation; a practice or belief for which there is no precedent in the Qur'an or the *sunna* (q.v.). Can be classed as good (*hasana*), praiseworthy (*mamduha*) or blameworthy (*madhmuma*).

Dar al-Harb: the House of War; the territory of the non-believers, against which there should be a state of perpetual war (*jihad*). A person from the Dar al-Harb is a *harbi*.

Dar al-Islam: the House of Islam, or Muslim territory.

Dhimmi: non-Muslim subject of a Muslim state, enjoying a pact or covenant (*dhimma*); generally, but not exclusively, they are the *Ahl al-Kitab* (q.v.).

Faqih: an expert in Islamic jurisprudence (*fiqh*).

Fatwa: a ruling or opinion on a point of law, given by a *mufti* (q.v.).

Fay': booty or spoils of war. Often land or the revenue from land, rather than moveable possessions.

Ghulam: a young male slave, used as a palace guard or attendant.

Hadith: tradition relating the words, deeds or decisions of the Prophet Muhammad. The corpus of hadith was a major source of authority for Islamic law.

Halal: lawful, permitted, in accordance with Muslim law.

Haram: illegal, taboo, prohibited (opposite of *halal*). Also denoted in the term *muharram*.

Hisba: the function of the *muhtasib* (q.v.).

'Id: festival. Two main Muslim festivals are the Feast of the Sacrifice (*'id al-adha*) and the festival of breaking the fast (*'id al-fitr*).

Imam: leader in prayer, and by extension political head of the Muslim community.

Isnad: chain of authority for the oral transmission of *hadith* (q.v.).

Jahiliyya: the age of ignorance, i.e. pre-Islamic Arabia.

Jihad: Holy War. A collective legal duty of the Muslim community. A fighter of Holy War is a *mujahid*.

Khawarij: members of an early religious sect who split from the main body of Islam.

194 GLOSSARY

Kohl: antimony, pulverized powder used for darkening the eyelids (hence the wo
alcohol).

Kufr: unbelief; the doctrines of the unbeliever (*kafir*).

Mafrud: incumbent, obligatory; one of the five categories used by Islamic law to defi
actions or beliefs. The opposite end of the scale from *muharram*, prohibited.

Makruh: disapproved, deplored (but not forbidden). One of the five categories used b
Islamic law to define actions or beliefs. The negative counterpart of *mandu*
recommended (but not obligatory).

Minbar: pulpit used by Muslim preachers.

Mozarab: Arabized Christian; applied to Christians who left al-Andalus and settled i
the north, or who came under Christian rule during the Reconquista.

Mu'ahad: someone who enjoys a covenant or pact (*'ahd*), whether whether inside th
Muslim state (cf. *dhimmi*) or outside it (cf. *aman*).

Mubah: permitted; one of the five categories used by Islamic law to define actions (
beliefs.

Mudejar: Muslim living under Christian rule.

Muezzin: the person who calls the Muslims to prayer.

Mufti: a jurisprudent who is competent to deliver a legal opinion (*fatwa*).

Muhajirun: those companions and adherents of the Prophet who emigrated with hir
from Mecca to Medina.

Muhtasib: an official entrusted with detecting and punishing offenses against th
shari'a (q.v.), and with maintaining public morals and standards in the markets

Mujtahid: a religious scholar competent to exercise individual reasoning (*ijtihad*), o
reasoning by analogy.

Mushrik: polytheist. Someone who associates God with "partners".

Mutatawwa'a: volunteer. Non-stipendiary fighter for the faith. Particularly used of th
Marinid volunteers fighting for Nasrid Granada.

Muwallad: someone born of non-Arab or non-Muslim parents; a neo-Muslim.

Nass: literal text, citation, quotation (e.g. of legal opinion).

Qadi: judge administering the law of Islam (*shari'a*).

Qa'id: leader, general, or commander-in-chief. Also denotes a military governor (=
Spanish, Alcaide).

Qibla: direction of Mecca, towards which a Muslim faces when praying.

Rak'a: bowing, i.e. the cycle of prayer, including the preliminary preparations
recitation, bowing and prostrating.

Shar', *Shari'a*: the Holy Law of Islam, lit. the path to be followed.

Sunna: the accepted practices and beliefs of the Islamic community, based on th
example of the Prophet Muhammad.

'Ulama: scholars of religious learning; theologians and jurisprudents (sing. *'alim*).

Vizier (*Wazir*): chief administrative official, generally head of the bureaucracy. Usually
a civilian. In Caliphal Spain, the powers of the vizier were often subordinate
to those of the *hajib* or chamberlain.

Index

TEXTS

MODERN EDITORS AND SCHOLARS

PLACES

Aris & Phillips
Hispanic Classics
published and forthcoming books

Afonso de ALBUQUERQUE
CAESAR OF THE EAST (edd. J. Villiers & T.F. Earle)

Antonio BUERO VALLEJO
THE SHOT (ed. David Johnston)
A DREAMER FOR THE PEOPLE (ed. M. Thompson)

Pedro CALDERÓN DE LA BARCA
JEALOUSY, THE GREATEST MONSTER (edd. Ann L. Mackenzie & K. Muir)
LOVE IS NO LAUGHING MATTER (ed. D.W. Cruikshank & S. Page)
THE PAINTER OF HIS DISHONOUR (ed. A.K.G. Paterson)
THE SCHISM IN ENGLAND (edd Ann L. Mackenzie & K. Muir)

Pere CALDERS
THE VIRGIN OF THE RAILWAY (ed. Amanda Bath)

Miguel de CERVANTES Saavedra
EXEMPLARY NOVELS
Vol 1. Preface to the Reader, The Little Gypsy Girl, The Generous Lover, Rinconete and Cortadillo, edd. B.W. Ife, R.M. Price, R. Hitchcock & Lynn Williams
Vol 2. The English Spanish Girl, The Glass Graduate, The Power of Blood, ed. R.M. Price
Vol 3. The Jealous Old Man from Extramadura, The Illustrious Kitchen-Maid, The Two Damsels, edd. M. & J. Thacker
Vol 4. Lady Cornelia, The Deceitful Marriage Marriage, The Dialogue of the Dogs, edd. Jones & J. Macklin
THE CAPTIVES TALE (ed. D. McCrory)

Christopher COLUMBUS
THE JOURNAL OF THE FIRST VOYAGE (ed. B.W. Ife)

José de ESPRONCEDA
THE STUDENT OF SALAMANCA (edd. C. K. Davis & R. A. Cardwell)

JUAN MANUEL
COUNT LUCANOR (ed. J.P. England)

LOPE DE VEGA
FUENTE OVEJUNA (ed. V. F. Dixon)

PERIBÁÑEZ (ed. J.M. Lloyd)

FERNÃO LOPES
THE ENGLISH IN PORTUGAL 1383–1387 (edd. D.W. Lomax & R.J. Oakley)

Federico GARCIA LORCA
GYPSY BALLADS (ed. R.G. Havard)
MARIANA PINEDA (ed. R.G.Havard)
YERMA (edd. I. R.Macpherson & J. Minett)

THE POEM OF MY CID (edd. P. Such & J. Hodgkinson)

Francisco de QUEVEDO
DREAMS AND DISCOURSES (ed. R.K.Britton)

Fernando de ROJAS
CELESTINA (ed. Dorothy Sherman Severin)

CHRISTIANS AND MOORS IN SPAIN
Vol I (711-1150) C.C. Smith
Vol II (1195-1614) C.C. Smith
Vol III ARABIC SOURCES (711-1501) (edd. Charles Melville & Ahmad Ubaydli)

TIRSO DE MOLINA
DAMNED FOR DESPAIR (ed. N.G. Round)
DON GIL OF THE GREEN BREECHES (ed. G.G. Minter)
TAMAR'S REVENGE (ed. J.E. Lyon)
THE TRICKSTER OF SEVILLE AND THE STONE GUEST (ed. G. Edwards)

Ramon Maria del VALLE- INCLAN
MR PUNCH THE CUCKOLD (edd. R. Warner & D. Keown)
LIGHTS OF BOHEMIA (ed. J. Lyon)

Roger Wright **SPANISH BALLADS**